Forging New Rights
in Western Waters

Forging New Rights
in Western Waters

Robert G. Dunbar

University of Nebraska Press
Lincoln and London

Manufactured in the United States of America

The paper in this book meets the guidelines for
permanence and durability of the Committee on
Production Guidelines for Book Longevity of the
Council on Library Resources.

Library of Congress Cataloging in Publication Data

Dunbar, Robert G.
    Forging new rights in western waters.
    Includes bibliographical references and index.

    1. Water-rights—West (U.S.)—History.
2. Riparian rights—West (U.S.)—History. I. Title.
KF5570.D86   1983   346.7304'691   82-13421
ISBN 0-8032-1663-7   347.3064691

To the memory of Charles A. Lory

*Ditch rider, teacher,
land-grant college president,
water statesman, man of vision*

Contents

Preface

I crossed the ninety-eighth meridian, that dividing line between the wet portion of the United States and the dry, during the night of September 9, 1937. I was en route from eastern South Dakota to Fort Collins, Colorado, to assume a teaching position at Colorado State College, now Colorado State University. I had boarded in Omaha the Union Pacific's deluxe City of Denver shortly after midnight and when I awoke in the morning the train was traveling through western Nebraska, with the level, brown, treeless plains extending toward the distant horizon on each side. I changed trains in eastern Colorado at LaSalle, near the site of James A. Michener's future Centennial, to take a spur to Fort Collins through the sugar beet fields and irrigated lands of the Cache la Poudre Valley. Beyond was the gray green wall of the Front Range of the Rocky Mountains, source of the snow water that fed the network of irrigating canals and ditches.

I had grown up on a farm in southern Wisconsin, but I discovered that farming under ditch in northern Colorado was very different from that back home in the humid East. I soon learned what Walter Prescott Webb meant when he wrote in *The Great Plains* that westward-moving farmers had been forced by the aridity of the region to make radical readjustments in their way of farming. First, they had to learn to dig canals and ditches. (Technically canals are larger than ditches, but westerners use the terms interchangeably.) The pioneer farmers had not had such experience. Moreover, their surveying instruments were usually crude. Consequently, their first ditches were usually too narrow, too shallow, and too steep, like Will Cedar's Canal Number One in Dorothy Gardiner's *Snow-Water*, a fictional account of irrigation development in the Cache la Poudre Valley. But through trial and error they learned. They learned to construct diversion dams, strong enough to withstand the force of rivers at flood stage and to install headgates at the intake of each canal. They learned also to construct large reservoirs in which to store those flood waters for the purpose of irrigating potatoes and sugar beets in the late summer. I had lived in Fort Collins for some time before I discovered that Terry Lake on the outskirts of the city was not a natural body of water but a storage reservoir for a large irrigation system.

Having constructed projects, the farmers next had to learn to irrigate, dig laterals, and apply the water to the land. They had to decide whether to irrigate by flooding, furrows, or the Spanish-American border method. That decided, they had to learn how much water to apply to the land, to determine the duty of water. In fact, in their new environment the farmers had to master a new vocabulary. To determine the duty of water the users had to think not in terms of pints, quarts, and gallons but in terms of miner's inches, cubic feet per second, and acre-feet. The miner's inch was a unit of measurement borrowed from the miners, who used streams to separate gold from the sand and gravel in the mountain gulches. It was the amount of water flowing through an inch-square orifice under a certain head. Among irrigators, the noun *head* has a variable meaning. As used in the preceding sentence, it means *pressure*, but it may also refer to the quantity of water flowing into a farmer's lateral, usually enough to irrigate a field. When the level of the stream pressing against the board in which the orifice has been cut is four inches above the top of that opening, it is said to be measured under a four-inch head. The head, however, may be more than four inches. Since it may vary, hydraulic engineers prefer the cubic foot per second, which is the volume of water flowing through a trough one foot wide and one foot deep with a mean velocity of one foot per second of time. An acre-foot is the quantity of water that will cover one acre one foot in depth.

The farmers likewise had to learn to divide the streams among the users. This could be done either by determining the share or fraction of the stream to which each ditch was entitled or by measuring the volume allotted to each user. The latter method necessitated the adoption, improvement, or invention of measuring devices. European and American engineers had developed weirs, such as the Cippoletti trapezoidal weir, invented by Cesare Cippoletti of northern Italy and popularized in this country by Louis G. Carpenter of the Colorado Agricultural Experiment Station. Another Italian invented the Venturi flume, which was improved in the 1920s by Ralph L. Parshall, who had an office on the floor below me in the civil engineering building at Colorado State College. In recognition of his achievement, the United States Department of Agriculture renamed it the Parshall Measuring Flume.

Not only did farmers need to divide the stream waters but they also needed to know how much there was to divide. This task was delegated to hydraulic engineers with current meters, but when the United States Geological Survey, under the direction of John Wesley Powell, undertook in the fall of 1888 the systematic gauging of streams there were neither sufficient engineers nor satisfactory instruments. Indeed, farming in the arid West was a new agriculture to migrants from the humid East, although old to the Hispanic Americans of the Southwest. New uses of water required new property rights for it. I had not been in Fort Collins long when I learned that in the late summer some farmers had their water supply cut off. To receive an explanation of this apparent injustice, I went to Charles A. Lory, president emeritus of Colorado State College and one of the architects of the Colorado-Big Thompson Reclamation Project. "First in time, first in right," he replied. The Coloradans had changed the law. They had done what James Michener's Hans Brumbaugh set out to do—replaced the Doctrine of Riparian Rights, with its emphasis on equality of use, with the Doctrine of Prior Appropriation.

This book is an account of how the Hans Brumbaughs, with the assistance of innovative lawyers like Michener's Joe Beck, forged new property rights in western waters, but, since diversions usually preceded consideration of rights, it is prefaced by brief histories of the construction of irrigation systems. The histories provide another story, one of institutional adaptation and creation, as farmers sought to borrow or invent agencies that could construct the dams, ditches, and reservoirs needed to irrigate the bench lands distant from the streams.

The narrative that follows has been many years in preparation, for it has been four decades since I sat at the feet of Charles A. Lory and he explained to me the mysteries of western water law. I am deeply indebted not only to him, but to many others. To the librarians, archivists, and state water resource officials who gave their assistance, I express my sincere gratitude and appreciation. I also wish to thank the historians who have assisted and encouraged me, especially Lawrence B. Lee of San Jose State University and Norris Hundley, jr., of the University of California at Los Angeles, for their critical reading of the entire manuscript. To my colleagues in the Department of History and Philosophy at Montana State University I express a special thanks for their consistent encouragement and support. Finally, I would like to acknowledge my indebtedness to Judge W.W. Lessley, "Chief Water Judge of the State of Montana," and to attorney H.B. Landoe of Landoe Brown Planalp Kommers and Lineberger in Bozeman. Again, many thanks.

Forging New Rights
in Western Waters

1
The First Irrigations

As one flies over the western contiguous states on clear summer days, one can usually look down on streaks of glistening water and circles of verdure spotting the landscape. The streaks and buttons are irrigation ditches and circular tracts of land watered by pivot sprinkler irrigation systems, evidences that the earth is dry and thirsty. Rainfall is limited west of the ninety-eighth meridian to less than 20 inches a year. The average annual precipitation in Lubbock, Texas, on the southern Great Plains, is 18.08 inches, paralleled by 12.17 inches at Miles City, Montana, on the northern plains. Similarly, an average of only 13.90 inches of rain and snow falls each year at Salt Lake City, Utah, in the Great Basin, while precipitation in the Southwest is even more limited—7.20 inches in Phoenix, Arizona, and 12.63 inches in Los Angeles, California. These are annual averages; some years there is more precipitation, some years less, as floods follow droughts in irregular cycles. Whatever the precipitation, it has usually been insufficient for agriculture as it is practiced in more humid regions, and today it is insufficient for the demands of bulging cities and the needs of expanding industries.[1]

Faced with insufficient rainfall, the first farmers of the Southwest supplemented it with diversions from the

streams—that is, they resorted to irrigation. They were the Hohokam Indians. Archaeologists, digging with a backhoe at Snaketown, in the desert southwest of Phoenix, Arizona, uncovered one of their irrigation canals, which dates back to 300 B.C. It was a broad, shallow diversion from the Gila River, excavated for a distance of five miles and provided with turnouts to supply water to the laterals servicing the fields.[2]

The Hohokam civilization reached its zenith about 1200 A.D. and disappeared approximately two hundred years later. During its heyday, its people extended their irrigation systems to water much of the area now included in greater Phoenix. Canals fanned out from both sides of the Salt River, totaling more than 135 miles and irrigating more than 100,000 acres—the original Salt River Project. Within its city limits Phoenix is preserving portions of two of these ditches on the grounds of the Pueblo Grande Museum. When they were in use, one of them was 30 feet wide, approximately 9 miles long, and partly lined with clay to reduce seepage. With a width of 18 feet and a length of 7 miles, the other canal was narrower, shorter, but somewhat deeper.[3]

The Hohokams were succeeded by the Subaipuris and the Pimas, whom the Spaniards found irrigating fields of corn, beans, and cotton. As Father Eusebio Kino's party advanced through the Santa Cruz Valley in 1697, the escort, Lieutenant Juan Matheo Mange, observed fields "irrigated by many ditches" where the Indians harvested "in abundance maize, beans, and cotton, with which they clothe themselves, as well as squash, cantaloupes and watermelons."[4] When the Jesuit missionary returned to the valley two years later in the company of his superior, Father Antonio Leal, the sown fields in the vicinity of the village of San Xavier del Bac "were so extensive and supplied with so many irrigation ditches running along the ground that the father visitor [Leal] said they were sufficient for another city like Mexico." So impressed were the fathers that they decided to establish a mission there.[5]

The Spanish records contain other references to Native Americans' irrigation. Seventy-four years after the founding of the San Xavier del Bac mission a member of Captain Juan Bautista de Anza's expedition en route to California noted, "[The Pimas] aided by irrigation . . . produce in plenty all sorts of crops."[6] Similarly, the Spaniards found the native inhabitants of the Rio Grande Valley irrigating their fields. On visiting the Indian pueblo of Acoma, Antonio de Espejo observed, "[The Acomas] have their fields two leagues from the pueblo on a river of medium size, whose water they intercept for irrigating purposes," while Caspar Castaño de Sosa on visiting San Ildefonso in 1591 found a considerable tract of land under ditch.[7]

The Spaniards were no strangers to irrigation. They had been diverting streams for this purpose since Roman times and under Moorish rule had developed sophisticated irrigation systems.[8] Consequently, as the frontier of New Spain moved northward into the Spanish borderlands, the padres and conquistadores constructed *acequias* (irrigation canals) to irrigate the mission and pueblo lands. Juan de Oñate, the pioneer colonizer of New Mexico, seems to have led the way. No sooner had he arrived at the pueblo of San Juan near the confluence of the Rio Chama and the Rio Grande in 1598 than he began the construction of an irrigation ditch. When Oñate's successor, Governor Pedro de Peralta, moved the headquarters of Spanish rule in New Mexico to Santa Fe in 1610, he situated the new settlement astride a little stream from which lands on both sides could be irrigated. Nearly a century later, Governor Francisco Cuervo y Valdez in founding Albuquerque located thirty-five families on the left bank of the Rio Grande and ordered the construction of canals to supply irrigation water. He reported to the reigning monarch,

Philip V of Spain, on April 23, 1706: "Irrigation ditches are in place and the water running. The fields are sown; everything is in good order, and there has been no expense to the royal treasury."[9]

The principal colonizers of California, the Franciscan friars, were careful to situate their missions near supplies of water for both domestic and agricultural purposes. In 1769, Junípero Serra located the first mission, San Diego de Alcalá, on a bluff high above the San Diego River, beyond easy access to the stream. Consequently, after several years of crop failures, the friars moved the mission six miles up the valley and with brush dams diverted water into ditches to irrigate their gardens and fields. When this diversion system proved inadequate, they went six miles farther up the river and built a solid masonry dam, 224 feet long and 12 feet high, so solid that it still survives.[10]

Learning from their experience at San Diego, the Franciscans constructed comparable irrigation systems at their other missions. To provide water for the irrigation of gardens, orchards, and vineyards as well as the operation of a grist mill and a fountain, the friars at the Santa Barbara mission constructed two mortared sandstone dams. The Mission Creek dam, which was about three miles distant from the mission, was one hundred feet long, seventeen feet high, and seventeen feet wide. Stone aqueducts conducted water from the dams to reservoirs; from them it was released to the mill, fountain, and gardens. So durable were these structures that the Mission Creek dam survives and one of the reservoirs, repaired and enlarged, still serves the city of Santa Barbara. Similar structures were built at Mission San Antonio de Padua, where water was conducted from diversion dams by clay pipes. When the San Gabriel mission founded another mission at San Bernardino, it dammed Mill Creek and constructed a twelve-mile canal to irrigate 536 acres.[11]

Besides the twenty-one missions, the Spanish established two pueblos in California. Governor Felipe de Neve founded San Jose in 1777 and Los Angeles in 1781. Selecting a site on the east bank of the Guadalupe River, the governor recruited settlers and formally founded the pueblo of San Jose on November 29, 1777. In preparation for the first crop, the settlers lost no time in digging a ditch and constructing a timber and earthen diversion dam. However, before a crop could be harvested the dam was washed away by the spring floods, and when a replacement was built it too was destroyed by the stream at flood stage.[12]

Four years after the establishment of San Jose, Governor Neve issued instructions on August 26, 1781, for the founding of Los Angeles. He directed that it should be located so that the maximum amount of land could be irrigated by a ditch from the Los Angeles River, or the Río de la Réina de los Angeles de Porciúncula as it was then called, and that each settler should receive two agricultural tracts which could be supplied with irrigation water. So important was water considered in the survival of the settlement that when the settlers arrived they constructed a dam and a ditch before they built their houses. When five years later another governor confirmed each settler in the possession of his town lot and cultivated land, he made it clear that the waters of the Los Angeles River were held in common for the use of the entire community. A century later the city of Los Angeles used this directive as a basis for its claim to the entire flow of the river. When this claim was affirmed, it became known as a *pueblo water right*.[13]

In Texas, as in California, irrigation provided the economic foundations of the missions and pueblos of New Spain. The first colony within the boundaries of the present state was a resettlement of Indian refugees following the suppression of the Pueblo revolt of 1680 in New Mexico. It was located at Ysleta on the Rio Grande below El Paso. By diverting the waters of the river, the transplanted farmers were soon irrigating three thousand acres. A Spanish visitor in 1726 noted that the "natural fertility of the land is improved by the number of irrigation ditches which carry water from the said Rio del Norte, making the farms independent of droughts."[14]

From the Rio Grande, Franciscan friars extended their influence to the north and east, locating missions on the banks of the Nueces, San Gabriel, Guadalupe, and San Antonio rivers, diverting them to irrigate the mission fields and gardens. They constructed the most successful systems at San Antonio, where they established five missions, the Concepción, San Antonio de Valero, San José, San Juan Capistrano, and San Francisco de Espada. To serve each mission, they dug five canals between the years 1718 and 1744 and diverted the waters of the San Antonio River into them. Their earliest *acequia* was the Alamo Madre, a canal six miles long, designed to irrigate nine hundred acres of the San Antonio de Valero mission, which years later during the Texan war of independence would become the site of the Alamo massacre. The waters of another ditch, the Espada, were diverted by a brush and stone dam and carried across an arroyo by means of a heavy, arched stone aqueduct. In 1731, the Spanish crown established a colony of families from the Canary Islands in San Antonio. These settlers dug a sixth ditch, six feet wide, two feet deep, and four miles long to irrigate four hundred acres. When another colony dug the seventh *acequia* in the 1770s, at least 4,000 acres were under ditch in eighteenth-century San Antonio.[15]

In addition to digging ditches and diverting streams, the American Indians and the Spaniards developed institutions for the administration of irrigation canals. Living in small agricultural communities, the water users elected a ditch superintendent, called a *majordomo* in the Rio Grande Valley, who superintended the construction of ditches and their repair, with each irrigator providing a share of the labor in proportion to his land holding. This official also distributed the water among the users, usually by a system of rotation, and arbitrated disputes. In organized municipalities, town officials either directly or indirectly managed the canals. In Spanish Los Angeles, the pueblo council maintained a ditch committee to administer the main ditch and divide its waters. Similarly, the town council of San Antonio appointed "commissioners" to assume duties of the same nature.[16] Consequently, when the United States acquired title to the Spanish colonized territories of the Southwest by the Treaty of Guadalupe Hidalgo with Mexico in 1848, it acquired cultures long experienced in the practice of irrigation.

2
The Mormon Experience

While American military forces were campaigning in Mexico, winning battles that would lead to the Treaty of Guadalupe Hidalgo, Brigham Young was piloting a harassed band of religious refugees across the plains and through mountain passes to a haven of safety on the shores of the Great Salt Lake. When they arrived, the area was a part of Mexico; within a year, by virtue of that treaty, it became a part of the United States.

Whoever possessed it, it seemed to be an inhospitable terrain; at least it was to Jim Bridger, who offered Brigham Young one thousand dollars for the first ear of corn grown there. The summer temperatures were warm and the annual precipitation limited, approximately fourteen inches. Moreover, the Mormons arrived during the driest season of the nineteenth century. As Orson Pratt, the leader of the migration's vanguard, surveyed the landscape on July 22, 1847, he noted that "the grass had nearly dried up for want of moisture," but that streams from the bordering Wasatch Mountains provided abundant supplies of water.[1]

The first irrigation by the Mormons occurred the day after Pratt made his observation. They camped in the morning on the banks of a stream which would soon be known as City Creek and with the temperature in the nineties they began to plow. The ground, however, "was like adamant," so hard "that neither wood nor iron was strong enough to make furrows in this soil." After breaking a plow-share or two, they went up the stream a short distance and, with spades, constructed a small earthen dam to divert its waters over the unyielding surface. With the ground moistened, the plowing was resumed with more success. The next morning, July 24, the Latter-Day Saints planted potatoes, and, again diverting City Creek, gave them "quite a soaking."[2]

Also on July 24, Brigham Young arrived with the main body of migrants. Four days later, on July 28, he announced his plans for the establishment of Great Salt Lake City, as the settlement was initially called. It would be laid out, he said, in a grid of ten-acre square blocks, with wide streets intersecting at right angles. Each block would be divided into residential lots of one and a quarter acres, enough for a house, barns, orchard, and garden. This announcement was followed in August by the construction of a fort and the survey and division of the city into 135 blocks. To provide the fort and later the city with household and irrigation water, the Saints diverted City and Red Butte creeks into a ditch that was extended the next spring along the streets of the city. When fully constructed the ditch bordered North Temple Street to the Jordan River, with laterals flowing into ditches around each ten-acre block. Mark Twain in *Roughing It* referred to the ditch with its laterals as a "street stream winding and sparkling among the garden beds and fruit trees," while another visitor writing in the *New York Herald* in 1858 referred to "the streets set as it were in a jewel of rippling brooks which glisten bright as silver in the sunlight."[3]

Brigham Young departed toward the close of August 1847 to join the remainder of the refugees, who were camped on the banks of the Missouri River near Council Bluffs. When he returned with them a year later, he ordered the distribution of the city lots among the settlers and the division of a "big field" of five thousand acres to the south of the lots into tracts of five and ten acres for farming purposes. At the same time he announced plans for the construction of a canal along the upper side of the field to irrigate these tracts. Construction began that autumn to divert Big Cottonwood Creek, but the Big Ditch, as it was called, never reached its destination. The Salt Lake City farmers, instead, relied on streams like Red Butte Creek, which were closer to their fields.[4]

As soon as the Saints arrived in Utah, they began to fan out to the north and south along the base of the Wasatch Range. Sometimes they came through individual initiative, like other settlers on the American frontier. At other times they came in groups organized by the Mormon church for the purpose of colonization. The settlements in the vicinity of Salt Lake City followed the first pattern. Peregrine Sessions drove his herd of cattle north of the city in the fall of 1847 and became the first settler in the community that was later named Bountiful. The next spring John D. Holladay with a company of Saints settled on Big Cottonwood Creek to the south. Others followed him, among them Alvin Green, who with members of his family dug the Green Ditch, and Nathan Tanner, who commenced the Tanner Ditch that fall.[5]

In March 1848, the church leaders decided to colonize the Utah Valley, where eight streams, among them the Provo, American Fork, and Spanish Fork, flow from the mountains into Utah Lake. The leaders made their decision at the home of Heber C. Kimball on March 10, 1849. They selected 29 persons, under the leadership of James S. Higbee, to make a settlement on the Provo River. Within less than a month the company was en route, arriving at their destination on April 1, 1849. The following year the church organized similar groups to found Lehi, Pleasant Grove, Alpine, American Fork, and Spanish Fork.[6]

Under the direction of church officials known as bishops (of which James Higbee was one), the settlements followed the pattern of Salt Lake City. A fort was built and a town, divided usually into ten-acre blocks, laid out with a field of larger tracts nearby for farming purposes. The bishops supervised the construction of dams and ditches to irrigate the lots and tracts. Most of these early ditches, whether in the Utah Valley or elsewhere, were short, shallow, and narrow, while the dams were crude obstructions, built of rocks and brush. As in the Spanish-American communities, each Utah Valley settler contributed labor in proportion to his holdings. Lacking sophisticated surveying instruments, the ditch builders sighted over a pan of water or determined the proper gradient by the use of a triangular frame with a plumb line suspended from its apex. Once the route of the ditch had been determined, the builders dug the ditch by plows, go-devils, shovels, and spades. The go-devil was an A-shaped implement made of logs, which, when drawn by oxen, pushed the plowed dirt to the sides and hollowed out the ditch. Within a decade there was a corridor of church-founded settlements extending the full length of the territory of Utah.[7]

Nor did the expansion of the Mormon irrigation frontier halt at the borders of the territory. As early as 1851 Brigham Young founded a colony in southern California. Its leaders purchased the Rancho San Bernardino and appropriated for their use the canal that the Franciscan friars had constructed out of Mill Creek. Nevertheless, this colony was abandoned six years later at the time of the invasion of Utah by federal troops under the command of Colonel Albert Sidney Johnston. More enduring were the colonies located in neighboring Arizona, Idaho, and Wyoming. Under the direction of the church, Mormons established colonies in the Salt, Upper Gila, and Little Colorado valleys of Arizona in the 1870s and 1880s. Those who settled in the Salt River Valley founded the community of Mesa and began using one of the prehistoric canals. The Little Colorado colonizers had a more difficult experience; one of their diversion dams washed out no less than eleven times. The Saints spilled over into Idaho from their communities in northern Utah and in the last decades of the century peopled the upper Snake River Valley, interlacing the valley floor with a myriad of canals, such as the Rexburg Irrigation Company Canal in Madison County and the People's Canal in Bingham County. In 1893, the Mormons extended their ecclesiastical empire into northern Wyoming, when fifty families settled near Greybull in the Big Horn basin and began the construction of two canals.[8]

As the Mormons diverted the stream waters, they devised distinctive institutions to govern their use. These institutions may be best understood by a realization that as members of the Church of the Latter-Day Saints the colonists believed that they were participating in a revival of egalitarian primitive Christianity, with its emphasis on the sharing of goods. They regarded the earth as belonging to the Lord, to be "inherited" by themselves as his chosen people. So they took possession of the land and their ecclesiastical leaders divided it among them in equal parcels. Similarly, they regarded the streams as belonging to the Lord and his people. Brigham Young declared on September 30, 1848: "There shall be no private ownership of the streams that come out of the canyons, nor the timber that grows in the hills. These belong to the people: all the people." Acting on this philosophy, the church leaders, usually the bishops, diverted the streams for the benefit of communities and divided their waters equitably among the users.[9]

With the creation of the State of Deseret in 1849, the theocratic government assumed control of the allocation of the public waters, although diversion by church officials continued for the benefit of groups of colonists. Since the waters belonged to the people, permission from the state was required for their use. Consequently, among the statutes of the State of Deseret may be found several legislative grants giving permission to use the streams. On November 23, 1850,

Brigham Young petitioned the General Assembly for "exclusive control" of City Creek "in order that the water may be continued pure unto the inhabitants of Great Salt Lake City," a petition that was approved eleven days later. On the same day that the grant to Young was approved, the assembly made a similar grant to Ezra T. Benson, the colonizer of Tooele Valley, with respect to the streams of that valley. A month later, the legislators granted Heber Kimball the right to use the waters of North Mill Creek for saw and grist mill purposes provided he did not interfere with the use of the stream for irrigation.[10]

Although the territorial legislature occasionally made comparable grants after the creation of Utah Territory in 1851, it delegated authority to control the streams to the county governments by an act dated February 4, 1852, which read, "The County Court has the control of all timber, water privileges, or any water course or creek, to grant mill sites, and exercise such powers as in their judgment shall best preserve the timber, and subserve the interest of the settlements, in the distribution of water for irrigation, or other purposes. All grants or rights held under Legislative authority shall not be interfered with." The county governments, composed of a probate judge and three selectmen, made numerous grants of water for irrigation purposes. Upon the receipt of applications, they usually determined the availability of the resource and approved them, but often with conditions. Occasionally, however, applications were denied, as in the case of a petition of a group of farmers to bring additional water out of Brigham Canyon. Other farmers protested; the court investigated, and, deciding that there was not enough water for all, denied the application. The courts also extended their jurisdiction over the construction of canals and dams, approving some, modifying others in the interest of the welfare of the community.[11]

After the water was diverted, it needed to be distributed equitably among the users. Distribution was initially undertaken by officials of the church. The colonists came as a church, they settled in the Great Basin as members of a church, the church allocated land to them, and the church through its appointed watermasters distributed the stream water among them. On August 22, 1847, the High Council, composed of twelve churchmen, appointed the first watermaster, one Edson Whipple, to distribute the waters of City Creek.[12]

Nevertheless, as soon as the 135 ten-acre blocks had been divided into nineteen wards, each under the jurisdiction of a bishop, the High Council delegated the task of water distribution to the bishops. They in turn delegated the task to specially appointed watermasters. The same procedure was followed in the outlying communities. Controversies over water use were decided in the bishops' courts, composed of the bishop and two counselors. If either party was aggrieved, the decision could be appealed to the High Council.[13]

In the cities, the water distribution responsibilities of the bishops were soon assumed by municipal governments. When the State of Deseret incorporated the cities of Salt Lake, Ogden, Provo, Manti, and Parowan early in 1851, it gave them control of the waters within their boundaries. The city council of Salt Lake City lost no time in assuming this responsibility and on March 21, 1851, created the office of watermaster with authority "to appoint one or more assistant watermasters in each of the bishops' wards." Other cities made similar provisions. When Utah Territory reincorporated these cities, it continued to delegate to the municipalities.[14]

In a similar manner, the bishops lost control of the water within their wards when the territorial government gave that control to the counties. The county governments of Davis, Salt Lake, and Weber counties responded by appointing watermasters in 1852, although in some other counties the bishops' authority over the distribution of water continued for a number of years.[15]

The role of watermaster, whether he was appointed by a bishop, municipal council, or county court, was a very responsible one. Like the *majordomo* in the Southwest, he was in charge of the distribution of the very life-blood of the community. As was the custom in the Southwest, he distributed water by a system of rotation, delivering to each user a "stream" of irrigation water for a certain length of time, depending on the user's needs. He was usually in charge of the repair of ditches in the spring, requesting the labor of each user in proportion to that person's use of the water. Maintenance during the irrigation season was also his responsibility. When controversies arose, he was the first "court" of arbitration, although his decision could be appealed to the county or municipal authorities.[16]

The Saints' system of water administration was created for a society based on subsistence agriculture. In the 1870s, with the growth of commercial agriculture and its demand for increased supplies of water, the system began to show signs of strain. As controversies became more heated and bitter, arbitration by the church and governmental authorities became more difficult. A controversy over the allocation of the waters of Big Cottonwood Creek resulted, in 1879, in the creation of a board of arbitration, which allocated to each user a fraction of the flow. At the same time a controversy between the communities of American Fork and Pleasant Grove over the waters of the American Fork River worsened.[17]

With disputes increasing and existing legislation unenforced, an all-Mormon legislature in 1880 rescinded the statute of 1852 and abandoned Utah's distinctive water-control institutions. In their place, the legislature adopted the laissez-faire, individualistic institutions of the other western states and territories, adding another episode to what Gustive O. Larson called the "Americanization" of Utah. The statute was a law of capture; it provided for a property right in water that was not to be acquired by a grant from the state—gone was the theory of public ownership—but by a prospective water user constructing a canal with "diligence" and diverting the stream "for any useful purpose"—in short, by seizure. Rights so acquired were claims to the use of water until they were confirmed by the county selectmen in a nonjudicial determination procedure; in other words, until they were "proved up." The selectmen, the law read, were "to receive, hear and determine all claims to the use of water, and on receipt of satisfactory proof of any right to the use of water having vested, to issue to the person owning such right a certificate . . . for recording." Unfortunately, this statute was enforced in only a few counties and Utah became, like the other western states and territories, a jungle of uncontrolled appropriations and undetermined water rights.[18]

3
Farmers, Investors, and Ditches

The Mormons were not the first people of north European derivation to irrigate in the western territories, although they were the first to demonstrate that an entire commonwealth could be maintained by the practice. The first to irrigate were the factors of the Hudson's Bay Company at Forts Okanogan and Nez Perces in the semiarid Columbia Basin. They did so, not by ditches, but by subirrigation, by taking advantage of water tables near enough to the surface to moisten the roots of the plants. The first in the Pacific Northwest to irrigate from ditches were Henry H. Spalding and Marcus Whitman, Protestant missionaries to the Nez Perces and Cayuses. Arriving in the valleys of the Snake and Columbia rivers in 1836, they too raised crops by subirrigation until drought convinced them of the desirability of irrigating from ditches. At his Lapwai mission near present-day Lewiston, Idaho, Spalding dug a ditch during the autumn of 1839 and recorded in his diary that he irrigated grain the following summer. When the traveler Thomas Farnham visited Marcus Whitman during September 1839, Whitman was still relying on subirrigation at the Waiilatpu mission. However, like Spalding he irrigated crops from a ditch in 1840, so successfully that the next year the Cayuses tried to steal the water in it for their crops.[1]

The Protestant missionaries were soon followed by the Catholic Black Robes. Those under the leadership of Father Pierre-Jean DeSmet established St. Mary's Mission in the Bitterroot Valley of present-day Montana. The date was October 1841. Surviving records do not record the season that the missionaries, with Indian labor, dug a ditch, but presumably in 1842 they diverted the Burnt Fork Creek to irrigate a plot of land that Father Nicolas Point referred to as "the farm."[2]

After the missionaries came the miners and the cattlemen, the miners to divert streams into sluice boxes, the cattlemen to irrigate an occasional meadow or maybe a garden. After them came the farmers to raise crops to sell in the mining camps or at the army posts. Like those of the Mormons, the farmers' first ditches were short and small, constructed to irrigate the bottom lands bordering the streams. Sometimes they were dug by individual farmers, sometimes by groups of farmers, usually with primitive surveying instruments. Consequently, these initial ditches tended to be crooked, steep, and subject to erosion.[3]

Several of these early ditches may be mentioned. The first diversion in central Colorado to supply the fifty-niners with vegetables was a short, narrow ditch to irrigate two acres. It was a profitable investment for its owner, David K. Wall, who confided to the editor of the *Rocky Mountain News* in February 1860 that the previous season he had realized two thousand dollars from the sale of his produce. Similarly the first ditches in Nebraska were small; that of Washington Hinman in Lincoln County, dug in 1863, furnished water for a plot of corn and vegetables, which he sold at Fort McPherson. Another early ditch was the Penwell Ditch, a diversion of the East Gallatin River in southwestern Montana. Constructed by the Penwell Brothers—Merritt and Oscar—during the spring of 1864, it was approximately two and a half miles long and provided moisture to raise wheat, which they sold to miners in Alder Gulch. The next spring fourteen other settlers banded together to make a somewhat longer diversion from the West Gallatin River. A member of the community, Albert Jerome Dickson, recorded its construction. "At the intake," he wrote, "a six or seven-foot cut was necessary and for nearly half a mile it was pretty hard digging, mostly pick and shovel work. Then we used the plows and a home-made scraper or 'stone-boat' [the go-devil of the Mormons], a v-shaped affair of timbers, constructed the width of the ditch and weighted. Several furrows were plowed and the stone-boat, drawn by six or eight horses, followed and threw the dirt out at each side."[4]

By the beginning of the twentieth century, myriads of these small ditches were extending from the western streams like the bones of a fish from its spine. In Montana in 1919, these ditches numbered 8,378, with an average length of 1.6 miles, and provided water for 58 percent of the state's irrigated acreage. Similarly, those in neighboring Wyoming numbered 4,782 with the same average length and irrigated 60 percent of this state's acres under ditch. Most of these small ditches have survived and provide irrigation facilities that are wasteful of water. Consolidation would conserve the resource, but water users fear the expense and loss of their water rights.[5]

The small bottom-land ditches, together with their crude diversion dams of brush and rock, could be constructed by individual water users or neighborhoods, but to irrigate the bench lands above them required greater resources. In imitation of the Mormons, these were supplied in a number of localities by colonies—that is, by cooperative communities.

The first of the irrigation-based colonies was organized by a group of German immigrants living in San Francisco, California. Under the leadership of George Hansen, they organized the Los Angeles Vineyard Society on February 24,

1857, to found a colony in the southern part of the state for the production of grapes and wine. A civil engineer, Hansen had two years earlier surveyed land bordering the Santa Ana River, some forty miles downstream from the Mormon colony at San Bernardino. It seems reasonable to assume that he was acquainted with that colony, although there is no evidence to support the theory. At any rate, in founding the colony for the society he adopted a pattern of settlement similar to that of the Mormons. He purchased 1,165 acres some miles distant from the Santa Ana and divided them into half-acre town lots and twenty-acre farm tracts, enough to accommodate fifty colonists. He then provided for the irrigation of the land by the construction of a seven-mile canal and distributing laterals.

The settlers named their colony Anaheim, but did not arrive until Hansen had finished surveying the site and constructing the ditches. While still in San Francisco, they selected their lots and vineyard tracts by lot, as the Mormons had in Salt Lake City. Then to operate and maintain the ditches they organized a cooperative irrigation company, with each colonist receiving one share of stock. Each share represented the amount of water necessary to irrigate a colonist's lot and tract. Moreover, the society, again following Mormon custom, declared the water appurtenant to the soil.[6]

A second irrigation colony was established in Colorado. It was organized by Nathan C. Meeker, the agricultural editor of Horace Greeley's *New York Tribune*. He had become familiar with the colony idea through his membership in a Fourier colony and his acquaintanceship with the Oneida community. Convinced that colony living provided a better quality of life, he proposed, in the columns of the *Tribune*, to found a colony in the West. In this proposal he had the encouragement of Horace Greeley, who in 1859 had visited Salt Lake City and was impressed by the cooperative aspects of Mormon colonization. In response to Meeker's call, a group of men met in New York City, organized the Union Colony, and selected a locating committee, composed of Meeker, R.A. Cameron, and W.C. Fisk. These men, who were joined by Henry T. West in Omaha, visited prospective sites in Colorado and then traveled on to Salt Lake City, where West had friends and relatives. Here they acquired valuable information regarding farming by irrigation. Returning to New York City, they announced in the spring of 1870 the selection of a site in northern Colorado, bordering the Cache la Poudre River, near its confluence with the Platte. Appropriately, they named the settlement Greeley.[7]

The new settlement was patterned after Salt Lake City. Like that community, it was surveyed and divided into lots comprising ten-acre blocks with outlying tracts for farming. "This land is to be furnished," read a circular dated May 16, 1870, "with water for irrigation. The Colony digs the ditches, and each member of the Colony is liable to assessment for cost of keeping the same in repair. It is estimated that the ditches for irrigating the lands of the Colony . . . will cost about $20,000, for which there is money in the Treasury."[8]

The Union Colony was a rather literate group—many of its members were business and professional people with college educations—but they were unfamiliar with irrigated agriculture. The organizers planned four canals, but only two were built. Canal No. 3, a short diversion from the south side of the Cache la Poudre, was a bottom-land canal, dug in the spring of 1870 to irrigate the town lots. Canal No. 2 was designed to irrigate the bench lands north of the river. Construction was supervised by Edwin S. Nettleton, the colony engineer. Nettleton, who was destined to play a major role in western irrigation development, was a native of Ohio, where he had attended Oberlin College. After leaving college, he was engaged in the lumber business for a while, then served as a county surveyor in Pennsylvania before deciding to move west in the spring of 1870. On the way, he met the Union Colony at Council Bluffs and joined it. He commenced the excavation of Canal No. 2 in the fall of 1870, but soon ran into difficulty. The colonists had greatly underestimated the cost of ditch excavation and the $20,000 they had appropriated was insufficient to build two canals, let alone four. So to complete No. 2, the farmers who used it had to pay an additional assessment of thirty-five cents an acre. Even so the canal was too small—it had to be enlarged and extended twice—and too crooked and steep. As a consequence, it eroded; as one farmer said, "it cut out on one side and silted on the other at every turn." The colony made repairs, but they added to the cost of construction. When in 1878 its ownership was transferred to the water users organized into a cooperative ditch company, the thirty-six-mile-long canal had cost eighty-seven thousand dollars.[9]

A second irrigation colony founded in Colorado encountered even greater difficulties. It was the Chicago-Colorado Colony, which founded Longmont. Organized in Chicago on November 22, 1870, it was patterned after the Union Colony. In fact, Meeker and Cameron were invited to Chicago to assist in its creation. A location committee selected a site on St. Vrain Creek and the colonists, on arriving in March of 1871, surveyed and divided the land into town lots and small farm tracts. At the same time, they commenced the construction of a ditch. Unfortunately, they made the same mistake as the Greeley people and underestimated the cost. In this case the colony failed to build the canal. Instead, five colonists organized a corporation known as the Highland Ditch Company, and undertook the construction. Since the canal was owned by them, they charged the other colonists for using the irrigation water.[10]

The construction of irrigation systems by corporations, frequently referred to as commercial companies, became popular in the West during the succeeding two decades.

Those who organized them saw, or thought they saw, opportunities to invest their money and to realize handsome returns by selling water to farmers. Capital was available, sometimes locally, but more often in eastern cities or in Great Britain. British money organized the Northern Colorado Irrigation Company, which constructed in the early 1880s the 85-mile High Line Canal, a diversion of the Platte, at a cost of $650,000. Joseph M. Carey of Wyoming in 1883 organized a corporation known as the Wyoming Development Company. It diverted the waters of the Laramie River by means of a 2,105-foot timber and stone dam and conducted them through a 2,380-foot tunnel into a neighboring watershed to irrigate more than fifty thousand acres near present-day Wheatland, Wyoming. Another corporation, the Pecos Irrigation and Investment Company of southeastern New Mexico, dug two canals, a northern one 30 miles long to irrigate lands south of Roswell and a southern one 50 miles long to supply moisture to lands in the vicinity of Carlsbad. The southern project involved the construction of two dams across the Pecos River; one created Lake McMillan and the other caused the formation of Lake Avalon. In Idaho, the Idaho Mining and Irrigation Company, organized with New York capital, commenced in the 1880s a large project under the supervision of an engineer named Arthur D. Foote, husband of the novelist Mary Hallock Foote. He constructed a diversion dam of rock and earth, 220 feet long and 43 feet high, in the canyon of the Boise River. To conduct water to 600,000 acres, he excavated a canal, 40 feet wide, with a carrying capacity of 2,585 cubic feet per second, a veritable river in itself.[11]

Projects of this magnitude were costly—costly to construct, costly to maintain and operate. Consequently, in order to defray these expenses and provide stockholders with dividends, the corporation managers imposed a charge on the use of irrigation water. The relationship that was established between the company and the user was embodied in a contract that described the land to be irrigated, the quantity of water to be delivered, and the charge for it. In case of a shortage of water, the contracts usually relieved the company of responsibility and provided that the water available be prorated among the users. The contract charges were for a "perpetual" right to the use of water in the company's ditch and an annual rental or service fee. The perpetual right charge was designed to pay for the construction cost and the annual rental to defray the costs of maintenance and operation.[12] These charges varied. Within the state of Colorado, the cost of a perpetual right varied from five dollars an acre to fifteen dollars. The Northern Colorado Irrigation Company charged ten dollars. The annual rentals likewise varied, although they were subject to regulation. The constitution of Colorado, written in 1876, empowered the county governments to regulate water rentals when specifically authorized by the legislature. Such authorization was not long in coming. Farmers under the corporation-owned Highland Ditch near Longmont became dissatisfied with its charges and requested relief from the 1879 legislature. This assembly responded by enacting a law authorizing county commissioners to fix irrigation water rates, a law that became a model for similar legislation in many other western states.[13]

Farmers under the High Line Canal, however, objected to payment for the perpetual right, the right to use water. They referred to it as a "royalty" or a "bonus" and sought to have it removed. One of the farmers, Byron A. Wheeler, requested water from the company, but refused to make the royalty payment. The company in turn refused to deliver the water. Wheeler responded by seeking a writ of mandamus from the courts, but while they considered his suit, his crops suffered during the dry summer of 1886. Thereupon, the farmers sought legislative as well as judicial action. They met in Denver on January 6, 1887, organized the State Farmers'

Irrigation and Protective Association, and appointed a legislative committee to draft a bill outlawing the perpetual right payment. The farmers contended that according to the constitution of Colorado the stream waters belonged to the people and that consequently a corporation-owned canal had no right to charge for the water. Like the railroads they were only common carriers and could only charge for the transportation service that they performed.[14]

The debate was lively, heated, and at times acrimonious. The farmers denounced the Northern Colorado Irrigation Company as the foreign, English company that was "choking the life" out of the agricultural industry, a monopoly that was imposing "an extortion which is unbearable." Waving the flag, one agrarian spokesman declared that the "idea of a royalty upon water was un-American. It was not the idea of an American brain or an American heart." The contest was especially bitter in the senate, where opponents tried to emasculate the bill by amendments, but the bill passed. Royalty was declared illegal and a few months later the state supreme court agreed. Nevertheless, agrarian harassment continued until the company sold the High Line Canal to the city of Denver in 1915.[15]

Other canal corporations experienced similar problems. Farmers in the Boise Valley of Idaho objected to the rates charged by the Boise City Land and Irrigation Company and asked their county commissioners to establish a reasonable rate. Believing that the rate set by the commissioners was too low, the company applied to a federal court for annulment. When the court refused, the company in desperation sold its project to the farmers organized into an irrigation district.[16]

Many canal corporations overestimated the rate at which the lands under their ditches would be settled by farmers. Too often the farmers were slow to arrive; or they arrived but refused to purchase water rights; or they were speculators, holding the land for resale. In any case, the expected revenues did not materialize and the companies were forced into bankruptcy. The lands under the canal of the corporation that built the Bear River Valley project in northern Utah were all filed on by speculators or by uncooperative farmers before the completion of the survey. Consequently, few water rights were sold and within four years of its organization the company went bankrupt. It was reorganized and submitted to a partial foreclosure sale and a second reorganization before the project was sold to the Utah Sugar Company in 1901 at a fraction of the original cost. After the construction of its two projects in New Mexico, the Pecos Irrigation and Investment Company, which was reorganized as the Pecos Irrigation and Improvement Company in 1890, went into the hands of the receiver in 1898. It then split into two companies—the northern one, controlled by James Hagerman, evolved into a user-owned company, while the southern company, organized as the Pecos Irrigation Company, solds its project to the United States Reclamation Service following the destruction of the Avalon Dam by a flood in 1904. After completion of its diversion works—dam and headgate—and only six miles of the main ditch, the Idaho Mining and Irrigation Company failed and the construction company recouped its expenses by purchasing the project at a sheriff's sale in 1894. Two years later it sold the unfinished project to the users, who completed it with the aid of the federal government. Similarly, the Grand River Ditch Company, organized in western Colorado in 1886 by the Traveler's Insurance Company, declared bankruptcy in 1894, and its project was purchased by the farmers.[17]

In general, the canal corporation as an institution could construct irrigation projects, but could not successfully operate them. By the turn of the century 90 percent of the companies were said to be in financial distress. One by one most of them disposed of their projects to the water users. Whereas in 1909 commercial companies were irrigating

44,872 acres in Idaho, that number had shrunk to 6,503 ten years later. By 1969, only ninety-six of these companies had survived in the seventeen western states, of which forty-two or nearly one-half, were in California. In Idaho, they numbered only four; in Wyoming, three.[18]

More numerous and certainly more permanent than the canal corporation are the mutual irrigation or ditch companies. A mutual irrigation company is a cooperative formed by a group of irrigators to provide water for their fields. Like other agricultural cooperatives they are private associations organized to provide services for members. Each member is a stockholder, and each share of stock represents a share of the water supply, expressed in fractions, quantity, or irrigated acreage.

The mutual irrigation companies grew out of neighborhood or community construction of ditches. After ditches were constructed it was necessary to determine the quantity of water to which each farmer was entitled and to create an institutional structure for the upkeep of the project and the division of water among the users. It has been assumed that this type of company originated in Utah among the Mormons, but similar groups were organized in other frontier communities in which men gathered to build small projects, as in the Boulder Creek drainage in Colorado. In Utah, community control of irrigation systems evolved into mutual irrigation companies under the stimulus of the Irrigation District Act of 1865. Enacted by the territorial legislature, it authorized the formation of companies within irrigation districts with the power to levy taxes for the construction and maintenance of irrigation projects. In response to this legislation many districts were organized, but their existence was short-lived. Established water users objected to being taxed for the construction of canals for newcomers and the districts were usually soon dissolved. In most cases, the companies organized under the authority of the act survived and were reorganized as mutual irrigation companies. In Colorado, these companies became so numerous by 1872 that their shareholders were able to persuade the territorial legislature to exempt from all "Territorial, county or municipal" taxation the ditches of mutual companies. Four years later the state's constitution makers incorporated this provision into the constitution of Colorado, and the privilege was later incorporated into the constitutions of Arizona, New Mexico, Utah, Idaho, and Wyoming. With the passage of the Capper-Volstead Act of 1922, Congress provided a similar exemption from federal income taxes.[19]

Farmers have organized mutual ditch companies by meeting together, electing boards of directors, and agreeing on the number and character of the shares of stock. Incorporation has been optional, but the companies owning the larger systems have usually incorporated in order that they may enter into contracts and assume legal obligations as corporate persons. The bylaws empower the directors to levy assessments either in money or labor for the construction and maintenance of the project and to employ ditch riders or watermasters to distribute the water equitably and fairly among the shareholders. Two examples will suffice to illustrate the nature of these associations, one in Arizona and the other in Montana.[20]

The Hardy Irrigation Canal Company was organized on December 6, 1870, by six Arizona pioneers to irrigate lands south of the Salt River near the future site of Tempe. A month or so later they changed the name to the Tempe Irrigating Canal Company. The organizers appropriated twenty thousand miner's inches of the Salt River and authorized the issue of 200 shares of stock, each share representing a fraction of the diversion. Later when they reduced the number of shares to 109 and the appropriation to eleven thousand inches, each share represented 1/109 of the appropriated water. Construction began the next spring. Shares could be purchased for two hundred dollars or acquired through labor at the rate of two dollars per man-day or three dollars a day for a man with a mule or a horse. Most, of course, chose to acquire shares through labor. Whatever the source of the funding, the project builders constructed a diversion dam in the Salt River and excavated a ditch that partly followed the trough of a prehistoric Hohokam canal. When completed with a number of extensions, the Tempe Canal was twenty-four miles long and irrigated more than twenty-four thousand acres. The shareholders elected the first ditch riders, but soon that authority was delegated to the board of directors. To pay for the maintenance, the board imposed assessments on each share of stock. Since these charges varied from ten dollars to one hundred dollars in the 1870s, collection was sometimes difficult.[21]

Another irrigation cooperative is the Big Ditch Company, which was organized in 1900 to purchase a corporation-owned project in southern Montana. A diversion of the Yellowstone River thirty-five miles west of Billings, the Big Ditch was constructed by the Minnesota and Montana Land and Improvement Company during 1882–83. Initially the corporation charged a rental of one dollar a miner's inch, but when with the consent of the county commissioners it doubled the rental, the farmers objected. One of them sought through the courts to force the company to furnish water at the former rate. When he lost the case he stole water from the ditch and was apprehended, fined, and jailed. After more than a decade of friction with the water users, the corporation agreed to sell. As a consequence, the farmers under the ditch met in Billings on May 15, 1900, organized the Big Ditch Company, and purchased the project. They divided the capital stock into sixty-four hundred shares, each share representing two miner's inches or sufficient water to irrigate five acres. Then they elected a seven-member board of directors, which in turn employed a ditch rider to keep the project in repair and to distribute the water among the share-holders.[22]

The identity of interest between the water users and the mutual irrigation company of which they are shareholders has made the institution a popular one for the management of irrigation projects. Of the 20,306,283 acres irrigated in the seventeen western states in 1969, 45 percent were supplied with water by mutual irrigation companies; in Montana they serviced 62 percent of the irrigated acreage; in Utah, 87 percent.[23]

Another institution adapted to the needs of western society was the development corporation, a cross between the corporation and the mutual irrigation company, devised by Californians. Capitalists transforming the southern California desert into communities organized corporations, purchased land, dug ditches, formed mutual irrigation companies, and with the sale of acreages transferred stock in the companies to the settlers. The development corporation grew out of controversies over the use of water in the corporation-owned canal at Riverside.[24] This community was founded by John Wesley North in the same year that Nathan Meeker established Greeley. Like Meeker, North was an idealist; he was also the father of two towns in Minnesota and a member of two state constitutional conventions. North organized with the financial assistance of a San Francisco capitalist the Southern California Colony Association, which purchased land near San Bernardino. This association, however, was not an association of settlers like the Union Colony, but a corporation that subdivided the land into lots and tracts and dug a ditch to irrigate them. It did not give the settlers water rights; instead it charged them a "royalty" and an annual rental. Consequently, friction between the corporation and the colonists was not slow in emerging.[25]

Although the Chaffey brothers—George and William—are usually credited with the invention of the development corporation, L. M. Holt seems to have been the originator of the idea. He had come to southern California in the middle 1870s as a member of the Pomona colony, but moved to Riverside to become editor of the *Riverside Press and Horticulturist*. Consequently, he was familiar with the conflict between the settlers and the Southern California Colony Association when the Chaffeys moved to Riverside from Canada and undertook the establishment of the Etiwanda Colony in 1881–82. They organized the California Land Improvement Company, purchased fifteen hundred acres lying fourteen miles west of San Bernardino, surveyed and divided the property into ten-acre tracts, and diverted water from a nearby stream. Then after conversations with Holt, the Chaffeys organized a mutual irrigation company (they are called mutual water companies in California) with fifteen hundred shares of stock, one share for each acre to be irrigated. Thereupon the brothers sold their water rights to the water company, receiving in return the fifteen hundred shares, which they transferred to the colonists, by giving the newcomers one share of water with every acre of land they purchased. When the colony lands had been sold, the colonists owned the water company.

No sooner was the Etiwanda venture successfully launched, than the Chaffeys purchased additional land and founded the community of Ontario. Again they organized a mutual company, the San Antonio Water Company, divided its stock into fifteen thousand shares, and distributed one share with each purchased acre of land. So successful was this system of project development that it became the pattern for the settlement of southern California, notably for the founding of Pomona, Pasadena, and Redlands.[26]

In addition to the development corporation, Californians also invented a viable irrigation district. The inability of either the corporation or the mutual ditch company to coerce those who refused financial support was a weakness of these institutions. To remedy this deficiency the California legislature in 1887 passed the Wright Act, authorizing the creation of irrigation districts. Passage of the law climaxed more than a decade of controversy over the nature of California's property right in water and the character of agencies to construct irrigation projects. The farmers of the San Joaquin in particular sought some way of constructing irrigation facilities that would enable them to increase the productivity of fields worn out by the continuous cropping of wheat. With a long-time interest in some form of irrigation district, the farmers of Stanislaus County elected to the state legislature in 1886 a young lawyer from Modesto, C. C. Wright, "for the express purpose of advocating some measure providing for the municipal control of water for irrigation."[27]

The Wright Act enabled a county board of supervisors to form an irrigation district on the receipt of a petition and a favorable vote by two-thirds of the electorate within the area. The statute gave authority to an elected board of directors to construct an irrigation project, funded by bond issues secured by taxes imposed on all the agricultural lands within the district. Like other taxes, district taxes constituted a lien on the land. If they became delinquent, the land could be sold by the district at a sheriff's sale. In other words, the districts had coercive powers.

Adopted by the other sixteen western states, the irrigation district went through several decades of testing and redesigning. Farmers with limited experience with irrigation enterprises overestimated the water supply, underestimated the cost, and fumbled at management. Too often they were the gullible victims of speculators and undertook unsound ventures. They issued bonds, borrowed money, and defaulted on repayment. Opponents not wishing to have their lands included in the districts challenged the constitutionality of the district legislation, although the U.S. Supreme Court gave a favorable decision to the proponents, in *Fallbrook Irrigation*

District vs. *Bradley* in 1896. Experience with the institution, however, led to improvements. Water users learned that the failure of the Wright Act to provide for state supervision was a mistake and after 1897, beginning with legislation in Idaho, this weakness was remedied. By 1969, there were 469 irrigation districts, irrigating 7,192,781 acres in the seventeen contiguous western states.[28]

Farmers organized irrigation districts to construct new projects or to improve or acquire old ones. The first two districts formed in California, the Turlock and Modesto irrigation districts, were organized to irrigate 250,000 acres of land on both sides of the Tuolumne River in Stanislaus County. The two districts constructed a diversion dam, costing half a million dollars, across that stream. The first irrigation districts in the Bitterroot Valley of Montana were created to construct reservoirs to provide supplemental water, while the farmers in Idaho's Snake River Valley used the district to acquire and manage projects built by corporations. One example is the acquisition by the Nampa Meridian Irrigation District in 1905 of the Boise City Irrigation and Land Company's project. Similarly, water users in the Imperial Valley of California organized an irrigation district in 1911 to assume ownership and control of the project of the bankrupt California Development Company. The United States Bureau of Reclamation also found the institution useful in organizing water users on its projects for repayment purposes.[29]

One weakness of the irrigation district is that farmers alone assume project costs, but people in the trade centers also benefit. This situation led to the invention of the water conservancy district. To conserve water in the Roswell Artesian Basin, state representative Clarence E. Hinkle introduced a bill into the 1931 New Mexico legislature enabling communities to establish artesian conservancy districts and to tax urban as well as agricultural properties. Under the authority of the legislation the citizens of Chaves and Eddy counties organized the Pecos Valley Artesian Conservancy District. The citizens of northern Colorado seem to have been unaware of the New Mexico organization when they created the Northern Colorado Water Conservancy District in 1937 to provide a broad tax base for the repayment of a portion of the costs of the Colorado-Big Thompson Project. Other states have followed the example of Colorado—notably Utah, Wyoming, Nevada, and Nebraska.[30]

4
Construction by States

As soon as streams became rather fully appropriated, irrigators began to observe that during the nongrowing season much water was flowing past them and going to waste. They concluded that if it could be stored it could be used to increase the amount of land under cultivation or to extend the irrigating season for the benefit of late-maturing crops. The problem lay in the cost of constructing storage reservoirs. Some farmers, however, were able to build small ones. A community of Mormons seem to have constructed the first reservoir for the storage of irrigation water. In 1871 the inhabitants of Newton in northern Utah dammed Clarkston Creek and built a reservoir to water their town lots and farming tracts during the late summer. Repaired and enlarged several times during the following fifteen years, it had a capacity of 1,566 acre-feet. Similarly, during the 1890s irrigators in the Cache la Poudre Valley of northern Colorado transformed natural depressions at the base of the mountains into storage reservoirs to irrigate potatoes and other crops that mature late in the summer. One of these structures, known as Terry Lake, was constructed north of Fort Collins by stockholders of the Larimer and Weld Irrigation Company to store 6,887 acre-feet at a cost of seventy thousand dollars.[1]

California land developers built larger reservoirs. To impound water for the irrigation of Redlands, Frank E. Brown erected a curved masonry dam in a narrow gorge of Bear Valley in the San Bernardino Mountains. It was built during 1883-84 at an estimated expense of $120,000, and had a capacity of thirty-six thousand acre-feet. A few years later the San Diego Land and Town Company built a similar reservoir to irrigate lands bordering the San Diego Bay. Created by a dam ninety feet high, it had a capacity of eighteen thousand acre-feet and cost $234,000. Although these structures demonstrated the value of the storage of irrigation water, they also revealed construction costs greater than most communities of farmers could afford. Consequently they initially sought the assistance of state governments.[2]

As early as the 1870s an articulate minority in California was demanding state construction and ownership of irrigation works. In 1873, James H. Budd, who would be the state's governor from 1895 to 1899, told a group of farmers in Stockton that the "sovereign power of the State must be invoked in some form to enable the necessary canals and works to be constructed." He added,

> The use of the waters of the valley is as essential to the farmer . . . as is the land which he cultivates, and he has the right to demand of the government, which he supports, to exercise its power and its credit to afford him that use. . . .
>
> It may be stated as a safe rule, that when works of internal improvements are vital to the prosperity of the people of the State, and such works cannot be constructed by private corporations . . . such works should be constructed by the State itself.

A number of newspapers echoed this demand, including the *Stockton Independent* and several San Francisco papers. When the constitution of 1879 was in the writing, advocates of state ownership introduced a provision requesting the legislature to "provide for the construction and maintenance of a system of irrigating canals and ditches in this State, said ditches and canals to belong forever to the State, and remain under its direct control," a proposal that was given scant attention.[3]

Within a decade the leaders of Colorado's antiroyalty movement, most of them officers in the state Grange, were also advocating state ownership. When the Grange met in annual convention in 1888, its members resolved: "That we . . . affirm our oft-repeated resolution in favor of state ownership of ditches for irrigation, domestic and drainage purposes and do hereby declare that we will vote for no man for a legislative office unless he shall favor and vote for a bill to that end." When two years later the Grange leaders helped to organize the Populist Independent party, they saw to it that the party platform included a plank requesting state ownership of ditches and reservoirs. The state legislature responded to this sentiment by authorizing the construction of three canals and five reservoirs. The reservoirs were completed by the state, but not the canals, which were to have been constructed with prison labor. The state penitentiary board commenced the construction of State Canal No. 1 near Canon City in the spring of 1890, but opposition forced its discontinuance. Enthusiasm waned, State Canal No. 2 was never started, and State Canal No. 3 was finished by the federal government.[4]

In the West in the late 1880s, there was a growing belief that if either the states or the corporations were to construct projects, particularly those involving reservoir construction, they needed the assistance of the national government, assistance in the form of cession of public lands to the states. The convention of the Colorado State Grange in 1888 that favored state ownership also requested "of the general government the donation of the arid lands of [their] state." When the next year the special committee of the United

States Senate under the chairmanship of Senator William M. Stewart of Nevada visited the western states, it found support for cession in Nevada and Wyoming, especially in Wyoming where the territorial engineer, Elwood Mead, made a "vigorous presentation" in behalf of the proposal. Support for the idea increased as the drought of these years continued into the 1890s. A series of drought-provoked conventions in Nebraska led to the calling of a national irrigation congress to meet in Salt Lake City, under the energetic sponsorship of Utah's Governor Arthur L. Thomas. It met September 15–17, 1891, and, with Elwood Mead playing an influential role in its deliberations, it memorialized Congress to cede the public lands within the western states to those states for the support of irrigation development. The next year, Senator Francis E. Warren of Wyoming incorporated the proposal into a bill that he introduced on March 9, 1892, into the Senate. It provided for the cession of "all public lands," except mining lands, to the western states and territories "for the purpose of aiding in the reclamation thereof." Although he was able to marshal little support for this bill, in 1894 his colleague, Senator Joseph M. Carey of Wyoming, introduced a compromise measure that Congress passed and President Grover Cleveland signed on August 17, 1894.[5]

Carey's legislation, which became known as the Carey Act, gave each of the eleven westernmost states and territories up to one million acres of the "desert lands" within their jurisdictions if they would reclaim and sell them to settlers in 160-acre tracts. No patents were to be issued until the settlers had irrigated one-eighth of their tracts. To construct the projects, states contracted with development corporations. Seeking to curb speculation, lands were not to be sold to settlers who had not purchased water rights of a corporation. Like settlers in the southern California communities, each purchaser of a water right gained a share in a mutual irrigation company. When the construction of the project was completed and the rights to the water sold, the corporation transferred management of the project to the mutual company. The states usually sold the land for fifty cents an acre, but the price of water rights varied from project to project.[6]

In spite of the hopes of its proponents, the Carey Act had limited use. Of the 3,897,860 acres that the Department of the Interior set aside for use by the states, 1,065,195 were patented by 1957. Only Wyoming and Idaho used the act extensively; California, Arizona, and Washington did not take advantage of the legislation at all. The Carey Act development corporations faced the same problems as the earlier corporations—miscalculation of costs, overestimation of the water supply, and a dearth of settlers to purchase the water rights. Too often they also failed.[7]

Wyoming was the first state to accept the provisions of the Carey Act. The acceptance legislation placed its administration in the state under the State Board of Land Commissioners, which in April 1895 began receiving applications. The first to be approved was an application by the Big Horn Basin Development Company, under the leadership of S. L. Wiley, for a diversion of the Greybull River near the Mormon settlement. The company constructed the irrigation works and attracted German settlers from Illinois and Iowa, but hesitated to turn the project over to them. Consequently, the settlers sought from the courts control of their water supply.

The commissioners awarded the second authorization to establish a Carey Act project in Wyoming to the Shoshone Land and Irrigation Company with William F. (Buffalo Bill) Cody serving as its president. The company dug a canal out of the Stinking Water River, soon to receive the more euphonious name of Shoshone, founded the town of Cody, and sold water rights for ten dollars an acre. Senator Carey took advantage of his act by extending its provisions to his Wheatland project. By 1938, Wyoming's Carey Act projects numbered thirty-two, with 222,071 acres patented.[8]

The largest Carey Act project in the nation is the Twin Falls South Side Project in Idaho. It has been very successful. To construct it, the state in 1903 entered into a contract with the Twin Falls Land and Water Company, organized by entrepreneurs from Pittsburgh, Pennsylvania. They built the Milner Dam across the Snake River and excavated a wide, eighty-mile-long canal. The company had little difficulty attracting settlers, who paid $25 an acre for water rights. With most of the rights sold, in 1910 the company transferred control of the project to the water users. By 1932, this project had 192,750 acres under ditch, after an expenditure of $3.6 million.[9]

Less successful was the neighboring Twin Falls Oakley Project, also built by financiers from Pittsburgh. They made the mistake of overestimating the water supply. The project was designed to irrigate 43,893 acres, but there was only enough water in the stream to irrigate 21,000. Launched in 1908, the development company attracted farmers with relative ease. Soon they had purchased water rights for 30,000 acres, most of them on the installment plan. Nevertheless, the company experienced construction delays and the project was not finished when it went broke in 1913. Lacking water, the farmers refused to pay their installment and assessment charges and, when the bondholders reorganized the corporation and sought to collect the money, there was trouble. There was more trouble when the project was completed in 1915 and droughts revealed the insufficiency of the irrigation system. The farmers demanded water and, when the company could not supply it, they appealed to the state land board in charge of the Carey Act projects. The board ordered the reduction of the project to 21,000 acres. The farmers whose farms were excluded from the project sought redress, but in vain. The bondholders lost more than 50 percent of their investment and the excluded farmers moved away. Today the Twin Falls Oakley Project survives, providing water for 11,000 acres.[10]

Unfortunately the troubles that bedeviled the Twin Falls Oakley Project were not unique. Of the 1,335,787 acres segregated for Carey Act projects in Idaho (Idaho was allocated an additional 1,000,000 acres in 1908), 614,894 were patented. Many projects were proposed but never built. Many development corporations failed, but even so, more acres were reclaimed under the Carey Act in Idaho than in any other state, three times as many as in Wyoming.[11]

The Carey Act was not the only congressional statute to subsidize state construction of irrigation projects. When Utah became a state in 1896, Congress ceded to it fifty thousand acres for "the establishment of permanent reservoirs for irrigation purposes." The new state placed the money from the sale of the lands in a fund and used it for the construction of two reservoirs and for loans to construct several others. In 1898, Congress made a similar grant to the territory of New Mexico for the same purpose.[12]

If the cession of public lands to the states to subsidize irrigation development was born of drought and depression, so was the launching in 1934 of a program of construction by Montana. The crop years of 1930 and 1931 had been especially dry and that of 1934 would be drier. Moreover, the Great Depression had caused unemployment and destitution, prompting Governor F. H. Cooney to call the legislature into special session to create an agency to conserve and utilize the waters of the state as well as to provide employment. The assembly responded by creating the State Water Conservation Board to construct, operate, and maintain small irrigation projects. With the aid of the Works Progress Administration and the Public Works Administration, which had been established by the New Deal, the board by

1966 had constructed 181 projects. They included 141 reservoirs to store 438,000 acre-feet of water and 815 miles of canals. One of the larger projects was the Deadman's Basin Project in the central part of the state, which diverted water from the Musselshell River. Built in 1934–41, it consisted of a diversion dam, a reservoir with a storage capacity of 57,000 acre-feet, and conveyance canals. Constructed in cattle country, it brought winter feed and stability to the area, as did the Ruby River Project to a valley in southwestern Montana.[13]

Droughts also played a role in the state of California's decision to undertake some project construction. A prolonged drought was beginning when in 1919 Robert Bradford Marshall proposed the transfer of water from the northern part of California, where the rainfall is abundant, to the southern part, where it is scant. Marshall was the chief geographer of the United States Geological Survey. He proposed the diversion of the headwaters of the Sacramento River into two canals, one on each side of the Central Valley, to irrigate lands in the San Joaquin Valley. He further proposed the diversion of the Kern River through canals and tunnels across the Tehachapi Mountains into the Los Angeles area. In scope and magnitude his plan was breathtaking, a proposal for the alteration of the geography of California, a blueprint for the utilization of the state's waters.[14]

The legislature responded in 1921 by authorizing the Department of Public Works to conduct a state-wide investigation of California's water resources. The study lasted for ten years. Each biennium the department made a progress report to the legislature until in 1931 state engineer Edward Hyatt presented the state water plan. It retained the general idea of the Marshall proposal, less the diversion across the Tehachapi Mountains. Submitted to the 1933 legislative assembly, it was enacted into law as the Central Valley

Project Act. It provided for the construction by the state of California of a large reservoir at the base of Mount Shasta on the main stem of the Sacramento River in northern California, canals and pumping plants to conduct the reservoir water southward to irrigate the lower San Joaquin Valley and the Friant Dam to capture the waters of the upper San Joaquin River for use on lands in the upper part of that valley around Bakersfield. To finance the gigantic project, the act empowered the state to issue $170 million in bonds. But during the depression the state could not find buyers for the bonds. So it approached the United States Bureau of Reclamation, which accepted the proposal in 1935 as the Bureau's Central Valley Project. When in 1944 the state had second thoughts about the transfer and offered to reacquire the project through purchase, the Bureau refused.

With another drought in the offing, California undertook in 1945 a new series of investigations, which resulted in the publication of several bulletins, culminating in 1957 in Bulletin No. 3, *The California Water Plan*. Following Marshall's plan more closely than Hyatt's proposal, it proposed to dam the headwaters of the Feather River tributary of the Sacramento and to transfer them southward through a long aqueduct extending across the Tehachapi range to the cities of arid southern California. To finance this new state project, the legislature passed the California Water Resource Development Bond Act, better known as the Burns-Porter Act, authorizing the issuance of $1.75 billion in general obligation bonds. Submitted to the people for approval, it precipitated a noisy controversy, north versus south. Led by the *San Francisco Chronicle*, the north sought to keep its water, but the voters on November 8, 1960, approved the California State Water Project by a majority of 3,008,328 to 2,814,384. The Oroville Dam impounding the Feather River waters was completed in 1967 and with the completion of the California Aqueduct in 1972 one million acre-feet of the waters of northern California were flowing southward, one-half for irrigation in the San Joaquin Valley and one-half to the water-short cities south of the Tehachapi Mountains.[15]

Indeed, water resource development by the states has been significant, but it has been eclipsed in the public mind by the spectacular engineering triumphs of the national government.

5

National Reclamation

In 1864 William N. Byers, editor of the *Rocky Mountain News* in Denver, appealed to the national government for assistance in irrigation development, but it was not until 1873 that Congress responded by authorizing an investigation of the irrigation possibilities in California's Central Valley. An appropriation of five thousand dollars enabled Colonel B. S. Alexander of the Army Corps of Engineers and George Davidson of the Coast Survey to conduct the survey and to issue a report, which was a forerunner of Robert Marshall's plan. Four years later, after experimentation in Lassen County, California, Congress increased its encouragement of irrigation by passing the Desert Land Act.[1]

The Desert Land Act offered a section of the public domain at $1.25 an acre to any U.S citizen who would claim it, make a down payment of $.25 an acre, and irrigate one-eighth of it within three years. The offer was restricted to the "desert lands" in what is now the eleven western states plus the Dakotas, although Colorado was not included until 1891. Payment of the remaining $1.00 for each acre was due at the time of presentation of proof of irrigation.[2]

There is no question but that the Desert Land Act encouraged irrigation. Although historians have contended that many settlers failed to comply with its provisions, some did and dug bona fide ditches. Canal corporations used it, sometimes as fraudulently as the settlers. The commissioner of the General Land Office referred in his annual report for 1888 to a canal company in Wyoming that had acquired seventy-eight desert-land entries through the use of absentee entrymen, most of whom lived in the eastern states. As might be expected, the company furnished the money to pay for the patents. In a similar manner the Arizona Canal Company in the Salt River Valley acquired forty thousand acres to include in its irrigation project. Unfortunately, the act was based on the false assumption that within three years the average pioneer could establish a farmstead, construct an irrigation project, and supply eighty acres with water. Moreover, by 1877, the bottom lands that could be irrigated by individual effort were rather well settled. The need now was for associational efforts to build high-line canals and reservoirs to irrigate the bench lands. Corporations and mutual ditch companies could construct the high-line canals, but reservoirs in the mountains were more difficult. Yet as irrigated acreage in the valleys expanded, the need for such reservoirs to store the winter and spring waters became the greater.[3]

Sensing this interest, Senators Henry M. Teller of Colorado and William M. Stewart of Nevada early in 1888 introduced into Congress resolutions directing the United States Geological Survey to study the feasibility of establishing storage reservoirs, measure the flow of the streams, and locate reservoir sites and irrigable lands. To protect the lands under study from acquisition by speculators, on October 2, 1888, Congress withdrew them from land office entry until they were reopened to settlement by the president.[4]

Quite by chance the solons placed the Irrigation Survey, as it was called, in the hands of the foremost authority on the aridity of the West, Geological Survey director John Wesley Powell. He stressed the need to adapt humid-country institutions to western aridity; ten years earlier he had written

Report on the Lands of the Arid Region of the United States, a blueprint for institutional adaptation. It stressed the importance of irrigation in the region and recommended the storage of "the waters of the non-growing season . . . that they may be used in the growing season."[5]

With a firm conviction about the nature of his assignment, Powell lost no time in beginning it. He organized three teams of scientists, one to continue the topographical mapping that the Geological Survey had underway, another to measure the flow of the streams, and still another to locate promising reservoir sites. Since there were few men skilled in stream gauging, he established a training camp during the winter of 1888–89 in New Mexico on the Rio Grande and placed it under the supervision of Frederick Haynes Newell, a mining engineer with a baccalaureate degree from the Massachusetts Institute of Technology. With the arrival of spring, Newell's students spread out into seven states and territories to begin the measurement of western streams, which continues to the present day. To locate the reservoir sites, Powell recruited Arthur D. Foote and Edwin S. Nettleton as well as other prominent irrigation engineers. Nevertheless, the Irrigation Survey was short-lived. When, in accordance with the congressional directive, the General Land Office closed to entry all of the public domain west of the 101st meridian until Powell could identify the reservoir sites and irrigable lands, such a howl went up from the arid region that Congress on August 30, 1890, rescinded the legislation of 1888, virtually terminating the Irrigation Survey and reopening the western lands to settlement. Nevertheless, Powell, with his topographical mapping, stream gauging, and reservation of reservoir sites, had laid the foundations for national reclamation.[6]

While Powell's work was progressing, the prolonged drought, the financial and management difficulties of the canal corporations, and the hopes aroused by the Irrigation

Survey convinced irrigation promoters that government construction was the next step. The question was, Which government, state or federal? Initially the proponents of state construction, subsidized by cession of the public lands, were the more numerous, so numerous that they constituted a majority at the first irrigation congress at Salt Lake City.

Nevertheless, there were individual promoters and groups in the western states and territories who were advocating, during the late 1880s and early 1890s, direct federal assistance. In a convention convoked by Colorado's Governor Alva B. Adams in March of 1888 to consider reservoir construction, those who advocated federal aid outnumbered the people who favored reclamation by the states. That same year two groups in Greeley petitioned Congress for "an appropriation . . . to construct a system of reservoirs," while the next year the territorial governor of Washington recommended federal construction. The delegates from Montana who attended the Salt Lake City congress so disagreed with its cessionist majority that they returned home and held a state convention in Helena, January 7–8, 1892, which anticipated the Newlands Act of a decade later by declaring:

It is the duty of the General Government to aid in the development of the arid lands in the several States and Territories where such lands exist; and while we do not deem it desirable that the control and title to such lands should pass from the General Government to the several states containing them, we do nevertheless urge that at least the proceeds arising from the sale of such lands shall be applied to the supplying of water for their development for the purpose of agriculture, and we urge our Senators and Representatives in Congress to use every effort to accomplish such legislation as will bring about this desirable result, not only for our State, but for all other States and Territories similarly situated.

When the state legislature convened a year later Governor John E. Richards urged it to memorialize Congress in a similar manner. Although there were also proponents of federal reclamation in New Mexico, Nevada, and elsewhere, they remained in the minority until Captain Hiram M. Chittenden made his influential reservoir report in November 1897.[7]

In 1896 Congress had directed the secretary of war to survey likely reservoir sites in Wyoming and Colorado, an assignment that fell to Captain Chittenden of the Corps of Engineers. The importance of his report lay not so much in his identification of five reservoir sites as in his recommendation that the reservoirs be built by the national government.[8] With the limitations of the Carey Act apparent, the West quickly espoused the proposed solution, the more so because Chittenden recommended that the responsibility of the federal government be restricted to the construction of the reservoirs, leaving to the states the construction of the canals and the distribution of water in accordance with state protected water rights. The report was printed and distributed in 1898 and the next year, Senator Francis Warren of Wyoming, the same senator who had introduced the cession bill in 1892, requested a congressional appropriation to construct three reservoirs in Wyoming and one in Colorado. In that same year, 1899, George H. Maxwell, a California water-rights lawyer, organized the National Irrigation Association, financed by the railroads and other corporate interests to arouse support for national reclamation. When Congress refused to approve Warren's reservoir appropriation requests as well as one of his own, Congressman Francis G. Newlands of Nevada resorted to an omnibus approach. On January 26, 1901, he introduced a bill providing for the construction of irrigation projects by the federal government in each of the sixteen western states and territories. Since the bill provided for the construction by the federal government of the distribution systems as well as the reservoirs, many westerners opposed it until Newlands included a paragraph safeguarding vested water rights. Then, with the support of President Theodore Roosevelt, it was enacted on June 17, 1902, with relatively little opposition and debate.[9]

The Reclamation Act of 1902, frequently called the Newlands Act, authorized the secretary of the interior to construct irrigation projects in sixteen western states and territories (Texas was added in 1905) and to pay for them from the proceeds of public land sales in these jurisdictions. Water users were to repay the construction costs within ten years and the repayments were to be returned to a revolving reclamation fund for reuse. Settlers seeking government land within the boundaries of a project could acquire it according to the provisions of the Homestead Act, but no water was to be supplied to tracts of more than 160 acres under one ownership. The acreage limitation was designed to effect a wide distribution of the benefits of the act among the small farmers of the nation.[10]

The Department of the Interior quickly assumed its new responsibilities. The day after the president signed the bill, the director of the Geological Survey presented the secretary with a plan to create the Reclamation Service within the Geological Survey. The plan was approved on July 8, and Frederick Newell was placed in charge of the Service. In the interim since the Irrigation Survey, Newell had become the agency's chief hydrographer and had assisted Newlands in the drafting of the reclamation act.[11]

Eight months after the organization of the Reclamation Service, on March 14, 1903, Secretary Ethan Allen Hitchcock authorized the construction of the first national reclamation projects, five of them on the same day. They were the Salt

River in Arizona, the Truckee-Carson in Nevada, the Uncompahgre in Colorado, the North Platte in Wyoming and Nebraska, and the Milk in Montana. However, his authorization of the latter was conditional, awaiting an agreement with Great Britain allocating the waters of the Milk River as it flowed through southern Alberta. Other authorizations soon followed. By 1907 the secretary had approved twenty-four projects located in fifteen states.[12]

Most of these projects provided storage reservoirs, diversion dams, and distributing canals. Typical was the Salt River Project. As early as 1888 a local surveyor had discovered a site in the mountains east of Phoenix that an official of the Geological Survey in 1897 thought was the best in the West. "It would probably be impossible," he wrote, "to find anywhere in the arid region a storage project in which all conditions are as favorable as for this one." Consequently, in 1903, the Reclamation Service chose it as a reservoir site and began construction of a curved masonry 280–foot dam, impounding 1,382,000 acre-feet of water to furnish, through the Granite Reef Diversion Dam and distributing canals, an adequate and dependable supply of water for the Salt River Valley. Named the Roosevelt Dam, it was dedicated by Theodore Roosevelt on March 18, 1911. Similar in makeup was the Shoshone Project in northern Wyoming, designed to irrigate lands in the vicinity of Buffalo Bill's Carey Act project. Constructed in 1905–10, its 325-foot concrete dam was wedged into a gorge of the Shoshone River, creating a reservoir with a capacity of 439,800 acre-feet. Seeking supplemental water for their Mormon-built irrigation systems, irrigators in the Spanish Fork drainage of central Utah persuaded the Service to construct the Strawberry Valley Reservoir on the east side of the Wasatch Range, 1908–13, and to divert its waters through a 3.8-mile tunnel to their lands. Somewhat more complicated, the Truckee-Carson Project, renamed the Newlands in 1919, was designed to irrigate lands in the Truckee and

Carson valleys by means of two storage reservoirs, two diversion dams, and a system of distributing canals. Construction of a dam to divert the Truckee commenced in 1903, followed in 1911–15 by the erection of the Lahontan Dam to impound the waters of the Carson. However, when the Service sought to use Lake Tahoe at the headwaters of the Truckee as a storage reservoir, it encountered opposition from industrial interests and shoreline property owners. In response, a federal court restricted the project's use of the lake.[13]

Some of the secretary's authorizations were designed to complete projects begun by other agencies. Arthur Foote saw his dreams come true as the majestic Arrowrock Dam rose to a height of 350 feet in the Boise Canyon. At the time of its construction it was the highest dam in the world. The state of Colorado was only too willing to turn over to the Reclamation Service the boring of the Gunnison Tunnel for the Uncompahgre Project, a feat that took the lives of fifteen workmen. Similarly, the Pecos Irrigation Company petitioned the Service to take over its project in southeastern New Mexico after the flood of 1904 destroyed the Avalon Dam. In the Yakima Valley the Service acquired the properties of the largest corporation-owned canal in Washington. This was the Sunnyside project, built by the Northern Pacific, Yakima and Kittitas Irrigation Company in the early 1890s. Later in that decade, the company suffered financial reverses and the project was obtained by another corporation, the Washington Irrigation Company, in 1900. Neither company, however, had developed the natural reservoirs of the Yakima Valley when the Reclamation Act of 1902 was enacted. Consequently, with its passage the irrigators of the Sunnyside system demanded federal construction, and after several years of controversy the company sold the project to the government on March 28, 1906. The Reclamation Service enlarged and extended the purchased project, built the Tieton unit with its diverted waters flowing through five tunnels, and provided the irrigation systems with six storage reservoirs. Today, the Yakima Project, with 450,000 acres under ditch, is one of the larger reclamation projects in the nation.[14]

The national reclamation projects were engineering triumphs, but economic and social headaches. The men who planned them made mistakes similar to those of their predecessors. They generally estimated correctly the water supply, but underestimated the costs. Both the legislative and the bureaucratic planners failed to anticipate the rising prices as well as the demand of the settlers for construction of lateral and drainage ditches. In 1903 the Reclamation Service judged that the Salt River Project would cost $5,650,000; twenty years later it had cost nearly twice that amount. Increased costs meant increased repayment charges, which were difficult, if not impossible, to pay within a ten-year period. Ten years proved too little time for project farmers to pay for construction costs on top of payments for the land, buildings, fences, and implements. In addition there were the costs of preparing the fields for irrigation. Settlers found that more than half of the land on many projects was in private ownership and held for speculative prices. Moreover, the Service did not screen the applicants and many farmers arrived without sufficient capital and irrigated farming experience. This situation prompted the farmers to demand an extension of repayment time. The government had required the farmers on each project to organize water users' associations, so as to have an agency with which to contract for the payment of costs. These associations formed a national association in 1911 and began to lobby for the improvement of project conditions. Their lobbying provoked the Service to appoint an irrigation adviser and Congress to extend the repayment time. To aid the settlers in solving the problems of farming in the desert, in 1913 the Service appointed I. D. O'Donnell of Billings, Montana, as supervisor of irrigation. O'Donnell was a farmer who had had years of experience as an irrigator under the corporation-built Big Ditch. Congress, on August 13, 1914, passed the Reclamation Extension Act increasing the repayment period to twenty years.[15]

The government's concessions seemed to meet the needs of the project farmers until the post-war depression of 1921–23 so depressed agricultural prices that the water users again requested relief. Congress responded with the approval of several moratoria on repayments, while the secretary of the interior, Hubert Work, transformed the Reclamation Service into the Bureau of Reclamation and appointed a committee of special advisers on reclamation to study the situation on the projects.[16]

The new committee, usually referred to as the Fact Finders' Committee, included Elwood Mead, whom Work later appointed the second commissioner of reclamation. Mead, through service in Wyoming, Australia, and California, had become convinced that the government should do more than build dams and canals, that it should also screen the settlers and provide them with land readied for planting, fences, farm buildings, credit, and agricultural advisers. Reflecting his influence, the committee, when it issued its report in 1924, urged economic reform and Congress responded by authorizing the screening of settlers, the appointment of a director of reclamation economics, and the extension of repayment time to forty years. It stopped short, however, of the appointment of project agricultural advisers and the preparation of farms for occupancy. When the Great Depression created new stresses on the projects, Congress in 1939 provided, where desirable, extension of repayments beyond the forty years.[17]

From the beginning, federal reclamationists had envisioned reclamation projects as more than irrigation projects. They saw them as also promoting navigation, flood control, and the generation of electric power—in other words, as multipurpose projects. The Reclamation Service built its first hydroelectric plant in connection with the Salt River Project to provide power to operate machinery used in building the Roosevelt Dam. Realizing that when the dam was completed power would be available for leasing to industries and communities, Congress in 1906 authorized its sale, with preference being given to municipalities. By 1914 the Service had eleven hydroelectric plants in operation, selling 38 percent of the power and using the income to reduce construction costs.[18]

Nevertheless, the heyday of multipurpose reservoir-building did not begin until 1928, when Congress authorized the Boulder Canyon Project. By this time others besides agriculturalists had become interested in water conservation. Cities were growing in the arid West, needing water and electricity. This was especially true in southern California, where the population of Los Angeles alone was approaching one million. Although the initial demand for the project came from the irrigators of the Imperial Valley, the major thrust came from the southern California municipalities. Supported by both rural and urban groups, Congressman Phil Swing and Senator Hiram Johnson introduced a succession of bills into Congress. They provided for the construction of a large reservoir on the main stem of the Colorado River and the diversion of a fraction of its waters into a canal to water lands in the Imperial Valley. After a series of legislative defeats, Congress passed the measure in 1928 and the Bureau of Reclamation commenced construction in 1931. During the next five years, a 726-foot concrete dam rose in the Black Canyon of the Colorado River, creating a reservoir, appropriately named Lake Mead, with a storage capacity of 32 million acre-feet. At the base of the dam, the Bureau installed two generating plants with a capacity of 1,332,300 kilowatts, available for sale to the communities of the Southwest. In addition, the Bureau built several dams on the Colorado

River below Lake Mead. One of them, Parker Dam, was built to divert water into the Colorado River Aqueduct for use by the cities of southern California. Another dam, the Imperial, diverted water into the All-American Canal.[19]

With the advent of the New Deal and the need to provide public works for the unemployed, Congress authorized several large projects in rapid succession—the Columbia Basin and the Central Valley in 1935, the Colorado-Big Thompson in 1937. The principal feature of the Columbia Basin Project is the Grand Coulee Dam, the largest concrete structure ever built by man, creating the Franklin D. Roosevelt Lake, which provides hydroelectric power and irrigation water for half a million acres in the Big Bend of the Columbia River. The Bureau of Reclamation took over the construction of the Central Valley Project from the state of California, building the Shasta Dam on the Sacramento and the Friant Dam on the San Joaquin during 1938–45. While Californians were seeking a solution to their problems, a series of dry years was revealing to the farmers of the South Platte Valley of Colorado the need for supplemental irrigation water. The need prompted a request to the Bureau to construct the Colorado–Big Thompson Project, a transmountain diversion of a portion of the Colorado River to the South Platte Valley. Built during 1938–59, its major component is the thirteen-mile long Alva B. Adams Tunnel through the Continental Divide, with accompanying reservoirs, canals, and power plants.[20]

These were large projects, but the Missouri River Basin and the Colorado River Storage projects, authorized during and after World War II, were larger. They involved entire basins and included many subprojects. Congress, by the passage of the Flood Control Act of 1944, approved the construction by the Army Corps of Engineers and the Bureau of Reclamation of more than one hundred storage reservoirs in the Missouri Valley. The Corps has built the Garrison, Oahe, and Fort Randall reservoirs on the main stream of the

Missouri in North and South Dakota, while the Bureau has dammed the tributaries at more than thirty places. In enacting the Colorado River Storage Act of 1956, Congress authorized erection of three large dams in that watershed, namely, the Flaming Gorge, the Navajo, and the Glen Canyon dams. The legislation initially provided for a fourth dam, Echo Park, but because its reservoir would flood a portion of Dinosaur National Monument, environmentalists forced its deletion from the act. Similarly, they forced the removal in 1968 of the Bridge and Marble Canyon dams from the act creating the Central Arizona Project. This project, now under construction, is designed to transport, by pumps, tunnel, and aqueduct, Colorado River water to the cities and farms of Central Arizona.[21]

In 1970, the Commissioner of Reclamation reported that in the sixty-eight years since the passage of the Reclamation Act the Bureau and the Reclamation Service had constructed 276 reservoirs with a combined storage capacity of nearly 134 million acre-feet of water. Nearly one-fifth of the dams creating these man-made lakes —49, to be exact—were equipped with power plants generating some 7 million kilowatts of electricity. Moreover, these reservoirs, diversion dams, and distributing canals furnished irrigation water to approximately 6 million acres. These acres, however, constituted only one-third of those irrigated in the seventeen western contiguous states by irrigation organizations. The other two-thirds were supplied by projects built by the states or by institutions of the private sector.[22]

6
Modification of
a Property Right

As soon as the first ditches were dug, the streams diverted, and droughts reduced the amount of water available for irrigation so that there was not enough for every user, the question of the character of the property rights in those streams arose. This question, of course, was an important one, although at first glance it seems not to have been too difficult to answer.

The courts of common law in England and the United States had developed a rule defining property rights to water, known as the Doctrine of Riparian Rights. The doctrine had presumably been adopted by the territorial or state legislatures of the West when they adopted the common law system.[1]

Pioneer lawyers found a classic statement of the riparian doctrine in Chancellor James Kent's *Commentaries*. The famous New York jurist wrote, "Every proprietor of lands on the banks of a river has naturally an equal right to the use of the water which flows in the stream adjacent to his lands, as it was wont to run . . . without diminution or alteration." It will be noted that this property right is restricted to riparian owners, that is, to those whose lands border a stream, the word *riparian* being derived from the latin word *ripa*, meaning the bank of a stream. Nonriparian owners cannot possess this right; it inheres only in riparian lands and may not be separated from them except by a legal process. Moreover, the right is correlative—it must be shared coequally with the other riparian owners. Finally, the doctrine prohibits alteration of the stream. Instead it requires that a stream be allowed to flow in its natural watercourse as it was accustomed to flow undiminished, unobstructed, and unchanged in quality.[2]

This rule is a very satisfactory one for humid areas where the rainfall is abundant and streams are used for navigation. In English jurisprudence it is as old as the thirteenth century, when Bracton declared that water must flow through a watercourse as it was "accustomed to flow . . . . [neither] in a lower or a higher, or a thinner, or a more rapid stream than before, or . . . diminished in any way." Of course, if the law were strictly applied, the provision would prevent all use; in practice, the courts allowed riparian owners to use streams for household and livestock watering purposes.[3]

However adapted the doctrine may have been to humid areas, it was ill-suited to arid areas where the rainfall is less than twenty inches. Its restriction to riparian lands would have prevented the irrigation of the extensive nonriparian lands in the arid West. The correlative nature of the riparian right required that the waters of a stream be divided equally, or at least proportionately, among the water users. This characteristic makes it a variable right, expanding and contracting with the number of users and with the varying flow of the stream. It does not give the security needed in agricultural enterprises. Moreover, the prohibition against alteration of the flow of a stream made it impossible to divert large quantities of water for irrigation. Faced with an unadapted water right, the western pioneers either rejected it or modified it. The Californians did both.

A year or two after the California legislature in April of 1850 approved the common law with its riparian property right as the "rule of decision" in judicial controversies, a new property right emerged in the goldfields on the tributaries of the Sacramento River. The discovery of gold in the tailrace of Sutter's mill triggered an avalanche of gold seekers. Arriving by land and by sea, they established mining camps in an area that only recently had been acquired from Mexico by the Treaty of Guadalupe Hidalgo. As yet there were no land offices and little local government; the miners were trespassers on the public domain. Nonetheless, they had need of government, of some form of association, to protect their mining claims. So in camp after camp they met and organized mining districts, adopting rules for the definition of their property rights in the gulches. These rules limited the size of claims, restricting one to each miner. They required miners to post notices of their claims and to record them with district recorders, following the pattern of the claims clubs in the Middle West. To retain their claims, miners had to work them with diligence; otherwise they were forfeited. When questions of right arose, they were settled by reference to priority. Since the miners were squatters on the public domain, they applied the law of the public domain, first in time, first in right. He who filed first on a quarter section of land in the land office had the better right to it. Similarly, the miners ruled that he who recorded a claim first had a prior right to that claim.[4]

After the days of the pan and shovel gave way to ditches and sluiceboxes, questions of right to use the streams arose. When they did, the miners applied the same rules to water as they had to the land—first in time, first in right. He who diverted water first had the prior right to it to the extent of his diversion for use on both riparian and nonriparian lands. To perfect the right, ditches had to be dug with diligence and the water applied to beneficial use. It was not to be wasted. As with the claims, when the use ceased, the right ceased. Here was the genesis of a new property right at variance with the riparian right.[5]

Nonetheless, no one seems to have initially objected, except the justices of the supreme court of California; certainly the federal government and the state legislature did not complain. In fact, by legislation in 1851 the California legislature accepted the miners' rules as the law of the diggings by a statute that declared, "In actions respecting 'Mining Claims,' proof shall be admitted of the customs, usages, or regulations established and in force at the bar, or diggings, embracing such claim; and such customs, usages, or regulations, when not in conflict with the Constitution and Laws of this State, shall govern the decision of the action."[6]

Although the state court rejected the new property right in *Eddy* v. *Simpson* in 1853, two years later the justices approved it in *Irwin* v. *Phillips*. The case dealt with a conflict over the diversion of a stream flowing through the public domain. In giving the opinion of the court, Justice Solomon Heydenfeldt noted that both the United States and the state of California had allowed settlers on the public lands to develop a new legal system governing the protection of property rights in land and water. These were "the rights of miners to be protected in the possession of their selected localities, and the rights of those who, by prior appropriation, have taken the waters from their natural beds, and by costly artificial works have conducted them for miles over mountains and ravines, to supply the necessities of gold diggers." He observed that these rights had become so "fully recognized . . . that without any specific legislation . . . they are alluded to and spoken of in various acts of the Legislature in the same manner as if they were rights which had been vested by the most distinct expression of the will of the law makers." Justice Heydenfeldt concluded that the state legislature had sanctioned the diversion of streams and that controversies arising from their use "must be decided by the fact of priority, upon the maxim of equity, *qui prior est in tempore, potior est in jure.*" And so the customs and regulations of the miners became the law of the commonwealth of California, those defining property rights in streams becoming known as the Doctrine of Prior Appropria-tion.[7]

Nevertheless, the legislature neglected to codify the customs of the diggings until 1872, when as part of the civil code it defined the appropriation right:

Section 1410. The right to the use of running water flowing in a river or stream or down a cañon or ravine may be acquired by appropriation.

Section 1411. The appropriation must be for some use-ful or beneficial purpose, and when the appropriator or his successor in interest ceases to use it for such a purpose, the right ceases.

Section 1412. The person entitled to the use may change the place of diversion, if others are not injured by such change. . . .

Section 1414. As between appropriators, the one first in time is the first in right.[8]

Having defined the right, the code provided a method for acquiring it. A would-be appropriator was to "post a notice, in writing, in a conspicuous place at the point of intended diver-sion," the notice to indicate the amount of water claimed, the purpose for which it was claimed, the place of intended use, and the means of diversion. Within ten days of posting the notice, the appropriator was to file a copy in the office of the county recorder and within sixty days of the posting was to commence construction of the project. The code required him to "prosecute the work diligently and uninterruptedly to completion, unless temporarily interrupted by snow or rain." If these rules were followed, the date of priority was to be the date of posting the notice.[9]

Notwithstanding the more recent legislative and judicial actions, the California Supreme Court continued to recognize the riparian right. In fact, the legislature inserted in its codification section 1422, which read: "The rights of riparian proprietors are not affected by the provision of this title." The courts, however, modified the right to allow a reasonable use for irrigation. In a contest in 1865 between two users of a stream in Solano County, the supreme court in *Ferrea* v. *Knipe* gave a riparian proprietor "a right to a reasonable use of the water," but added that he had "no right to so appropriate it as to unnecessarily diminish the quantity in its natural flow." The court was recognizing two property rights in water, often in the same stream—the appropriation and the riparian. The question was, Which would prevail?[10]

The question did not become a live issue until in the 1870s the *ranchos* in southern California gave way to orange groves and colonies based on irrigation. Since these developments were based on the assumption that the Doctrine of Prior Appropriation was the law of California, the colony leaders became concerned in 1879 when the state's supreme court decided in favor of the riparian right in *Pope* v. *Kinman*, a case that had come to it from San Diego County. The southern Californians responded to this threat to their property rights in water by drafting a bill to limit the rights of riparian owners to household and livestock uses, adding that such rights might be condemned if water was needed for irrigation. The bill was introduced in the 1880 legislature by J. W. Satterwhite, state senator representing San Diego and San Bernardino counties. The senate debated and approved it, but it was defeated in the assembly, where it met opposition from representatives of the northern counties. There the annual precipitation was greater and cattle-raising and wheat culture still predominated.[11]

Undaunted, the southern California irrigationists supported a bill in the next session of the legislature that, if it had passed, would have divided the state into two districts, each with its own water right. Riparian rights would prevail in the north, appropriation rights in the south. Introduced by Senator Grove L. Johnson of Sacramento, the bill met a fate similar to the Satterwhite bill. The senate approved it, the assembly defeated it.[12]

The irrigationists decided that greater organization of their efforts was needed. So they arranged a convention that met in Riverside, May 14–16, 1884. This convention was primarily a gathering of leaders from southern California. John Wesley North, founder of the Riverside colony, was elected president; L. M. Holt of the same community was chosen secretary. North spoke at length in defense of the appropriation right, arguing that it had the approval of both state and national governments. He proposed the rejection of riparian rights and the repeal of section 1422 of the civil code. The convention agreed with him, embodying his proposal in a resolution that read, "It is the duty of the legislature of this State to repeal Section 1422 of our Civil Code in order that there may be, upon our statute books, no *seeming* recognition of the English common law of riparian rights, which has not, and never had, an existence in this State." After considering a number of other reforms, the conference adjourned to meet later in the year in Fresno.[13]

Coincident with these events, a major legal contest was occurring in the upper San Joaquin Valley, a contest over rights in the Kern River. The litigants on one side were Henry Miller and Charles Lux; on the other, James B. Haggin and Lloyd Tevis. Miller and Lux, the cattle kings of the San Joaquin Valley, had acquired one hundred thousand acres of swamp lands along the Kern River. Haggin and Tevis had acquired lands above them along with two canals to irrigate their properties. They extended one of the canals, constructed a diversion dam, and diverted the entire river. Miller and Lux sued, contending that as riparian owners they had a right to have the Kern River flow through their lands undiminished and unaltered. The defendants countered by asserting that the Doctrine of Prior Appropriation prevailed in California, that it was an integral part of the common law rather than the riparian doctrine. When the trial court agreed with the defendants, the plaintiffs appealed to the state supreme court. On October 27, 1884, the court reversed the decision of the lower court and favored the plaintiffs.[14]

Consequently, when the appropriationists met in Fresno later that fall, they found that they had gained an ally. William B. Carr, an associate of Haggin, was in attendance. After several days of discussion, in which Carr participated, the Fresno convention appointed a committee to draft bills for presentation to the 1885 legislature. The committee drafted four bills, one of which, Assembly Bill 410, was patterned after the Satterwhite bill of 1880; it would repeal section 1422 of the civil code and give builders of irrigation projects the power of eminent domain. The bill passed the assembly, but opponents killed it in the senate. Again the southern Californians were thwarted.[15]

In the meantime, the state's high court granted a rehearing in the legal contest known as *Lux* v. *Haggin*. On April 26, 1886, it issued a second and final decision, the longest in California legal history. The court rejected neither doctrine; rather it accepted both as definitions of property rights in water in the state of California. In writing the majority opinion, Justice E. W. McKinstry assumed that, since common law was the legal system of the United States, riparian rights inhered in lands bordering streams on the public domain. Overlooking this fact, the federal government had allowed miners and agricultural settlers to develop the appropriation right on that domain in the West without objection; in fact, with approval. "Recognizing the United States as the owner of the lands and waters," wrote the jurist, "the state courts have treated the prior appropriator of water on the public lands of the United States as having a better right than a subsequent appropriator, on the theory that the appropriation was allowed or licensed by the United States." He was referring to contests, like those between Irwin and Phillips, that had arisen between appropriators on the public domain.

Nevertheless, he continued, land granted by the United States to individual settlers carried with it common-law riparian rights. The riparian doctrine governed property rights in water on private lands, the appropriation doctrine on public lands. Riparian rights, however, were limited by appropriations made to water public lands prior to their transfer to private individuals, but were superior to appropriations made after the transfer. In declaring that the riparian doctrine was a law of waters in the state of California, the court recognized that it allowed a reasonable diminution of a stream for irrigation and other consumptive uses. A majority of the justices ruled, "By our law the riparian proprietors are entitled to a reasonable use of the waters of the stream for the purpose of irrigation." And so the supreme court of California, in *Lux* v. *Haggin*, saddled the citizens of the state with a dual system of water law, a system that the legal profession dubbed the "California Doctrine."[16]

It was a strange arrangement, yoking into one system two discordant rights. One gave first appropriators preference to the waters of a stream for beneficial use on both riparian and nonriparian lands. The other right restricted the use of water for irrigation to riparian lands, giving each riparian owner a reasonable, coequal use of a stream flowing in its natural channel. As a consequence of this antithetical situation, controversies over rights in California's water were many, so many that in 1927 the California state engineer could report that in a sixty-year period "about seven hundred State Supreme and Appellate Court decisions on water matters" had been given.[17]

It is true, as Samuel C. Wiel, the noted authority on western water rights, observed, that the *Lux* v. *Haggin* decision was in the mainstream of American jurisprudence. Earlier decisions in the eastern states had allowed reasonable alterations of streams to provide power for the use of textile mills. Citing precedents, the California courts allowed reasonable diversions of stream waters, restricting their use to riparian lands and in case of scarcity allocating that use coequally or proportionately. Nonetheless, the modified riparian right was poorly suited to irrigation-based communities. In limiting use to riparian lands, it deprived millions of prospective farms of irrigation water. Cities deriving their water from streams found themselves prohibited from servicing their nonriparian residents. Irrigators found their water rights variable, varying with the flow and number of riparian neighbors.[18]

Yet, in spite of the problems caused by the California Doctrine, economic development continued, in fact, accelerated. Californians were able to surmount these problems for several reasons. In the first place, the Californians who had championed condemnation of riparian rights gained a signal victory when the passage of the Wright Act in 1887 gave irrigation districts the right of eminent domain and the power of condemnation. In the second place, the court recognized the acquisition of rights to water on nonriparian lands by prescription or adverse use. Irrigators who appropriated water and used it continuously for five consecutive years without protest from riparian owners were given a right to that use by the courts. Since diversions for the irrigation of nonriparian lands were usually made near the emergence of the streams from the mountains, they were frequently not noticed until the prescriptive right had matured. In the third place, although its decisions affected only two cities, the California Supreme Court awarded Los Angeles and San Diego pueblo rights to the entire flow of the Los Angeles and San Diego rivers on the basis of grants made to them by the Spanish and Mexican governments. Other cities gained water rights by the exercise of eminent domain and condemnation.[19]

The key problem in enforcing the modified riparian right lay in defining *reasonableness*. Whether a usage was reasonable or not was decided by judges on the basis of their convictions and prejudices. Nor were any effective limits placed on this legal subjectivity until the 1920s, when Californians were formulating a state water plan. The case that led to the limitation was *Herminghaus* v. *Southern California Edison Company*. The Herminghaus ranch consisted of eighteen thousand acres of riparian grazing land bordering the San Joaquin River for a distance of twenty miles. Annually the river flooded this property, soaking it and depositing a thin layer of fertilizing silt. The Southern California Edison Company, on the other hand, acquired small storage reservoirs in the mountains upstream and sought to enlarge them in order to store the flood waters and to use them for hydroelectric power. When the owners of the Herminghaus ranch realized that this development would terminate the flooding of their lands, they sought an injunction to prevent the impounding of the flood waters.

The California Supreme Court favored the plaintiffs. Even though the owners of the ranch were using only 1 percent of the flood waters and allowing the remaining 99 percent to flow wastefully into the ocean, the court declared that such use was reasonable. The use of the "flow and underflow and overflow" of the San Joaquin River to flood the plaintiffs' lands, it said, constituted a "reasonable use." The court added that, since the proprietors of the ranch as riparian owners had the right to have the river flow over their lands as it was accustomed to flow, the Southern California Edison Company was forbidden to construct storage reservoirs and retain the waters "to the inevitable detriment of not one but all of the lower riparian owners and users."

If the court's decision were the law, the state would be unable to implement the emerging state water plan and to utilize the flood waters of the Sacramento and San Joaquin rivers. Justice John W. Shenk dissented. He thought that "to employ this tremendous flow as a booster or a means of conveyance ... to lift the very small percentage of the flow" was an "extravagant and wasteful use of water." Thousands of Californians agreed. When in a few weeks the 1927 legislature met, it organized a joint committee of the assembly and senate to consider a remedy. Although the committee considered a proposal to nullify all riparian rights dating back to 1850, it decided instead to submit to the voters a constitutional amendment that would better define *reasonable use*. This amendment as enacted by the legislature read: "The right to water ... from any natural stream ... in this State is and shall be limited to such water as shall be reasonably required for the beneficial use to be served, and such right does not ... extend to the waste or unreasonable use or ... unreasonable method of diversion of water." It was approved by the voters by a two to one margin. Since the state's supreme court interpreted this amendment as allowing stream storage to prevent waste, it made possible the construction of the big storage reservoirs of the Central Valley and the California State Water projects.[20]

California was not the only state to modify the riparian right to permit the diversion of streams for irrigation. It was accompanied by Oregon, Washington, and the Great Plains states. Like California, sizable fractions of these states were humid; in fact, in each one the more humid areas were the first settled. The courts of first one and then another recognized irrigation as possible under the riparian doctrine, but emphasized that the use of streams for this purpose must be correlative and reasonable. Frequently, they supported their decisions by reference to *Lux* v. *Haggin*. The Oregon court in *Low* v. *Schaffer* declared that each riparian proprietor had "the right to use

a reasonable quantity of a stream for irrigating his land."
"A diversion of water for irrigation," it emphasized, "can
only be exercised reasonably, and with proper regard to the
rights of the other proprietors." In *Benton* v. *Johncox* and
numerous other decisions, the Washington court agreed.
The legislature of Dakota Territory, meeting in 1866 in
Yankton, some miles east of the ninety-eighth meridian,
approved the riparian doctrine by a statute that the supreme court of South Dakota construed as permitting
"riparian owners to use a reasonable quantity of the water
flowing over or along their lands for irrigating the same."
The Nebraska court in 1903 felt that in the organization of
Nebraska Territory "the common-law rule of riparian proprietorship was established as a part of its laws," that the
exercise of the riparian right for irrigation "must be reasonable." Two years later the supreme court of Kansas, in
Clark v. *Allaman*, noted that the doctrine of riparian rights
in that state had "been modified by various statutes enacted for the laudable purpose of encouraging irrigation."
The first territorial assembly of Oklahoma borrowed the
Dakota statute of 1866, while the Texas court consistently
safeguarded the riparian right, but allowed its modification
for the purpose of irrigation. In *Watkins Land Co.* v.
Clements, the Texas Court announced, "Each riparian owner
is entitled to use the water of a stream which flows by or
through his land for the purpose of irrigation, provided such
use is reasonable."[21]

Among the Rocky Mountain states, Nevada, in *Vansickle* v. *Haines*, initially recognized riparian rights in the
stream waters of that state, while Montana, one half in the
plains and one half in the mountains, favored the California precedents and accepted the modified riparian rule.
Chief Justice Decius S. Wade in *Thorp* v. *Freed* said he
preferred the riparian to the appropriation right because of
its equality rule. He feared that priority of appropriation

would lead to a "monopoly of water."[22] There is little question that, at least at one time, modification of the riparian right was a popular method of developing a satisfactory property right in western waters.

A New Property Right
in Western Waters

The discovery of gold in California aroused hopes of similar discoveries elsewhere. So as soon as the tributaries of the Sacramento were "panned out," miners began to disperse, seeking gold in gulches throughout the mountains of the West. They found it first in Nevada in 1850 and the next year in southwestern Oregon in the watershed of the Rogue River. They found it also in northeastern Washington in the vicinity of Fort Colville in 1855, but these placers yielded only moderate amounts of gold. More momentous was the discovery of William Green Russell in the vicinity of present-day Denver, Colorado. With experience in the goldfields of California, Russell headed a party of a dozen prospectors who found a placer in Dry Creek, rich enough to provide each of them with an income of ten dollars a day. This find, which occurred in July of 1858, triggered the Pike's Peak gold rush. While the rush was in progress, John H. Gregory and George A. Jackson made richer finds in the mountains on the north and south forks of Clear Creek. The fact that it was midwinter, January 1859, did not deter them. Jackson had to thaw the gold-bearing ground with a fire and Gregory nearly lost his life in a snowstorm returning from his discovery. Later that year prospectors discovered the Comstock silver lode in Nevada and the next year Elias D. Pierce struck it rich in Idaho on the Orofino tributary of the Clearwater. Then, in quick succession, other prospectors found pay dirt in the gulches of the Salmon River, followed by even richer finds in the Boise River gulches.

John White precipitated a similar rush by his discovery on July 28, 1862, of gold in Grasshopper Creek in what was to become southwestern Montana. The next year Bill Fairweather and Henry Edgar, seeking enough gold dust to provide them with "tobacco money," made a rich strike in Alder Gulch, which was followed during the summer of 1864 by another rich find in Last Chance Gulch, where the community of Helena promptly mushroomed. While these events were taking place in Montana, prospectors were making parallel finds in the Southwest, where in 1863 Jack Swilling, Henry Wickenburg, and their companions made finds of gold-bearing placers in the vicinity of Prescott, Arizona.[1]

Like their counterparts in California, miners in other western states found pay dirt in gulches on the public domain far from organized governments. When they organized mining districts and adopted rules and regulations to protect their claims in both dirt and water, quite naturally they patterned these rules after the laws they had known in California. Sometimes they indicated that priority of claim gave the better right; more often they omitted reference to priority, leaving that to the unwritten law of the gulches. Some of the Colorado miners, however, were explicit in their declarations of prior rights in water. When the organizers of the Downeyville Mining District met on July 29, 1859, to write their code, they included an article that read: "In all gulches or ravines where water may be scarce the oldest claimants shall have preferance [sic] and priority of right to water." Two months later, on September 26, 1859, the miners who formed the Illinois Mining District gave those using water on their claims "priority of right." Similarly in Gregory Gulch the rules provided that in case of scarcity of water, "priority of claim" would prevail.[2]

While the Pike's Peak gold-seekers were organizing mining districts in the mountains, they were creating in Denver
the Territory of Jefferson. During October 1859, they held a
constituent convention, adopted a constitution, and organized a government. Its territorial legislature convened on
November 7, 1859, and enacted a statute that legalized the
diversion of Clear Creek by David K. Wall for the irrigation of
his two-acre garden. This statute, which applied the rules of
the diggings to agriculture, authorized the use of stream
waters for irrigation of both riparian and nonriparian lands
and recognized that priority of appropriation gave the better
right. Section two read: "No person or persons making subsequent claims above said first claimant, shall turn out of its
original channel the waters of such stream in such a manner
as to deprive said first claimant of . . . irrigation privileges."[3]

Congress rejected the territory of Jefferson and replaced it
on February 26, 1861, with the territory of Colorado. This
territory's legislature in its first session approved "the records,
laws and proceedings of each mining district" and enacted a
statute of its own regulating irrigation. The statute, dated
November 5, 1861, may have been influenced by either Spanish-American or Mormon experience. It authorized the
diversion of water for use on both riparian and nonriparian
lands and granted irrigators the right to construct ditches to
their farms across the lands of others. In addition it provided
for the division of a stream in case of scarcity. In that even-
tuality, "the nearest justice of the peace" was to appoint three
commissioners "whose duty it shall be to apportion, in a just
and equitable proportion, a certain amount of . . . water upon
certain or alternate weekly days to different localities, as they
may, in their judgment, think best for the interests of all
parties concerned, and with a due regard to the legal rights of
all." Whether those rights were riparian or appropriative, the
statute did not say, but the supreme court of Colorado

regarded them as appropriative. The 1864 and 1868 sessions of the territorial legislature seemed to agree, for they specifically protected "priority of right" in the streams.[4]

Colorado's legislature was not the only western legislative assembly to validate the rules and customs of the miners. California's general assembly approved them in 1851 and Oregon's legislature did the same in 1864, but the federal government, the owner of the public domain, remained silent, giving neither its approval nor disapproval, until 1866. Then it took notice, in response to proposals for the sale of its mineral lands. The Civil War had been an expensive struggle and the Union government emerged from it deeply in debt.

To many people in the eastern states, including the secretary of the treasury, one way of reducing the debt was to sell the western mineral lands and deposit the proceeds in the federal treasury. When bills to effect this sale were introduced into Congress, Senator William M. Stewart of Nevada, who had been involved in litigation over the Comstock Lode, countered with a measure to protect possessory rights in western mines. Introduced by Senator John Sherman of Ohio, it was passed by Congress through an adroit legislative maneuver and became law on July 26, 1866.[5]

The Act of 1866 gave federal sanction to property rights in mines and waters as defined by the western mining districts. Secton 1 declared the mineral lands of the public domain to be "free and open to exploration and occupation by all citizens of the United States . . . subject to such regulations as may be prescribed by law, and subject also to the local customs or rules of miners in the several mining districts." Then after providing procedures whereby lode claims might be patented, the statute expressly gave its approval in section nine to appropriative rights in water: "Whenever, by priority of possession, rights to the use of water for mining, agricultural, manufacturing, or other purposes, have vested and accrued, and the same are recognized and acknowledged by

the local customs, laws, and decisions of courts, the posses-
sors and owners of such vested rights shall be maintained and
protected in the same."

To provide additional protection to the appropriative
right, Congress four years later, in July of 1870, amended the
act to read, "all patents granted, or pre-emption or home-
steads allowed, shall be subject to any vested and accrued
water rights, or rights to ditches and reservoirs used in connection with such water rights, as may have been acquired
under or recognized by the ninth section of the act of which
this act is amendatory."

Congress gave further approval to the appropriative right
when in the passage of the Desert Land Act of 1877 it included a provision which provided

> that the right to the use of water . . . on or to any tract of
> desert land of six hundred and forty acres shall depend
> upon bona fide prior appropriation; and such right shall
> not exceed the amount of water actually appropriated . . .
> for the purpose of irrigation and reclamation; and all
> surplus water over and above such actual appropriation
> and use, together with the water of all lakes, rivers and
> other sources of water supply upon the public lands and
> not navigable, shall remain and be held free for the appro-
> priation and use of the public for irrigation, mining and
> manufacturing purposes subject to existing rights.[6]

Through the passage of these legislative acts, Congress
made two important decisions in regard to property rights in
western waters. First, it approved the evolving doctrine of
prior appropriation and, second, it delegated to the states and
territories the authority to determine the character of the
property right in water within their jurisdictions. The U.S.
Supreme Court in *Kansas* v. *Colorado* stated, "Each State
has full jurisdiction over the lands within its borders, including the beds of streams and other waters. It may determine for

itself whether the common-law rule in respect to riparian rights or that doctrine which obtains in the arid regions of the West of the appropriation of waters for the purposes of irrigation shall control. Congress cannot enforce either rule upon any State." The way was now open for the Coloradans to perfect the appropriative right and develop it into a distinctive part of American water law.[7]

The territorial supreme court laid the theoretical basis of the Colorado water right by its *Yunker* v. *Nichols* decision in 1872. The controversy concerned the right of Yunker to construct a ditch across Nichols' property and to transmit irrigation water through it, a right that had been guaranteed by the territorial statute of 1861. Disregarding humid-country precedent, Chief Justice Moses Hallett declared that the right grew out of man's relation to his environment. The Colorado climate was so arid that irrigation was necessary to raise agricultural produce. "The principles of the decalogue," he contended, "may be applied to the conduct of man in every country and clime, but rules respecting the tenure of property must yield to the physical laws of nature, whenever such laws exert a controlling influence." His colleague, Justice Ebenezer Wells, concurred and added, "The right springs out of the necessity, and existed before the statute [of 1861] was enacted, and would still survive though the statute were repealed." Yunker's right was created by the aridity of the region.[8]

Three years later, on December 20, 1875, thirty-nine citizens assembled in Denver to write a constitution for the state of Colorado. Aware of controversies over the use of water in several localities in the territory, they incorporated into the document four paragraphs dealing with the problem. Article sixteen, section five read, "The water of every natural stream, not heretofore appropriated, within the State of Colorado, is hereby declared to be the property of the public, and the same is dedicated to the use of the people of the State, subject to appropriation as hereinafter provided." The first version of this paragraph, as submitted by the committee on irrigation, agriculture, and manufacturing, stated that the stream waters of the state were "the property of the people," but the phrase was altered by the committee of the whole to read "property of the public."[9]

The concept of stream waters as public property had its origin in Roman law. Roman lawyers divided streams into those that were private and those that were public. Public waters belonged to no one; rather, they were *res communes,* the common property of everyone—that is, of the public. Since the concept had been incorporated into the common law, the Coloradans were familiar with it. By its inclusion in their constitution, they sought to establish a legal basis for the appropriative right. Whereas the Californians found the source of the riparian right in a grant from the federal government, the Colorado constitution makers sought the source of the prior appropriation right in a grant from the state of Colorado. Consequently, they declared that the streams of the state belonged not to the federal government, but to the people of Colorado and subject to appropriation by them. Later Coloradans were of the opinion that, when President Ulysses S. Grant approved the constitution by the admission of the state into the Union, the federal government relinquished its ownership of the state's waters and its control over property rights in them.[10] Section six defined these rights:

The right to divert the unappropriated waters of any natural stream to beneficial uses shall never be denied. Priority of appropriation shall give the better right as between those using the water for the same purpose; but when the waters of any natural stream are not sufficient for the service of all those desiring the use of the same, those using the water for domestic purposes shall have the preference over those claiming for any other purpose, and those using the water for agricultural purposes shall have preference over those using the same for manufacturing purposes.

In this manner the framers of the Colorado constitution approved the appropriative right as the water right of the state of Colorado, giving preference first to domestic use, then to agriculture, and finally to manufacturing.

The two remaining sections related to irrigation: section seven guaranteed rights of way for ditches across the lands of others and in this manner affirmed the decision of the territorial court in *Yunker* v. *Nichols,* and section eight delegated to the boards of county commissioners the authority to establish the rates that would be charged for irrigation water in their respective counties.

Still there remained the question of the status of riparian rights within the new state. Did they still exist, as they did in California, along with the appropriation right or had they been extinguished? The supreme court of Colorado answered that question in 1882 by its decision in *Coffin* v. *Left Hand Ditch Company.* A group of farmers, organized into the Left Hand Ditch Company, had diverted the South Fork of the St. Vrain Creek for use on their lands in an adjoining watershed. Below the confluence of the South and North forks another neighborhood of farmers were irrigating fields lying along the main stem of the stream. A dispute arose between the two groups when during the dry season of 1879 the company diverted so much of the creek that the crops of the farmers below the confluence withered for lack of moisture. Thereupon the latter tore out a section of the ditch company's dam; the company then went to court, contending that as prior appropriators they had a prior right to the waters of the stream. The lower appropriators, led by George Coffin, countered with the argument that as riparian owners they had a right to have the St. Vrain flow as it was wont to flow down to their premises, the riparian doctrine having been in force in Colorado when they made their diversions. The lower court heard the case and decided in favor of the upper appropriators. Coffin and his neighbors then appealed.

In writing the opinion of the Colorado Supreme Court, Justice Joseph C. Helm used the philosophy of *Yunker* v. *Nichols*, without referring to the case. The climate was so dry, he wrote, that the irrigation of fields to produce food was an "absolute necessity." As a consequence, men had diverted streams, moistened their farms, produced crops, built houses, and established communities with the understanding that their investments would be protected by the rule that priority of appropriation gave the better right. Although Coffin and his neighbors contended that this rule had prevailed in the state only since the adoption of the constitution, the judge thought that it had existed from the date of the earliest appropriations in the state. He concluded:

The common law doctrine giving the riparian owner a right to the flow of water in its natural channel upon and over his lands, even though he makes no beneficial use thereof, is inapplicable to Colorado. Imperative necessity, unknown to the countries which gave it birth, compels the recognition of another doctrine in conflict therewith. And we hold that . . . the first appropriator of water from a natural stream for a beneficial purpose has . . . a prior right thereto, to the extent of such appropriation.[11]

And so by legislation, constitutional provision, and court decisions the state of Colorado abrogated the riparian right in surface waters and established prior appropriation as the exclusive water right within its borders. Since Colorado was the first state to take such action this legal system became known as the Colorado Doctrine.

Eventually all of the mountain states, including Alaska, followed Colorado's example, justifying their departure from common law by the argument of necessity. Nevada in 1885 was the first, overruling *Vansickle* v. *Haines* in *Jones* v. *Adams*. According to Samuel Wiel, the Vansickle decision was so unpopular that it stimulated the rejection of riparianism in Colorado and in several other of the Rocky Mountain states and territories. In rejecting its earlier decision, the Nevada court quoted *Coffin* v. *Left Hand Ditch Company* and justified its action by reference to the aridity of the climate and the necessities of the people. In a similar manner, the Idaho court in 1890 regarded the Doctrine of Prior Appropriation as "the lineal descendant of the law of necessity," while the Utah court the following year declared that riparian rights had "never been recognized in this territory," that if they had Utah "would still be a desert." *Yunker* v. *Nichols* was casting a long shadow. The supreme court of Wyoming, in *Moyer* v. *Preston* (decided in 1896), paraphrased the Coffin decision and concluded: "The common law doctrine relating to the rights of a riparian proprietor . . . is unsuited to our requirements and necessities, and never obtained in Wyoming."[12]

Utah's appropriative right, developed by the Mormons, was somewhat different from that in Colorado. It was molded by the Mormons' sense of ecclesiastical brotherhood. They divided rights in streams into two categories, early and late rights, or, as they called them, primary and secondary. Within these categories water was divided coequally or proportionately among the water users. Division was not by measurement in miner's inches or cubic feet per second, but by fractions of the stream flow, delivered by rotation. When the flow of the stream decreased, so did the delivery to each one. None were cut off, unless the stream went dry. All the "brothers" within each category were treated alike; their rights were correlative. In other words, the Utah water right was a blend of the appropriation and the riparian.[13]

In the Southwest, the pattern of abrogating the riparian right differed from that in the central states and territories. There the courts regarded the appropriation right as having existed under Spanish and Mexican dominion, if not before. Since the Kearny Code, promulgated by the military government of General Stephen W. Kearny in 1846, recognized this right, the New Mexico court concluded that the "common law doctrine of riparian rights was not suited to an arid region, and was never recognized by the people of this jurisdiction." In Arizona, the Howell Code of 1864 gave similar approval to the appropriation doctrine. Based on existing customs and laws, it declared "rivers, creeks and streams of running water . . . public, and applicable to the purpose of irrigation and mining." In times of scarcity, the code provided that "owners of fields shall have precedence of the water for irrigation, according to the dates of their respective titles or their occupation of the lands, either by themselves or their grantors. The oldest titles shall have precedence always." With these rules in force, the territorial legislature in 1887 formally abrogated the Doctrine of Riparian Rights and twenty-three years later the Arizonans incorporated the abrogation into their constitution.[14]

Not until 1921 did Montana follow in Colorado's footsteps. Anna Mettler owned a stock ranch near Helena, through which the Prickly Pear Creek flowed. As a riparian owner, she utilized the creek as a source of water for her household and livestock. In the vicinity, the Ames Realty Company farmed agricultural lands with water diverted from the creek below the Mettler ranch. During the drought of 1919, it changed the point of its diversion to a place above Mettler's property and drained the creek dry. Thereupon, the woman sued, contending that as a riparian proprietor she had a right to have the creek flow as it was accustomed to flow "without diminution in quantity or deterioration in quality." The company countered with the claim that as an appropriator it had a prior right to the waters of Prickly Pear Creek. The supreme court of Montana agreed and in *Mettler v. Ames Realty Co.* announced, "Our conclusion is that the common law doctrine of riparian rights has never prevailed in Montana since the enactment of the Bannack Statutes [the first territorial laws] in 1865; that it is unsuited to the conditions here."[15]

Still to join the Colorado Doctrine states was Alaska. Although the state has never formally abrogated the riparian doctrine, a federal court in 1910 announced that it was inapplicable to the territory, and the territorial court agreed. So did the framers of the 1956 constitution, for they incorporated into the document a sentence that read: "Priority of appropriation shall give prior right." When ten years later the legislature repealed the existing riparian legislation and designated appropriation as the exclusive method of obtaining a water right, Alaska was solidly in the Colorado camp.[16]

On the other hand, the Pacific Coast and Great Plains states followed the example of California and accepted both rights. After the extension of the mining frontier into the Pacific Northwest, the courts of Oregon and Washington recognized the existence of appropriative as well as riparian rights. Following the Black Hills Gold Rush, the legislature of Dakota Territory gave its approval to the priority principle, as did the Nebraska solons in 1889. Similar legislation in Kansas in 1886 and Oklahoma in 1897 validated prior appropriations on the public domain. Texas, bisected by the ninety-eighth meridian, authorized in 1889 the appropriation of water for beneficial uses, but restricted the authorization to the western, semiarid half. There was, however, an important difference in the implementation of the dual system of water rights in most of these states from the method used in California. Whereas in the Bear Flag State the courts consistently enforced the riparian right, in the other California Doctrine states, with the exception of Texas, the courts and legislatures have whittled away that right until there is not much left. Each state, however, has done its whittling in its own way. The Oregon Supreme Court discovered in 1908, while considering *Hough* v. *Porter*, that the Desert Land Act had nullified the riparian doctrine on the public domain and replaced it with its rival. The following year the legislature limited riparian rights to the ones then existing and ruled that thereafter only the appropriation right could be acquired in the state's waters. The Washington legislature and courts solved the problem by restricting riparian rights to beneficial uses. On the Great Plains, four states—North Dakota, South Dakota, Nebraska, and Kansas—have established appropriation as the exclusive method of acquiring rights to the use of water after certain dates. By these same statutes, however, the legislatures have validated and perpetuated riparian rights that had accrued and become vested. In Oklahoma the legislature and the courts have restricted the exercise of riparian rights to the use of water for household, livestock, and garden purposes. In Texas, where the courts have rather consistently protected the common law right, riparianism is more robust, although grants of state lands have not carried the riparian right since 1895.[17]

Since Colorado became a state in 1876, the Doctrine of Riparian Rights has been in retreat in most jurisdictions. Instead westerners have favored the indigenous Doctrine of Prior Appropriation, annulling the rival doctrine in the nine mountain states and greatly restricting its existence in a similar number of dual-system states. The customs of the miners have become the law of western waters.

8

The Colorado System
of Water-Right Enforcement

The creators of the appropriative right regarded it as real property, separate and distinctive from the land. This assumption caused problems of acquisition and enforcement that had not arisen in connection with the riparian right. Since it was considered part and parcel of the land abutting a stream, the riparian right was acquired with the land and enforced or protected by the courts.

The miners solved the problem of the acquisition of an appropriative right by requiring the appropriator to post a notice at the point of intended diversion, construct the project, divert the water, and put it to beneficial use. The priority of the right dated from the date of posting. The agriculturists in borrowing the miner's right frequently did not bother with the posting. In that case, priority dated from the date of the commencement of the project, the survey, or the actual construction.

As the miners' customs spread from California throughout the West, they remained the principal method of acquiring an appropriative right into the closing decade of the nineteenth century. They had, however, several weaknesses, one of which was lack of provision for public record. It was to remedy this deficiency that the California legislature, in codifying the miners' customs in 1872, required that notices be recorded in the county courthouse within ten days of posting.

As previously mentioned, the codification also provided for posting of notices and commencement of construction within sixty days of the posting. Construction was to be pursued with diligence until completion. This legislation proved so popular that before the close of the century every western state and territory, with the exception of Nevada, had enacted statutes modeled after it. Some, like the Montana law, were virtual copies of the California statute; others were modifications requiring the commencement of construction before filing in the county courthouse. In no state or territory did the statutory method supersede the nonstatutory. Reflecting the individualism of the frontier, the miners' method of appropriation remained a valid way of acquiring a water right.[1]

Neither method placed any restrictions on the number of appropriations that might be made of a stream, nor did they provide for recordation of the completion of projects. Since frontiersmen preferred freedom of action, they wanted few or no restrictions on their freedom to utilize the streams. In fact, the Colorado constitution expressly declared that the right of appropriation "shall never be denied." Enjoying this kind of freedom, many pioneers planned projects and filed notices, but never completed them. As a consequence, it was impossible to determine the number and priorities of the appropriations of a stream except through an expensive adjudication lawsuit. Nor was there any method in times of scarcity, with the exception of that provided by the Colorado statute of 1861, of dividing the waters among the users according to their priorities. Those situated along the upper part of a stream took what they wanted, depriving the downstream appropriators of their legitimate supply of irrigation water. These problems provoked institutional innovation in northern Colorado along the tributaries of the South Platte.

The Union Colony, under the leadership of Nathan C. Meeker, founded Greeley in 1870 and constructed two diversions from the Cache la Poudre River. These were Colony Canal No. 3, designed to water lands south of the river, including the town lots, and Colony Canal No. 2, dug with a capacity of 280 cubic feet per second to irrigate the farms north of the stream. Two years later John C. Abbott, a member of the colony, joined forces with Benjamin H. Eaton to construct a ditch known as the Lake Canal, twenty-five miles up the river near Fort Collins. About the same time, General R. A. Cameron, vice-president of the Union Colony, established another colony at Fort Collins and excavated a ditch during 1873 and 1874 to serve it.[2]

No sooner was Cameron's canal completed than the valley experienced a drought. By the first week in July, there was not enough water in the Cache la Poudre to supply both of the Greeley ditches and so little water was flowing into Canal No. 3 that crops, gardens, and fruit trees were perishing. Thereupon Meeker and two colony associates went to Fort Collins and found the Abbott and Cameron canals full of water. Since the water was coming to them first, they were taking their fill, even though their ditches were constructed after those of the Union Colony. Believing that they had prior rights to the stream, the colonists sought a court-ordered injunction to close the upstream headgates. In response to this action, Cameron, Abbott, and Eaton came to Greeley and proposed a conference at a schoolhouse located midway between the two communities.

At the conference the Fort Collins people proposed the appointment of a commission to divide the waters of the stream in accordance with the amount of land under cultivation. The representatives of the Greeley colony refused to consent to the proposal unless the upstream appropriators recognized their prior rights. The ensuing deadlock was broken when the Fort Collins irrigators agreed to let more water flow down the river in return for the Greeley colonists dropping their request for an injunction. Since the conference did not provide a solution to the problem, the Greeley people did not relinquish their search for one.[3]

Benjamin Eaton, who would become Colorado's governor in 1885, dreamed of a much larger canal than any yet constructed in the valley. Obtaining financial assistance from the British-owned Colorado Mortgage and Investment Company, he commenced construction in 1878 of a canal with a capacity more than two and a half times that of the Colony Canal No. 2. The *Colorado Sun*, published in Greeley, reported in its October 12, 1878 issue that the new canal would be fifty-three miles long and would irrigate nearly fifty thousand acres. The colonists became alarmed, as did the Fort Collins irrigators; there was an imperative need now to establish rights to the Cache la Poudre and to create institutions to protect them. At the same time water users in other valleys, such as Lorin C. Mead and C. A. Pound of the Highland Ditch Company in the St. Vrain Valley, became concerned about their rights to water.[4]

Again the Greeley people assumed the initiative. Shortly after the state elections that fall, Jared L. Brush, who was elected to the house of representatives, and Judge Silas B. A. Haynes, who was elected to the senate, issued a call for a meeting in Greeley on October 19, 1878, to consider legislation regarding irrigation. Although not many attended, those who did according to the *Colorado Sun*, were "earnest and intelligent." They included Mead, who had also been elected to the house, and two other men from the St. Vrain Valley. After some preliminary discussions, the meeting agreed that legislation was needed on three subjects; namely, (1) clarification of the priority provision of the state constitution, (2) measurement of the streams to determine the amount of water flowing in them, and (3) appointment of a state official to supervise the distribution of water by "commissioners" elected in the various valleys. Because of the slim turnout, the group agreed to call a state-wide meeting for a more representative discussion of the subject, the meeting to be held in Denver early in December.[5]

The irrigation convention met in Denver, December 5–7, 1878. It was attended by about fifty men, representing twenty-nine ditch companies and agricultural communities in the South Platte Valley. Twelve of those who attended came from the Cache la Poudre communities, six from Greeley, and six from Fort Collins. As it had earlier in Greeley, the discussion centered on the triple problems of determination of priorities, distribution of water according to those priorities, and stream measurement. Toward the close of the convention, the chairman, Mead, appointed a committee to prepare a memorial to the legislature, summarizing the agreements that had been reached and urging it to enact them into law. After the adoption of the memorial, the chair appointed another committee to incorporate it into a legislative bill.[6]

The second committee was composed of five men: a farmer, a doctor, a ditch builder, a lawyer, and an agricultural journalist. The farmer was David Boyd, a member of the Union Colony, who was a graduate of the University of Michigan and a veteran of the Civil War. Dr. Isaac L. Bond of Longmont had come west with the Chicago-Colorado Colony and for several years had practiced medicine. Ill health, however, had forced him to give up his practice and move to a farm, where he had assisted in the organization of a mutual irrigation company. The ditch builder was John C. Abbott; he had attended college in Michigan, joined the Union Colony in 1870, and in 1872 moved to Fort Collins, where he had helped to build two canals and was about to begin a third. Daniel Witter, a Denver lawyer, had come to Colorado from Indiana with the fifty-niners. Fellow miners had elected him judge of a miners' court and then member of the first territorial legislature. Admitted to the bar in 1862, he had gained recognition as a lawyer specializing in public land cases. In the convention he was representing the Platte Water Company, which supplied the city of Denver with irrigation water. The agricultural journalist, John S. Stanger, was editor of the *Colorado Farmer*. He was educated at Allegheny College in Pennsylvania and later became a captain during the Civil War. Although these men had varied backgrounds, they had in common better-than-average formal education, humid-country experience, and familiarity with the problems of irrigation.[7]

In drafting the bill the five men sought to solve the problem of protecting the appropriation right by creating a system of public officials to divide the streams according to the users' prior rights. These officials, or water commissioners, were to be appointed by the county commissioners to serve for one year and to be on duty during the irrigating season. One water commissioner was to be appointed in each irrigation district, which usually conformed to a hydrographic basin. The convention had considered the protection afforded by the statute of 1861 and thought it inadequate. "The trouble with the law," the conferees concluded, "was that too much delay would occur—at least two weeks."[8]

The water commissioners were to determine the priority of rights in the streams, and these rights were to be attached to the lands, rather than to the ditches. Each commissioner was to obtain a record of the lands irrigated from each ditch within his district, together with the initial dates of irrigation. Water users were required under oath to supply this information; failure to comply would result in loss of priority. In case of dispute, the commissioner had the right to enter the premises of the contestants, "to call for persons and papers, administer oaths, take evidence and render decisions in regard to the rights of claimants to the use of water." Appeals could be made to the district courts.[9]

It is likely that Daniel Witter suggested the idea of administrative determination on the basis of his familiarity with the role of land office registers and receivers in the settlement of public land disputes. These officials frequently received testimony, interrogated witnesses, and determined rights to public lands. Without question, Isaac Bond was responsible for the attachment of water rights to the land. He came from the St. Vrain Valley, where a conflict between the corporation canal companies and the farmers was in the offing. There the irrigators were objecting to the control of their water by the Highland Ditch Company, and Bond believed that the right should appertain to the land and its priority date from the initial use of the water on it. The St. Vrain farmers were also objecting to the company's charges for water, and Bond was responsible for the inclusion in the bill of a provision authorizing the county commissioners to fix the price of irrigation water.[10]

Whatever the origin of the water-right provisions of the bill, they were rejected by the irrigation committee of the house, chaired by Lorin Mead. The lawyers regarded the determination of property rights as the province of the courts rather than of an administrative officer. As a consequence, one of them, Henry P. H. Bromwell, rewrote the section on water-right determination and placed it in the domain of the courts. The judge of the district court within each irrigation district was authorized to appoint a referee, who would take testimony and receive proofs to substantiate claims to water. Each claimant was to present proof of the dates of the construction and enlargements of ditches, together with their capacity and the amount of water carried in them. Using the evidence gathered by the referee, the judge was to issue a decree establishing the priorities of each ditch within the district. The customary lawsuit was not involved, since the judge was to act as an administrative officer. It should be noted in this recasting of the determination procedure that an appropriation dated from the construction of a ditch rather than from the application of the water to the land. In this manner the idea of Isaac Bond was discarded, but it would surface again during the antiroyalty movement of the 1880s.[11]

Mead's committee, however, did approve Bond's proposal concerning rate-fixing; and the bill that emerged from it and was enacted by the 1879 legislature empowered the country commissioners to establish the rates that corporation canal companies could charge their water users. The committee also approved the creation of irrigation districts and the appointment of a water commissioner in each one, selected not by the county commissioners but by the governor. This official was to divide the waters of a stream among the ditches according to prior rights. In case of scarcity of water, he was authorized "to shut and fasten . . . the head-gates of any ditch . . . which . . . shall not be entitled to water by reason of the priority of the rights of others below them on the same stream."[12]

The Coloradans did not delay implementing their system of water-right enforcement. Since the crop season of 1879 was another dry one, the farmers on the St. Vrain River in Irrigation District No. 5 petitioned Governor Frederick W. Pitkin to appoint a water commissioner, which he did on June 9, 1879. Later that year he made similar appointments for Boulder and Bear creeks, while in the Cache la Poudre drainage, Judge Victor A. Elliott of the Second Judicial District appointed, on August 24, Harry N. Haynes, son of the state senator, as referee for Irrigation District No. 3. Immediately, the younger Haynes posted and published the required notices and began taking testimony on September 29, 1879, first in Fort Collins and later in Greeley. The ditch owners appeared, presented their claims, and in turn were questioned by rival ditch owners. Remembering the earlier controversy, irrigators near Greeley, critical of the claims of irrigators near

Fort Collins, employed David Boyd and a local attorney to safeguard their interests.[13]

Returning to Fort Collins in December, Haynes gathered the rest of the testimony in January and on April 9, 1880, submitted his report to the court, but Judge Elliott refused to issue the decree. Elliott was convinced that the adjudication procedure was illegal because it did not provide for the usual lawsuits initiated by complaints and summons. He also objected to judges serving as administrative officers and exercising police powers. He declared:

> I cannot bring myself to depart from the English and American systems of jurisprudence. In the administration of justice in an English court there are always parties, and sometimes four: the *actor*, the plaintiff; the *reus*, the thing; the *judex*, the court; and the *juratta*, the jurors; and each have their separate and proper functions to perform. I cannot consent . . . to bring myself to leave the judicial position in which I have been placed by the constitution . . . and take the position of any *actor*, to go around to determine, without being solicited, what are the rights of the respective owners of ditches in these several water districts.

He concluded,

> I shall . . . insist that someone who may desire to have a decree entered in any particular water district, shall become an *actor* by serving out process, and bringing others in to answer; and that when that shall have been done . . . and the case shall then be regularly before the court upon the testimony taken by the referee . . . together with a simple complaint and a simple answer, the court shall then enter upon the investigation of the rights of the

parties at their solicitation and enter a decree determining their rights in the premises.[14]

The farmers were disappointed and angry. No doubt most of them agreed with David Boyd when he referred to Judge Elliott as "a narrow-minded, conservative lawyer, who fears to proceed upon any ground not covered by a precedent." They were seeking to invent institutions new to Anglo-American culture in order to define and enforce a new property right. Lacking precedent, they were groping, aware that "a situation wholly unique could not be met by ordinary remedies," yet opposed by most members of the legal profession. Frustrated, Boyd lashed out against them as "men of hidebound precedents . . . of blind conservatism" who were "looking ahead to endlesss fat jobs about to come to them from the wasting and ceaseless litigation likely to arise in reference to the establishing of priority of claims to the use of water." Yet the farmers had to rely on the legal profession for relief.[15] In response to Judge Elliott's refusal to issue a decree, they petitioned the Colorado Supreme Court for a writ of mandamus to compel his cooperation, but it agreed with the judge. By this time two years had elapsed, another legislature was in session, and from it the farmers sought assistance.[16]

During the elections in the autumn of 1880, the voters of Weld County, of which Greeley is the seat, elected James M. Freeman to the state senate. Freeman was a native of New York state, where he had studied law. In 1873 he migrated to Greeley and began a distinguished legal career. Named chairman of the senate irrigation committee in Colorado's Third General Assembly, he introduced three bills, senate bills numbers 93, 124, and 121, which when enacted and later amended constituted, along with the legislation of 1879, the Colorado system of water-right enforcement.[17]

Senate Bill No. 93 provided an adjudication procedure that met Judge Elliott's requirements. As he desired, it was initiated by a petition of one or more ditch owners to a district court, requesting it to adjudicate the priorities of rights within a water district. Throughout this bill and Senate Bill No. 124, irrigation districts were referred to as "water districts," a nomenclature that has been retained to the present day. Upon receipt of the petition, the district judge was authorized to appoint a referee, who would notify all claimants of the dates and places within the district that he would take evidence of the dates of the commencement and enlargement of ditches, the diligence with which they were constructed, and the original sizes and carrying capacities. When he had completed taking evidence, he would prepare a draft decree that after a hearing and possible modification, the judge would issue to establish the priorities of right to the waters of the stream. Thereupon the clerk of the court would issue to each ditch owner a certificate showing the date and amount of each appropriation. Since the need for this legislation had become apparent, the solons approved it without serious opposition and Governor Pitkin signed it, February 23, 1881.[18]

With a procedure at last acceptable to the legal profession, three ditch owners of the Cache la Poudre watershed petitioned Judge Elliott on June 28, 1881, for an adjudication of rights. The judge in turn appointed Henry Bromwell as referee, with authority to take testimony and prepare a draft decree. Bromwell was an appropriate selection inasmuch as he was the principal author of the 1879 and the 1881 procedures. Using both the testimony that he took in November of 1881 and that taken by Harry Haynes, the new referee prepared a draft decree which, after hearings, Judge Elliott issued on April 11, 1882, as a legal record of property rights in the waters of the Cache la Poudre River. Within the next two and a half years similar adjudications were conducted in the other valleys of the South Platte, giving water users there similar determinations of their prior appropriation rights.[19]

Freeman's second bill, Senate Bill No. 124, authorized the governor to appoint a state hydraulic engineer to supervise the distribution of water throughout the state and to measure the flow of the streams. The name of the official came from California, where in the spring of 1878 the legislature had created the office of state engineer and the governor had named William Hammond Hall to the position. The idea, however, may have been indigenous, for the farmers who met in Greeley on October 19, 1878, at the call of Jared Brush and Silas Haynes, proposed the appointment of a state officer to supervise the distribution of irrigation water.[20]

Freeman's state engineer was to appoint the water commissioners in the water districts and to supervise their work. In addition to gauging the streams, he was to participate in water-right adjudications by measuring the capacity of each claimant's ditch and sharing the information with the referee in the form of testimony. By performing this service, the state engineer would provide a check on the exaggerated claims of many of the ditch owners.[21] But the senator's colleagues badly mutilated his bill, and the official came out of the legislative process deprived of the power to appoint and supervise the water commissioners and without authority to intervene in the adjudications. His duties were limited to supervision of "water companies" and to the measurement of streams and ditches. Nevertheless, in practice many of the water commissioners made periodic reports to the state engineer.[22] To coordinate the allocations of the water commissioners, the act designated the South Platte, Arkansas, and Rio Grande valleys as water divisions and the 1887 legislature placed a superintendent in charge of each one.[23]

Freeman's third bill, Senate Bill No. 121, was a recordation measure similar to those enacted in other states. Within ninety days after the commencement of the construction of a project, the owner was to file a notice and a map in the county courthouse. In 1887, this statute was amended to require registration in the state engineer's office as well as in the county courthouse.[24]

These legislative acts, together with that of 1879, provided Coloradans with a method of acquiring, determining, and administering the appropriation right, but the system was not without deficiencies. Reflecting the individualism of the state's post-frontier era, they placed minimal restrictions on a citizen's freedom of appropriation. Since the constitution promised that the right of appropriation "shall never be denied," the only limit placed on the number and amount of appropriations was beneficial use and what was beneficial was a subjective judgment of the court. It made no difference that the stream was overappropriated; one could commence a ditch, file a notice and a map, divert the waters, and use them until rights were proved up in an adjudication procedure. Then the ditch owner could successfully claim more than he needed since the judges and referees were usually unfamiliar with the duty of water and the measurement of streams. The state engineer, representing the public that was granting the use of the water, was not allowed to participate in the adjudication and question the accuracy of the claims. As a consequence, the courts awarded rights to water in excess of the capacity of the streams. Elwood Mead, a young professor at the Colorado Agricultural College, situated on a tract of land adjacent to the village of Fort Collins, concluded that there was a better way.[25]

9
Creating the Wyoming System

Elwood Mead was the architect of the Wyoming system of water-right enforcement. He had studied agriculture at Purdue and civil engineering at the Iowa Agricultural College. In December 1882, he was offered a position at Colorado's agricultural college as an instructor of mathematics. He accepted, began teaching the next month, and remained there until the spring of 1884. It was during the mid-1880s that Coloradans reformed their water-rights laws, and from their proposals Mead fashioned the Wyoming system.[1]

Coloradans were not slow to detect weaknesses in their system. During the winter of 1883–84, Bryant S. La Grange prepared a paper on irrigation, which Mead read at a farmers' institute in Fort Collins on February 24, 1884. La Grange had come to Colorado in 1870 with the Union Colony. He had helped to construct the two colony canals and on July 9, 1980, had been appointed the first water commissioner to divide the waters of the Cache la Poudre in Water District No. 3. Consequently, in writing his paper he relied on four seasons of experience as commissioner.[2]

La Grange revealed that Judge Elliott in adjudicating the Cache la Poudre had awarded rights to more water than there was in the stream. Specifically, he declared "The discharge of the river at the period of its greatest flow was not equal to the actual capacity of our present canals and was not over three-fifths of the intake granted the canals in their decrees." In short, he contended that both the actual and the decreed appropriations were excessive. To prevent the development of this situation on other streams, he thought, "[The state has] the urgent and imperative duty . . . to take such control of our streams as will prevent the building of additional canals or enlargements of the present ones until it has been ascertained that there is a surplus of water in the stream." He sought to realize his objective through the creation of a "Board of State Control." No canal construction would be allowed until the projectors had received a "permit" from the board, which would "issue . . . water privileges in proportion to the water supply in each stream." In addition, he proposed "a State water-right register of all existing legal claims to the use of water; and also a state register of all permits or water privileges that may be hereafter granted." Here was a radical proposal for state control of the appropriation right; here in the paper read by instructor Mead was the Wyoming system in embryo.[3]

La Grange's ideas did not go unnoticed. Later that year, Edwin Nettleton, now the state engineer, espoused them in his first biennial report to the governor. He recommended the creation of a "Board of Commissioners for Water Divisions" to formulate uniform rules for the guidance of the water commissioners in the various districts. He thought the board might also "be invested with the power to grant or refuse water appropriation from a stream, all water of which is supposed to be fully appropriated, and to settle the order of priorities on the whole stream, when that stream is covered by two or more Water Districts."[4]

As for Elwood Mead, he soon had an opportunity to learn first hand the accuracy of La Grange's observations regarding excessive grants of water by the court adjudications, for during the summers of 1884, 1885, and 1886 he was employed by Nettleton to gauge the irrigation ditches in the South Platte Valley. He soon noted a wide discrepancy between the decreed and the actual carrying capacity of many of the ditches. "So great was this in some instances," Mead wrote in a report submitted December 1, 1886, "that the results of the gaugings and the decreed capacity seemed to have no connection with each other. Ditches were met with having decreed capacities of two, three and even five times the volume they were capable of carrying. . . . It needs no argument to show the worse than uselessness of these decrees as a guide to the Water Commissioner in the performance of his duties."[5] As Mead wrote he was becoming involved in another irrigation issue; the antiroyalty movement in Colorado was reaching a crescendo.

The antiroyalty movement was provoked by the construction of three large canals in the South Platte Valley by the British-owned Colorado Mortgage and Investment Company and its subsidiaries. These canals were the Larimer and Weld, the High Line, and the Loveland and Greeley, diversions respectively of the Poudre, South Platte, and Big Thompson streams. The first two were begun in 1879 and all three were completed by 1883. Their construction touched off a speculative boom during which many corporation canals were projected, although few were constructed. Whether they were dug or only projected, they were threatening. The farmers were concerned about the overappropriation of their streams and the proposals to place them under state control grew out of this concern. Once the ditches were constructed the companies charged for a "perpetual" right to use them as well as for annual operation and maintenance. As described in Chapter 3, the irrigators objected to the perpetual right fee and dubbed it royalty, but when they did not pay, the companies refused to supply water and crops withered.[6]

The Colorado State Grange served as a vehicle for expressing agrarian grievances. As early as January 1881, the state master, Levi Booth, sounded a note of alarm. "Vast ditch companies are being formed," he declared, "controlling a large amount of foreign capital—capital that has no sympathy for us or ours. These companies are taking possession of our waters, without any regard to prior rights or prior use of such waters." Five years later one of the Grangers, Byron A. Wheeler, refused to make the perpetual right payment. When the company cut off his water, he requested a writ of mandamus from the Colorado Supreme Court. The court, however, refused to issue the writ, declaring that it did not have original jurisdiction over disputes between private parties, and directed him to seek relief from a lower court. He did so during the summer of 1886, and when this court favored the company, Wheeler again sought action by the higher tribunal. But since relief from the courts was slow and uncertain, he and his fellow Grangers decided to seek legislative assistance.[7]

As the Colorado legislature was about to meet, the Grangers gathered in Denver on January 6, 1887, and formed the State Farmers' Irrigation and Protective Association. After the election of officers, Wheeler presented the report of a committee on needed legislation, a report that requested the creation of a board of water commissioners "having entire control of the appropriation of water," the appropriation of water by the land rather than by persons, and the recognition of canal corporations as common carriers. Significantly, Wheeler acknowledged the help of state engineer Nettleton in the preparation of the report. After some discussion, the meeting authorized the selection of a legislative committee to draft legislation. To this seven-man committee, the chair appointed Elwood Mead.[8]

After measuring the capacities of ditches during the summer of 1884, Mead had returned to Indiana, studied for a master's degree at his alma mater, and read law in his father-in-law's office. When the governing board of the Colorado

Agricultural College created a professorship of irrigation engineering—the first in the nation—he returned to the campus on September 14, 1886, to fill the position.[9]

We can assume that when Mead returned to Fort Collins, he was sympathetic to the Granger cause. He had been tramping the banks of streams all summer, talking to irrigators, gauging ditches, noting discrepancies between actual capacities and those determined by the courts, and realizing beyond doubt the need for state control. Whatever may have been his views then, during the winter of 1887 he became an active participant in the antiroyalty crusade. Sometime before that he had read William Hammond Hall's *Irrigation Development*. This was the first book-length description of irrigation in other countries to be published in the United States. Aside from a report to Congress by George Perkins Marsh, who was U.S. minister in Italy from 1861 to 1882, Americans had had few descriptions of irrigation institutions in foreign countries to guide them in creating their own system. In his treatise the state engineer of California provided western settlers with an account of the irrigation institutions of France, Italy, Spain, and ancient Rome. Mead learned that in these countries the streams were considered the property of the state and could be utilized only by a grant from the state. He learned that in Spain, peace prevailed in communities where water was tied to the land, whereas exploitation and dissension prevailed in localities where water was separated from the land and sold in the market. He also learned of tribunals, like the *tribunal de aguas* in Valencia, that allocated stream waters and enforced rights in them. Hall sometimes referred to these tribunals as boards of control. Certainly, reading Hall's book helped to convince Mead of the soundness of the views of the antiroyalty agitators.[10]

The legislative committee prepared three bills for presentation to the legislature—namely, house bills numbers

294, 271, and 119. The latter was also introduced in the senate as Senate Bill No. 115. That Mead played an influential role in the writing of these bills is likely; it is also likely that Nettleton was consulted. House Bill No. 294 created a "State board of water control," consisting of the state engineer and two persons "well known and experienced in practical irrigation" from each of the state's water divisions. To this board was given the control and supervision of the streams of the state and the power to make rules regulating their diversion, distribution, and use. No diversion in any water division was to be allowed without the permission of a subcommittee of the board, composed of the state engineer and the two members from that division. A person seeking to appropriate water was to submit to the subcommittee an application, which was to include a description of both the ditch and the land to be irrigated. On approval, the appropriator could construct his project. When completed, he was to submit a notice of completion, and the subcommittee would then issue him a "certificate of concession." The bill was intended to curb the individualism of Colorado appropriators and subordinate their actions to the welfare of the community.[11] House Bill No. 271 tied the water to the land and made the farmer the appropriator rather than the canal corporation. If enacted, it would achieve the objective favored by Isaac Bond eight years earlier. The key provision read: "Every right to water by priority of appropriation shall be deemed to be attached to and to be a part of the realty upon which the same has been used for beneficial purposes."[12] House Bill No. 119 outlawed royalties, or perpetual right fees, and provided penalties for their imposition.[13]

Shortly after the introduction of the bills, Elwood Mead addressed a meeting of farmers in Fort Collins. He contended that the Colorado system was defective in that it made the construction of a ditch the act of appropriation rather than the application of the water to the land. This provision in the law had separated the title to the land from that to the water and encouraged the current boom in canal construction. Corporations constructing canals were establishing monopolies in water, burdening farmers with exorbitant charges. Capitalizing on Hall's *Irrigation Development*, he referred to the contentment of those communities in Spain where "land appropriates the water," in contrast with the economic stagnation of "those districts where individuals gained control of the water supply." To clinch his argument, he quoted the advice of John Wesley Powell, expressed in the *Report on the Lands of the Arid Region of the United States*, that the "right to use water should inhere in the land to be irrigated, and water rights should go with land titles." He closed his address by urging his audience to support the proposed legislation of the antiroyalty movement.[14] Nevertheless, of the three bills, only the antiroyalty bill was enacted into law. The movement concentrated its attention on the passage of that measure (see Chapter 3). House Bill No. 271 was reported out of the house committee on agriculture and irrigation "without recommendation" and tabled by the house in the committee of the whole, while House Bill No. 294 never reached the house floor for debate.[15]

A year later, Governor Thomas Moonlight of Wyoming invited Mead to serve as that territory's first territorial engineer. He accepted and arrived in Cheyenne to assume his new responsibilities in April of 1888, carrying with him, if not copies of the discarded bills, at least memories of them.[16] If the new territorial official had any doubts about the weaknesses of the Colorado system, they were removed during the first seventeen months of his service. In 1886 and 1888 Wyoming had copied, with some alterations, Colorado's legislation of 1879 and 1881—its method of acquiring the appropriation right, its adjudication procedure and administrative system. He soon found the same defects in Wyoming as he had found in Colorado. There was no central register of appropriation claims; instead they were recorded in the county seats throughout the territory. Many of the streams were overappropriated, and few had been adjudicated. Of those that had been the decreed rights were excessive and inconsistent. On one stream one claimant was given four and a half cubic feet per second for one hundred acres, while a neighbor was given only three for the same acreage. The territorial government exercised no control over ditch construction; as a consequence it had been haphazard, inefficient, and unnecesarily expensive. "The public waters of our streams," Mead wrote Senator William M. Stewart of Nevada, "are conferred upon parties who . . . build ditches regardless of its effect on the conservation of the water supply or the expense of regulating its distribution." Happily, a vehicle for reform was at hand.[17]

On June 3, 1889, Francis Warren, the last territorial governor of Wyoming, issued a summons for the election of a constitutional convention. The delegates were elected in July and the convention met on September 2. Several members were aware of the water-right situation and the need for reformation at a time when the open-range cattle industry was declining and agriculture was gaining in importance. One of those members was James A. Johnston. He had been the engineer in charge of the construction of Wyoming Development Company's irrigation project near Wheatland, Wyoming. Earlier he had lived in Colorado, where he became acquainted with Edwin Nettleton. As a member of the territorial legislature in 1888, he had introduced the bill creating the office of territorial engineer and, on the recommendation of Nettleton, had recommended to Governor Moonlight the appointment of Elwood Mead to the position. Another knowledgeable member of the convention was Charles H. Burritt of Buffalo, Wyoming, in the Powder River basin, where he had had considerable experience in water-right litigation. Both men were named members of the agriculture, irrigation and water rights committee, with Johnston serving as chairman.[18]

The committee sought the assistance of Elwood Mead in writing a constitutional provision on water rights. He did not neglect the opportunity. Reportedly he met nightly with the committee while they wrote an article with five sections, which on September 10 they presented to the convention. The article declared the streams to be the property of the state, placed them under the supervision of a board of control, affirmed the appropriation right as the water right of the proposed state, divided Wyoming into four water divisions, and provided for the office of state engineer. There can be little doubt that Mead was the principal author of these provisions, for typewritten copies of first drafts with revisions in his handwriting are preserved among his papers in the Wyoming state archives.[19]

The committee was worried about the convention's reception of the proposal. Burritt, who was selected as floor manager, referred to it as in "some respects . . . radical and different from anything that any state or territory in the union now had," as indeed it was. To ease its reception, Mead prepared a statement "as to the principles which should control the constitutional provisions affecting irrigation." Summarized, the principles were state contrc. of its waters, adaptation of irrigation institutions to the geography and needs of the state, construction of efficient ditches, determination of water rights by persons knowledgeable in hydrology, and the centralization of stream administration in one office under one official. As the debate commenced, Burritt read Mead's memorandum to the convention.[20]

The opponents attacked the article, but the proponents defended it so skillfully that is was altered only once. The alteration occurred after a prolonged debate over the nature of an appropriation, whether it was constituted by application of water to the land or by the construction of a ditch. Burritt settled the question by moving that an appropriation be "for beneficial uses." Over the question of state ownership there was little debate. Judge Asbury B. Conway of Green River, Wyoming, wondered about the constitutionality of state ownership. He reminded the convention that the "United States, as the owner of public lands, [was] the owner of the water also," and then, prophetically, he raised the question whether Wyoming's "claim as a state to the ownership of all this water [might] not conflict with the rights of the United States." But that was a question for the future.[21]

On September 30, 1889, the last day of its deliberations, the convention incorporated the proposal into the constitution as article eight. Captioned "Irrigation and Water Rights," it read as follows:

Section 1. The water of all natural streams, springs, lakes or other collections of still water, within the boundaries of the state, are hereby declared to be the property of the state.

Section 2. There shall be constituted a board of control, to be composed of the state engineer and superintendents of the water divisions; which shall, under such regulations as may be prescribed by law, have the supervision of the waters of the state and of their appropriation, distribution and diversion, and of the various officers connected therewith. Its decisions to be subject to review by the courts of the state.

Section 3. Priority of appropriation for beneficial uses shall give the better right. No appropriation shall be denied except when such denial is demanded by the public interests.

Section 4. The legislature shall by law divide the state into four (4) water divisions, and provide for the appointment of superintendents thereof.

Section 5. There shall be a state engineer who shall be appointed by the governor of the state and confirmed by the senate; he shall hold his office for the term of six (6) years, or until his successor shall have been appointed and shall have qualified. He shall be president of the board of control and shall have general supervision of the waters of the state and of the officers connected with its distribution. No person shall be appointed to this position who has not such theoretical knowledge and such practical experience and skill as shall fit him for the position.[22]

Article eight provided a constitutional framework within which to develop an operational system. This was provided by a statute written by Mead and enacted by the first state legislature on December 22, 1890. The statute and the constitutional provisions formed the Wyoming System,[23] the essence of which lay in the subordination of the appropriator to the welfare of the state. The interest of the state or the community came first, that of the individual irrigator second. Gone were the days in Wyoming when an appropriator, without anybody's leave, could post a notice, dig a ditch, install a dam, and divert the waters of a stream. Water was too limited a resource to be diverted and wastefully used without regard for the rights of others. Since it was the property of the state, rights to its use were to be granted by the state, adjudicated by the state, and protected by the state.

The law of December 22, 1890, provided an exclusive method of obtaining a water right. A person intending to appropriate water applied for a permit from the state engineer, giving a description of the proposed project and the land to be irrigated by it. If unappropriated water was available and the diversion was not "detrimental to the public welfare," the permit was granted; otherwise it was refused. If granted, the applicant constructed the project. Upon completion and the application of water to the land, he notified the board of control, which issued him a certificate of appropriation. This procedure generally followed the one outlined in Colorado's House Bill No. 294 and provided the control over appropriations that Mead desired.

The statute assigned the adjudication of streams to the board of control rather than to the district courts, although irrigators could appeal board decisions to the courts. To initiate an adjudication, the state engineer measured the flow of the stream and gauged the capacities of the ditches; this procedure provided the state control that was eliminated from the 1881 state engineer's bill in Colorado. Then the divisional superintendent took testimony, inviting claimants to submit records of construction and beneficial use. On the basis of this evidence, with the measurements of the state engineer serving as a check on the claims of the appropriators, the board determined priorities, granting no more than one cubic foot per second for each seventy acres. The adjudication procedure achieved another of Mead's goals—determination of rights by men familiar with hydrology and the measurement of water. Although the law was not as explicit as House Bill No. 271, Mead regarded the law as attaching the water to the land and thereby implementing the recommendation of John Wesley Powell. Not the least of the advantages of this procedure was its minimal costs, in contrast to those of adjudication by the courts. On one stream, the total expense to each appropriator was $1.75, the fee for the issuance and recordation of the certificate of appropriation.[24] To protect rights obtained from the board, the statute created an administrative hierarchy patterned after that of Colorado. The hierarchy was headed by a state engineer who supervised four superintendents, one for each of the four water divisions into which the state was divided. The superintendents in turn supervised the water commissioners who divided the streams among the entitled users.

So created, the Wyoming system soon came under attack in the courts. The leading case was *Farm Investment Company v. Carpenter*. When the board of control adjudicated the rights to French Creek in 1893, the plaintiff failed to submit a claim for an appropriation dating from 1879 and consequently had not received a certificate of appropriation, confirming his right to use the waters of the stream. In its complaint, the company challenged the constitutionality of the 1890 statute, charging that in vesting the board of control with judicial functions the law violated the separation of powers provision of the state's constitutions. The company also questioned the constitutionality of state ownership of waters.[25]

The chief justice of the Wyoming Supreme Court, Charles N. Potter, wrote the opinion. An eminent jurist and a member of the court for thirty-three years, he had been a member of the constitutional convention and had participated in the debate concerning article eight. He denied that the separation of powers provision had been violated. The functions of the board of control, he declared, were "primarily administrative rather than judicial in character," since determination of the relative rights of the claimants was a step toward effective distribution of water. "The board," conceded Potter, "acts judicially; but the power exercised is quasi judicial only, and such as, under proper circumstances, may appropriately be conferred upon executive officers or boards." In support of this conclusion, he referred to the judicial power exercised by the public land offices.[26]

In response to the question of state ownership, the chief justice thought that the federal government had approved it when, by the act of admission, Congress had "accepted, ratified and confirmed" the state's constitution. Moreover, he contended that state or public ownership of water was part of the Doctrine of Prior Appropriation and had been approved by Congress in the Act of 1866. With this approval by the state's high court, Elwood Mead's Wyoming system was secure, giving greater protection to the appropriative right than the Colorado system.

10
Diffusion of
the Wyoming System

The spread of the Wyoming system was slow, accompanied by controversy. Its most controversial aspect was the determination of property rights by an administrative board rather than by the courts. The engineers liked the system because it provided determination by men versed in hydrology, men who were familiar with miner's inches and cubic feet per second. The members of the legal profession, on the other hand, opposed it because they regarded the board's determination as an exercise of judicial powers, in violation of the separation of powers principle of the American constitutional system. With memories of executive justice in Stuart England and in the English colonies, they considered the maintenance of the principle a safeguard of American liberties and property rights. As a consequence, when the Wyoming system was adopted, it was usually with significant modifications, but not always.

Nebraska in 1895 was the first state to adopt the Wyoming system and it did so with few changes. Most of her citizens were not interested in irrigation and water rights until the late 1880s, when several dry years prompted the St. Raynor Act of 1889, which legalized appropriations. The severe drought of the following year encouraged William E. Smythe to organize a series of irrigation conventions, first at Ogallala in January 1891, and then in McCook and Lincoln.

Although above average rainfall in 1891 tended to dampen enthusiasm for irrigation, 1893 was dry and 1894 drier. Crops withered, settlers departed, and many of those who stayed accepted relief food and clothing shipped from eastern cities. In the midst of this distress, a group of citizens met in North Platte and formed the State Irrigation Association, which promptly authorized the appointment of a committee on legislation. To it were appointed J. S. Hoagland of North Platte, R. B. Howell of Omaha, and William R. Akers of Morrill in the Nebraska Panhandle. Of these men, Akers was the most influential. He had farmed under ditch in the Cache la Poudre Valley, was familiar with the Colorado system, but was impressed by the merits of the Wyoming institutions. Under his leadership, the committee drafted a bill modeled after the Wyoming law of December 22, 1890. Akers, a member of the Nebraska senate, introduced it and a receptive legislature enacted it.[1]

The Nebraska water-right act of 1895 declared the unappropriated waters to be the "property of the public . . . subject to appropriation," preferring in this instance the language of the Colorado constitution to that of Wyoming. Otherwise, it was essentially a copy of the Wyoming legislation. It created a board of control in the form of a state board of irrigation, composed of the governor, attorney general, and commissioner of public lands and buildings. The act authorized these officials to appoint a "hydraulic engineer" to serve as secretary. It divided the state into two water divisions, with an officer in charge of each. It also empowered the board to divide the divisions into water districts with appropriate officials.

The statute provided for the Wyoming method of acquiring water rights—an application for a permit, approval or disapproval by the hydraulic engineer, notice of completion, and the issuance of a certificate. It attached the water to the land, restricting, as in Wyoming, a maximum of one cubic foot per second to each seventy acres. The act also provided for adjudication of priorities by the state board of irrigation rather than by the courts. When in *Crawford Co.* v. *Hathaway* the plaintiff questioned the constitutionality of the procedure, the Nebraska Supreme Court cited *Farm Investment Co.* v. *Carpenter* and agreed that the board's functions were "clearly administrative in character, and not judicial."[2]

The next adoptions, although partial, occurred in Nevada, Utah, and Idaho, under pressure from the federal government. When Nevada's congressman Francis Newlands and his associates wrote the Reclamation Act of 1902, they included a section guaranteeing respect for western water rights. Section eight read in part:

> That nothing in this Act shall be construed as affecting or intended to affect or to in any way interfere with the laws of any State or Territory relating to the control, appropriation, use, or distribution of water used in irrigation, or any vested right acquired thereunder, and the Secretary of the Interior, in carrying out the provisions of this Act, shall proceed in conformity with such laws, and nothing herein shall in any way affect any right of any State or of the Federal Government or of any landowner, appropriator, or user of water in, to, or from any interstate stream or the waters thereof.[3]

Although the act protected state and territory laws, some interference seemed necessary. Frederick Newell, chief engineer of the new Reclamation Service, noted, "The laws of many of the States and Territories relating to water are in a more or less chaotic condition." Because of this condition, the Service in many jurisdictions was unable to determine the amount of unappropriated water available for its projects. Consequently, Newell warned that a reformation of water-right laws would be a condition for the approval of some projects. In September 1902, his superior, Charles D. Walcott, director of the United States Geological Survey, came west and told a group of farmers in Nevada that construction of reclamation projects in the state would not begin until the water rights on the major streams had been adjudicated.[4]

Nevadans quickly responded to the warning. When the legislature met the following January, the house and senate appointed irrigation committees, which invited Newlands to assist them in drafting a bill. He accepted and with the assistance of Leon H. Taylor, a Geological Survey hydrographer in Nevada, wrote the 1903 water-rights act.[5] This act was influenced by the Wyoming statute, but it was no copy. It created the office of state engineer, outlined a rights determination procedure, and authorized an administrative system, but did not prescribe a method of acquiring new rights. The method was provided by the 1905 legislature, when it instituted the permit system patterned after that of Wyoming.[6]

The rights determination procedure was unique in that it was conducted not by a board or a court but by the state engineer. It resembled adjudication by water commissioners, which was proposed by the bill-drafting committee of the 1879 Denver irrigation convention, and like that procedure the Nevada method may have been suggested by the settlement of disputes in the public land offices. However that may be, the act directed the state engineer to "prepare for each stream in the State of Nevada a list of the appropriations of water according to priority." He was to make a hydrographic survey of the stream and to collect the claims of the appropriators. Having gathered this information, the state engineer was to prepare a list of priorities and to issue each appropriator a certificate of appropriation.[7]

The first two state engineers assembled lists of rights to three streams, but, hampered by inadequate funding, they did not act fast enough for the Reclamation Service. The 1913 legislature rewrote the act, but did not change its character. The constitutionality of the new statute was immediately questioned and the supreme court of Nevada declared adjudications by a state engineer unconstitutional. The court declared that it was illegal for a "nonjudicial officer" to exercise "judicial powers." The West was still groping for a satisfactory solution to the rights determination problem.[8]

The citizens of Utah responded to the same pressures as the Nevadans. Having scuttled their indigenous public control institutions, they created the office of state engineer in 1897, patterning it after the office in Colorado and limiting its functions to stream measurement and dam inspection. The first man to fill that office, Robert C. Gemmell, favored the Wyoming system. After complaining of the expense involved in court adjudications, he recommended adopting the Wyoming method in his first three biennial reports, but, when a bill for this purpose was introduced into the 1901 legislature, it was defeated. The following year, however, officials of the Geological Survey made it clear that reformation of water-right laws was a prerequisite to federal reclamation.[9]

Since Utahans were interested in several projects, Governor Heber M. Wells responded by urging the 1903 legislature to revise the state's water-right laws in line with the recommendations of the state engineer. "We cannot too soon," he advised, "place our State in a position to realize the benefits" of national reclamation. The solons responded with the Utah water code of 1903.[10] In drafting this legislation they patterned the acquisition of rights after the Wyoming system, the determination of rights after the Colorado system, and their administration after both systems. Moreover, in declaring the waters of the state "to be the property of the public," they followed the language of the Colorado constitution.[11]

Yet the rights determination procedure was no copy of the Centennial State's system, for the state engineer was given a role that the Colorado legislation of 1881 did not allow. According to the Utah code, the state engineer initiated the adjudication proceedings by making a hydrographic survey of the stream and filing a report of it with the district court. Thereupon the clerk of the court was to order the submission of claims, which were to be tabulated by the state engineer. Then, as in Colorado, the court was to appoint a referee, who was to take additional testimony. This evidence together with that collected and tabulated by the state engineer he was to use in the preparation of a provisional decree for submission to the court. After reviewing it, the court was to issue a final decree and certificates of appropriation.

After the procedure became law, the state engineers conducted hydrographic surveys and reported them to the courts, but nothing happened. The courts failed to respond and continue the adjudication. In 1914, eleven years after the passage of the act, the state engineer complained, "[Over] $75,000.00 has been spent in hydrographic surveys on the Weber, Logan, Virgin, San Rafael, and Sevier river systems. The hydrographic survey of the Weber river system has been in the hands of the court since 1908, the Logan river system since 1912. So far not a single water right has been adjudicated as the result of these surveys."[12]

What went wrong? In the first place it is obvious that Utah farmers were relatively satisfied with the definition of rights by the Mormon system, which had been in existence for half a century before the passage of the 1903 act. Under the supervision of the church, rivers and creeks had been apportioned by arbitrators, conferences, agreements, and court decisions. As a consequence, the average farmer did not feel the need of the imported institution. In the second place, the legislature failed to appropriate money to fund the adjudications—to pay for the services of the judges, referees, and stenographers — and the average farmer did not wish to pay for something that he believed he did not need. So the situation remained unchanged until legislation in Oregon influenced the Utah system.[13]

Interested in the Minidoka and the Boise projects, Idahoans also responded in 1903 to federal pressure. Having established the office of state engineer in 1895 to supervise Carey Act projects, the Idaho legislators adopted the Wyoming permit system for the acquisition of new rights, retained judicial determination of old rights, and divided the state into three divisions with a water commissioner in each one for the administration of both rights. Borrowing from Wyoming, the solons created a state board of irrigation, composed of the state engineer and the three water commissioners. This board was empowered to divide the water divisions into water districts and to appoint water masters in each one, but it was given no role in rights determination. That was reserved for the courts. The procedure, however, differed from Colorado's system in that the court was required to request the state engineer to make a hydrographic survey and to prepare a map showing the stream and ditches and the lands irrigated by them. Submitted to the court, the statute directed that this information should be "accepted as evidence in the determination of . . . rights" by the court.[14]

The Idaho act, like those of 1903 in Nevada and Utah, declared the water to be attached to the land. This provision reflected not only the influence of Elwood Mead, but also that of the Reclamation Act, which declared that "the right to the use of water acquired under the provisions of this Act shall be appurtenant to the land irrigated, and beneficial use shall be the basis, the measure, and the limit of the right," a phrase attributed to George Maxwell.[15]

The legislators of neighboring Oregon and Washington responded to Geological Survey proddings by requesting that their governors appoint commissions to draft water-right codes. Nonetheless, Governor Henry A. McBride did not appoint the Washington commission until the Reclamation Service made reform of water-right laws a condition of approval of projects within the state. The two groups met in joint session in Walla Walla, Washington, to which meeting they invited Frederick Newell. When members inquired about the character of the reformation that Newell desired, he suggested a code patterned after that of Wyoming. After some discussion, the commissions requested his legal expert, Morris Bien, to draft a model. Hoping that this action might lead to greater uniformity in state water-right legislation, Bien consented.[16] The code that he wrote during the summer of 1904 was like the Utah and Idaho codes, a variant of the Wyoming system. It contained the Wyoming permit method of acquiring rights and the Wyoming administrative hierarchy, but not the Wyoming adjudication procedure. Like the Utah code it left adjudication to the courts, but sought to improve the Utah determination by requiring that the state engineer submit the report of his hydrographic survey to the state's attorney general, who within sixty days was to initiate a suit in the district court. Like the Idaho statute, the Bien code declared streams and lakes the property of the public and the water appurtenant to the land.[17]

The Washington commission took the Bien code, slightly altered it, and, after adding sections of rate fixing and the abolition of riparian rights, had it introduced, with McBride's blessing, into the 1905 legislature. Its opponents were many. Riparian owners, especially those west of the Cascades, disliked the bill. Canal corporations opposed its rate-fixing feature. One such corporation was the Washington Irrigation Company, owner of the Sunnyside Project in the Yakima Valley. This company sought to prevent the federal government from constructing reservoirs and taking control of the project. Other opponents claimed that a state

engineer was unnecessary and that the adjudication procedure would provoke interminable lawsuits. In short, the
bill's enemies in the legislature outnumbered its friends and
it did not pass.[18] Nor did its counterpart in the 1905 Oregon
legislative assembly fare much better. Section after section
was whittled away until only the provisions creating the
office of state engineer were left. On the Great Plains, however, the Bien code received a more favorable reception.[19]

The 1905 legislatures of North Dakota, South Dakota,
and Oklahoma adopted the code with minimal modifications. These adoptions, however, were somewhat hasty, for
institutions created for use in the arid Rocky Mountain states
were not well adapted to the semihumid plains, where rainfall frequently made irrigation unnecessary. The permit system proved useful, but the state engineers conducted few
hydrographic surveys and initiated fewer adjudications.
Moreover, with limited irrigation there was little need for a
hierarchy of water commissioners and watermasters to
divide the streams. As the North Dakota state engineer wrote
in his 1905 report, the provisions for the appointment of
these officials were not "directly applicable to this state" and
so they were never appointed. The state engineer of South
Dakota did not appoint a water commissioner until 1950, and
then to apportion the waters of Rapid Creek in the western
part of the state.[20]

The territory of New Mexico also adopted the Bien
system. In 1901, after Congress granted new Mexico five
hundred thousand acres of the public domain to finance the
construction of reservoirs, the territorial legislature authorized the appointment of a commission of irrigation to select
sites for the reservoirs and to designate lands capable of
irrigation from them. A year later, the Congress passed the
Reclamation Act of 1902 and the commission turned some of
its attention to implementing that statute. Aware of the
interest of the Reclamation Service in better water-right

enforcement, the Commission members, under the presidency of Granville A. Richardson of Roswell, prepared a bill embodying the Wyoming system. As enacted in 1905, it created the office of territorial engineer, divided the territory into six water divisions, and established a board of control with authority to determine rights.[21]

The act never became operative. The legislature failed to fund it and in 1907 it was replaced by the Bien code, minus provision for a hierarchy of administrative officers. Instead the territorial engineer was given the power to create water districts and on "the written application of a majority of the water users . . . to appoint a water master" in each one. In declaring water appurtenant to the irrigated land, the statute incorporated into law the custom of communities irrigating from *acequias* in the Rio Grande Valley, dating back to Spanish times and perhaps before.[22]

In the Pacific Northwest, the Oregonians tried again to enact a code in 1907, with even less success than in 1905. The Portland Board of Trade appointed a committee composed of citizens from both sides of the Cascades. Late in 1906 it drafted a bill, which was introduced into the 1907 legislature. Although Governor George Earle Chamberlain, a progressive, conservation-minded Democrat, recommended its passage, lack of interest from the humid section of the state doomed the bill to defeat.[23]

Not willing to give up, the governor requested the state engineer to prepare a report on the need for water-right reform. Issued in December 1907, the greatest demand for it came from members of the Oregon State Grange. Those in Multnomah County (of which Portland is the seat) read it, discussed it, and adopted a resolution favoring reform, which they distributed to every one of the 120 subordinate granges in the state. As a consequence, when the state organization met in its annual convention in Eugene on May 14, 1908, it approved resolutions that began:

Whereas, titles to water are of equal importance with titles to land, and it appears that a water right should be as easily ascertained, as clearly defined, as secure, and in all respects as definite as a . . . title to land, and

Whereas, it is apparent that without a definite system of water right titles and adequate protection by the State, our water users are burdened with costly, and apparently, unending litigation; our present constructed works are depreciated in value; the United States hesitates to construct irrigation systems; private capital declines to invest; homeseekers go to other States and countries, where the purchase of an irrigated farm does not mean the purchase of a lawsuit, and thus our development is seriously retarded.

Following this statement of need, the Grangers demanded that the state of Oregon "codify and enact a complete, concise, and definite water law . . . based upon the best experience of other States and countries, such as Wyoming, Idaho and Canada." Rights, they declared, should be granted by the state, recorded in a central office, and determined by adjudications based on hydrographic measurements. Water in turn should be distributed by "efficient" administrators, limited by beneficial use and tied to the irrigated land.[24]

It so happened that as the Grangers were meeting in Eugene, President Theodore Roosevelt was meeting in Washington, D.C., with the governors of the states. He had called them together to consider the conservation of the nation's natural resources, a gesture that was the apogee of the Roosevelt conservation crusade. The governors recommended the creation of a national conservation commission with similar ones in each state. The president responded with the appointment of the national commission, divided into four sections —water, forests, lands, and minerals. Governor Chamberlain lost no time in returning home and appointing the Oregon

Conservation Commission. It turned its attention immediately to the water-rights problem and issued a report in November 1908.[25]

The report reiterated the weaknesses of posting notices and relying on court adjudications. It noted the inability under that system to determine perfected rights without costly litigation, which was usually prolonged and invariably inconclusive. The report praised the Wyoming system and repeated the recommendations of the state Grange. One month after the issuance of this report, the commission held a public hearing at the Portland Commercial Club, December 14, 1908. Citizens attended from all parts of the state. Clarence T. Johnston, the state engineer of Wyoming, was present and described the Wyoming system. After the meeting, the commission prepared a code patterned after that of Wyoming and submitted it to the 1909 legislature. Governor Chamberlain, soon to begin an illustrious career in the United States Senate, urged that it be given "careful consideration."[26]

The solons took his advice. The senate irrigation committee, objecting to administrative determination, promptly amended the bill to provide for submission of the determination to a court for review and approval. On the floor of the senate, its members altered the method of selecting the state engineer and the divisional superintendents, providing for their election instead of for their appointment. Amended also to protect vested riparian rights, the measure passed both houses with ease.[27]

The principal difference between the Oregon and Wyoming systems lies in the role of the courts. In the Oregon system the determination of the board of control must "be filed with the clerk of the circuit court." Within "thirty days from the filing . . . any party may file exceptions to the determination. If no exceptions shall be filed, the court shall on the day set for hearing enter a decree affirming the determination of the board." Had he known, Colorado's Judge

Victor Elliott would have been pleased.[28] The National Irrigation Congress, which had been meeting annually since 1891, promptly hailed the new system as a model for other states, and Nevada and Utah revamped their adjudication procedures afer it, the former in 1915, the latter in 1919. The Arizona legislators also thought it good and in 1919 adopted it with modifications.[29]

As in most western states and territories, water rights in Arizona were initially adjudicated by the courts, especially by the district court of Maricopa County. In 1892, in a contest over the use of the Salt River, Judge Joseph H. Kibbey interpreted the Howell Code of 1864 to mean that priorities were determined by the dates that the water was first applied to the land, to which it became attached. In keeping with this interpretation, he issued a decree ordering the allocation of the disputed water to the ditches in accordance with the dates of initial use. After issuing the decree, the judge appointed a water commissioner to execute it. When the canal corporations circumvented it, the Salt River Valley Water Users' Association brought suit and Judge Edward Kent in 1910 affirmed his predecessor's decision.[30]

Since court adjudications were prolonged, expensive, inconclusive, and confined to the streams of one county, some Arizonans looked for a better way. The severe drought of 1897–1900 provoked the introduction into the 1901 territorial legislature of the Ivy bill by James P. Ivy of Maricopa County. It provided for the adoption of the Wyoming system, but opponents in the house killed it by a vote of seven to sixteen. So unpopular was the system that it was ridiculed in the constitutional convention of 1910 during a debate on water rights.[31]

As the territory entered statehood, the principal proponent of water-right reform was George E. P. Smith, professor of irrigation engineering at the University of Arizona. His principal interest was the construction of the San Carlos storage reservoir on the overappropriated Gila River, a stream that flowed through eight counties. Since this project could not be undertaken until rights in the stream were determined, he urged reform. To achieve it, he drafted a bill incorporating the Oregon system for introduction into the 1915 legislature, but the Arizona solons failed to consider it. The principal opposition came from members of the Salt River Valley Water Users' Association, who wanted to safeguard their court-decreed rights. Consequently, not until Smith altered the bill so as to respect those rights did the association approve it. Rewritten to eliminate the board of control and the elaborate administrative system, the bill was enacted by the 1919 legislative assembly. It provided Arizona with a state water commissioner, who was authorized to divide the state into water districts as needed. It also provided for the Wyoming method of acquiring new rights, the Oregon system of adjudicating vested ones, and Arizona's traditional appurtenance of the water to the irrigated land.[32]

Neighboring California retained its allegiance to the system of posting notices, required by the 1872 statute, until 1914, in spite of a thirty-year effort on the part of reformers to replace it. State engineer William Hall advocated state regulation of water rights—state recordation of existing rights in a central office, their adjudication by the state, state issuance of new rights, and state administration of all rights. The legislature, however, did not agree with him and failed to fund his office adequately. In frustration, he resigned in 1888 and the solons discontinued the office.[33]

Eleven years later, in 1899, a group of citizens requested Elwood Mead to undertake an investigation of the water-rights situation within the state. The previous year Mead had left Wyoming to take charge of investigations conducted by the United States Department of Agriculture into the irrigation laws and practices in the western states and territories. He responded with studies made by a team of irrigation engineers during 1900. They found that the streams were overappropriated—six claims to the entire flow of the San Joaquin River—and that rights determinations by the courts had been lengthy, inconclusive, and costly. As a remedy they recommended the adoption of the Wyoming system. Thereupon, the newly organized Water and Forest Association appointed a committee of prominent citizens to draft a bill for introduction into the legislature. The committee met and delegated the drafting to one of its members, John D. Works, a former justice of the California Supreme Court and author of a treatise on water law.[34]

The Works bill followed in general the recommendations of the Department of Agriculture investigators. It provided for the Wyoming permit system of acquiring rights, adjudications by an administrative board, and the distribution of the appropriated waters by state officials. As soon as it was presented to the public, it aroused a storm of protest, especially in the southern part of the state, where rights had been adjudicated by the courts. Again, as in 1884, the southern California irrigators assembled in Riverside. Among them was John Wesley North's son, John Greenleaf North. No longer were they radicals trying to overturn the laws of California; now they were conservatives seeking to protect their court-adjudicated rights. One speaker attacked the bill as "autocratic, dictatorial and nagging," another as "one of the most vicious bills relating to the question of irrigation, which [he had] ever seen attempted in this State." They regarded the bill as a threat to their decreed rights. North spoke for the assembled water users when he declared, "The general purpose of the proposed act . . . is to interfere with and unsettle and confuse rights already vested, established and adjudicated." He opposed administrative determinations and favored the status quo. The southern Californians also opposed the creation of a costly hierarchy of state officials to distribute the waters, preferring local management. In the face of such determined opposition, the Works bill was introduced into the 1903 legislature, referred to a committee, and reported adversely.[35]

Water-rights reform in California had to await the triumph of the progressive movement in that state. In 1910, the people elected a reform governor, Hiram Johnson, and a reform legislature. Urged by the governor, this legislature created the California State Conservation Commission, which drafted a water-rights bill. Introduced into the 1913 legislative assembly, it was enacted as the State Water Commission Act. Nonetheless, the opposition was strong enough to refer it to a vote of the people, who approved it in November of 1914.[36]

The State Water Commission Act of 1913 declared the unappropriated waters of the state "public waters . . . subject to appropriation" under the supervision of a commission consisting of five persons. It provided for the Wyoming system of acquiring rights and the Oregon system of adjudication. Although the statute gave the commission "power to supervise the distribution of water in accordance with the priorities," California has never developed a hierarchy of administrative officials similar to that of Wyoming.[37]

In the same year that California enacted the water commission act, Texas adopted the Wyoming permit system, placing the acquisition of appropriative rights under the control of a board of water engineers. When four years later the legislature gave the agency the power of adjudication, the supreme court of Texas declared in 1921 that the grant of judicial power to a member of the executive branch was unconstitutional. Adjudications remained the exclusive domain of the courts until, with the passage in 1967 of the Water Rights Adjudication Act, Texas adopted the Oregon system.[38]

Adjudication by the courts was also favored by the state of Washington, where riparian proprietors west of the Cascades and electric power companies blocked reform until

1917. Four years after the defeat of the Bien Code, Governor M. E. Hay appointed another code commission, headed by Professor O. W. Waller of Washington State College. The commission drafted a code modeled after the Oregon system, only to have it rejected by the 1911 legislature. Undismayed, the governor appointed a third code commission, whose draft, which eliminated the board of control feature of the Oregon system, was likewise defeated by the next legislature. By this time it had become apparent to the Reclamation Service officials in the state that a greater mobilization of support for reform was needed. As a consequence, they invited Washington irrigators to a conference held in North Yakima, January 14–16, 1914, where the Washington Irrigation Institute was organized. Although the first bill sponsored by this organization was defeated, the second was enacted in 1917. It provided for an adjudication procedure similar to that of the 1903 Idaho statute, with the state engineer serving as a referee of the court.[39]

More loyal than the Washingtonians to the institutions of local control were the Montanans. The state's water-right reformers made no less than five attempts during the first third of this century to replace local control with state control. They made their first attempt in 1903, when E. C. Kinney, who had recently directed the construction of the Low Line Canal in the Gallatin Valley, drafted a bill modeled after the Wyoming code. When it was introduced into the legislature, opponents prevented its enactment, although supporters were able to salvage the office of state engineer with limited functions. They returned to the legislative halls again in 1917 with another facsimile of the Wyoming statute, only to suffer another defeat.

The proponents of the Wyoming system did not give up. Believing that they needed to mobilize greater popular support, they followed the example of Washington and organized the Montana Irrigation and Drainage Institute. Meeting first in January 1920, its legislative committee drafted another copy of the Wyoming code, which like its predecessors was rejected by the legislature. Since one of the objections to it was adjudication by an administrative board, the leaders of the institute incorporated into their next bill the Oregon adjudication procedure. Submitted to the solons in 1923 and again in 1925, these compromise measures were each time defeated. Montana water users preferred enforcement by local officials with whom they were familiar.[40]

Montanans soon had reason to regret their failure to establish centralized recordation of their water rights. When in the mid-1930s they undertook to negotiate the Yellowstone River Compact with Wyoming, they found themselves at a disadvantage. Wyoming had a record of all its water rights in a central office. Montana, where the miners' method of appropriation still prevailed, did not have a complete record of any kind, not even in the county courthouses. In an attempt to remedy the situation, the 1939 legislature hastened to demand that "the waters of this State and especially interstate streams arising out of the State, be investigated and adjudicated as soon as possible in order to protect the rights of water users in this State." To implement the request, the state engineer, Fred E. Buck, initiated the Montana Water Resources Survey. This was a program of cataloguing, county by county, irrigation projects and of mapping the lands irrigated by them, but it was in no way an adjudication of rights. Although the legislators in 1953 directed that all appropriations of the waters of interstate streams made after January 1, 1950, be recorded in the state engineer's office in Helena, the law usually was not obeyed and Montana remained without a complete registry in a central office of its surface water rights.[41]

In fact, Montanans retained unaltered local administration of those rights until 1973, when change was provoked by water needs of the Southwest. Water planners proposed to divert the waters of the Columbia and Missouri rivers. In 1966 congressmen from the area amended the Central Arizona Project authorization bill to empower the secretary of the interior to investigate the feasibility of importing water from the Columbia, and a Texas plan to divert some of the flow of the Missouri onto the High Plains was nearly approved by the state's voters in 1969. Again it was evident that Montanans needed a complete record of their water rights. Again bills to adopt the Wyoming system or portions of it were introduced into sessions of the legislature and again in 1967, 1969, and 1971 they were rejected.[42]

A few months after the adjournment of the 1971 legislature, the people of Montana chose delegates to a constitutional convention. When these delegates assembled, they incorporated into the state's 1972 constitution a provision directing the legislature to "establish a system of centralized records, in addition to the present system of local records."[43] The Department of Natural Resources and Conservation then prepared a draft bill. With some alterations, it was another copy of the Wyoming code! When it was submitted to the legislature as the Montana Water Use Act of 1973, the holders of adjudicated rights in the southwestern valleys forced revisions. They persuaded the solons to amend the rights determinations sections of the act to provide for the Oregon procedure and to retain administration of the streams by the district courts. The permit system of acquiring rights was the only part of the Wyoming system to survive the legislative hatchet.[44]

The Department of Natural Resources and Conservation selected the Powder River in southeastern Montana as the first stream for adjudication under the new system, but when the department had adjudicated only that stream by 1977, Montanans became concerned. At this rate, they said, it would take one hundred years to complete the determination of water rights in the state, and since they were in competition with other states for the use of interstate stream waters Montana didn't have that long to assemble a central registry of rights.[45]

One of the impatient citizens was state representative John P. Scully of House District No. 76 in Gallatin County. Seeking to speed up the adjudication process, he incorporated a proposal for the creation of a number of specialized water judges into a bill and submitted it to the 1977 legislature as House Bill No. 809. The house approved it by a unanimous vote, but the senate, instead of passing it, proposed the appointment of a joint house-senate interim study committee. Chaired by Scully, it revised the bill after holding informational meetings throughout the state and introduced it as Senate Bill No. 76 in the 1979 legislature. The act, which was passed, required all claimants to the use of water in Montana to submit their claims to the Department of Natural Resources and Conservation by January 1, 1982, and the adjudication of those claims by four water judges. Montanans remain loyal to adjudication of water rights by the courts.[46]

Not so loyal were the water users of Alaska. Five years after gaining statehood, the new commonwealth employed Frank J. Trelease, dean of the college of law at the University of Wyoming, to serve as consultant in the drafting of the Alaska Water Use Act of 1966. As might be expected, it provides for the Wyoming system of acquiring new rights and administrative determination of existing ones, although by an administrative official rather than by a board. This official has the authority to divide the streams, but the act creates no hierarchy of officials.[47]

Little could Elwood Mead have dreamed, when he advised the constitutional convention of Wyoming, that he would have such great influence on the irrigation institutions of the western states.

11
Rights to
Interstate Waters

Rivers frequently cross the boundaries of states or flow between them. When this situation occurs west of the ninety-eighth meridian, irrigators in different states use the same stream; initially when they quarreled over that use they sought enforcement of their rights in the federal courts. If the dispute was between individual irrigators or canal companies, it was adjudicated by a federal lower court. If it was between states, then the U.S. Supreme Court decided the case.

When irrigators on Sage Creek, which arises in Montana and flows into Wyoming, quarreled in the 1890s, the aggrieved party, who lived in Wyoming, brought suit in the Ninth U.S. Circuit Court. He claimed that appropriators in Montana, who had diverted the creek subsequent to his diversion, were depriving him of sufficient water to irrigate his crops. Consequently he petitioned the court to enjoin them from their excessive and illegal use of the stream. The judge, the veteran Montana jurist Hiram Knowles, complied. A few years later, forty-eight appropriators of the west fork of the Carson River in Nevada failed to receive enough water to irrigate their crops. In response, they sued in federal court some thirty irrigators in California, where the stream originates. After hearing the case, the federal judge imposed a system of rotation on both the plaintiffs and defendants. The firm of Miller and Lux, with properties along nearby Walker River, protested in the same court diversions by Thomas B. Rickey and others in California. A federal judge heard the arguments in the dispute and on January 4, 1904, favored the plaintiff. By this time, Kansas and Colorado were in court.[1]

The Arkansas River rises in the mountains of central Colorado and flows southeast 280 miles before entering Kansas. It continues through that state, turning southeast again, near Great Bend, Kansas, toward Oklahoma. During the last decades of the nineteenth century the Coloradans diverted a considerable portion of it for the purpose of irrigation, lessening its flow in Kansas. As a consequence, residents of the valley in the Jayhawk State prevailed on their legislature in 1901 to instruct the attorney general of Kansas to institute a suit in the Supreme Court. In his petition he requested that the tribunal enjoin the Coloradans from diverting the waters of the river. Although the state recognized the appropriation as well as the riparian right, he contended that the valley's riparian owners had a right to have the Arkansas River flow as it was wont to flow without diminution or alteration.

In their defense, the Coloradans argued that as citizens of "a sovereign and independent state," they could, if they wished, "deprive Kansas and her citizens of any use . . . or share" of the river. They relied, they said, on the rules governing relations among nations and pointed out that their state occupied "toward the state of Kansas the same position that foreign states occupy toward each other." If they needed the water, they could use it to the detriment of downstream residents.

The Court rejected the contentions of both parties. Regarding "equality of right" as the "cardinal rule, underlying all the relations of states to each other," it sought to determine an "equitable apportionment of benefits between the two states resulting from the flow of the river." Taking note of the productive agricultural economy created by the diversions in Colorado, the justices could not find that these diversions had injured southwestern Kansas to any great extent. When they compared this limited injury "with the great benefit which has obviously resulted to the counties in Colorado," they concluded "that equality of right and equity between the two states forbids any interference with the present withdrawal of water in Colorado for purpose of irrigation." It was a victory for Colorado, but a tentative, inconclusive one, for the justices allowed Kansas to return to the Court in case Colorado increased its diversions and upset the balance.[2]

The Kansas-Colorado suit worried western water users. As they counted the number of streams crossing state lines, they could foresee as many interstate lawsuits, many of them as expensive and unsatisfactory as this one. The testimony of 347 witnesses had filled 8,559 typewritten pages and produced 122 exhibits, all at a cost of $200,000. Yet, aside from establishing a rule for the apportionment of interstate streams, the decision had settled nothing. Kansas could reopen the dispute at will.[3]

Elwood Mead was one of those concerned. While attending the National Irrigation Congress meeting in Boise, Idaho, in 1906, he proposed the appointment of a committee to determine the administrative measures needed to protect both intrastate and interstate water rights. The assembly accepted the proposal and the chair appointed a committee consisting of Mead; Morris Bien; John H. Lewis, the state engineer of Oregon; and two others. The men met and proposed the creation of a "Federal administrative system corresponding in character to that needed for the establishing and protection of rights within a state." In other words, protection of interstate water rights on a national scale required a version of the Wyoming system.[4]

A number of years later, at meetings of the American Society of Civil Engineers, John Lewis described the proposal in some detail. It would, he said, establish a national interstate commission with authority to plan the development of rivers. It would have authority to determine and record rights to water in states where they had not been determined and the power, like that possessed by the Wyoming board of control, "to refuse any permit where the proposed use was a menace to the safety or welfare of the public." Such an infringement on state control of water rights was too much for most westerners to accept, and the proposal was stillborn. The solution to the problem lay in another direction.[5]

A few years after the announcement of the Kansas-Colorado decision in 1907 the Coloradans were assailed, not by one, but by three neighbors. The Kansans renewed their attack in 1910, Wyoming initiated a prolonged suit in 1911, and Nebraska irrigators joined the assault in 1913.

A Kansas ditch company, not the state, resumed the attack in 1910. The United States Irrigating Company sued the Graham Ditch Company and other Colorado defendants in a federal district court, demanding a determination of priorities between users on both sides of the state line. When after six years of litigation the case was settled out of court, the attack on the Graham Ditch Company was immediately renewed by another Kansas company.[6]

Wyoming sued the state of Colorado and two corporations to prevent the diversion of the Laramie River through a tunnel into the Cache la Poudre to irrigate fields in that valley. The river originates in northern Colorado and flows across the state boundary to join the North Platte in the vicinity of Wheatland. Wyoming objected to the diversion, asserting that it would injure irrigators in that state. Filed in the Supreme Court on May 29, 1911, the case was argued in 1916 and reargued in 1918, when the federal government intervened, claiming ownership of the unappropriated waters in western unnavigable streams. It was argued again in 1922, when it was finally decided.[7]

The third suit was initiated by the Pioneer Irrigation Company of Nebraska in an effort to obtain a greater allocation of the waters of the Republican River. It was directed against the Colorado state engineer and his subordinates. Argued in a federal district court and appealed to the U.S. Supreme Court, its litigation continued for nearly a decade.[8]

To assist in the defense of the state's interests in the Wyoming and Nebraska cases, the attorney general of Colorado selected an attorney from Greeley, Delph E. Carpenter. A graduate of the law department of the University of Denver, he had engaged in general practice until 1908, when he began to specialize in water-right cases. As the three suits dragged on, costing hundreds of man-hours and thousands of dollars, he concluded that there was a better way of apportioning interstate streams—namely, by treaty or compact.[9] Borrowing from the assumption of the Colorado attorneys in the *Kansas* vs. *Colorado* suit that the states of the Union are "sovereign and independent," Carpenter noted that before nations go to war they try to achieve their objectives by diplomacy, by the negotiation of a treaty; so, he argued, should the states of the Union before they went to court. The Constitution authorized the states, with the consent of Congress, to enter into compacts. The device had been used since 1780 to settle disputes over boundaries and fisheries. If compacts were useful for these purposes, they could be used to apportion interstate streams. The United States had used treaties to allocate the waters of three western international rivers. In 1906, it had negotiated a treaty with Mexico to grant annually sixty thousand acre-feet of the Rio Grande to that nation, while in 1909 it had reached an agreement with Great Britain concerning the use of the St. Mary and Milk rivers. Moreover, alarmed by the claims made by federal lawyers during the Wyoming-Colorado litigation, the Greeley attorney thought that to resort to negotiation and compact making would reduce opportunities for federal encroachment on state control of streams.[10]

Carpenter's views soon found acceptance. During the summer of 1920 water statesmen of the Colorado River Basin were at loggerheads over its development. Those from southern California favored the construction of a large storage reservoir on the lower Colorado and a California congressman had introduced a bill into Congress for that purpose. Fearing the perfection of prior rights by lower basin appropriators, the upper basin states opposed the project. To prevent a deadlock at a meeting of the seven basin states in Denver and a possible suit, Delph Carpenter proposed that the dispute be settled by the negotiation of a compact. His view prevailed and the assembly resolved,

> That it is the sense of this conference that the present and future rights of the several States whose territory is in whole or in part included within the drainage area of the Colorado River ... should be settled and determined by compact or agreement between said States ... with consent of Congress, and that the legislatures of said States be requested to authorize the appointment of commissioners for each of said States for the purpose of entering into such compact or agreement for subsequent ratification and approval by the Legislatures of each said States and the Congress of the United States.[11]

Carpenter promptly drafted a model bill for introduction into the state legislatures to authorize the appointment of commissioners. During the winter and early spring of 1921, the legislatures acted and the governors made the appointments. Appropriately, the governor of Colorado selected Carpenter as the commissioner for his state. On May 10, the seven governors met in Denver to request the approval of the federal government. Representative Frank W. Mondell of

Wyoming introduced a bill in Congress authorizing the states to negotiate "a compact . . . providing for an equitable division and apportionment . . . of the water supply of the Colorado River" and the president to appoint a representative on the commission. Congress approved the bill and President Warren G. Harding appointed his secretary of commerce, Herbert Hoover, to represent the federal government in the negotiations.[12]

The Colorado River Commission met in Washington, D.C., on January 26, 1922, and, after electing Hoover as chairman, they began their compact making. They initially sought to divide the waters of the river among the seven states in proportion to the irrigable acreage in each state, but they were unable to agree on the number of acres capable of irrigation. Although the meeting in Washington adjourned without agreement, Delph Carpenter did not despair. In August, three months before the commissioners reconvened, he proposed an allocation between the upper and lower basins of the river rather than among the states. He suggested that the demarcation line between the two basins cross the Colorado River at Lee's Ferry in the canyons of northern Arizona and that each basin receive one-half of the total flow across that line.[13]

When the commission reconvened at Bishop's Lodge near Santa Fe on November 9, 1922, Carpenter's proposal became the basis of agreement. The Reclamation Service had estimated that the average annual flow of the Colorado River at Lee's Ferry, from 1899 through 1920, had been 16.4 million acre-feet. To give some leeway, Herbert Hoover suggested that the conferees accept a figure of 15 million acre-feet, with 7.5 million going to each basin. This division of the waters was acceptable to the other commissioners, with the exception of W.S. Norviel of Arizona. He demanded the exclusion of the flow of the Gila, which supplied water to the irrigated fields of central Arizona, from the lower basin's allocation. To mollify him, his colleagues voted to give the lower basin an additional one million acre-feet. This decision having been made, along with another concerning the allocation of water to Mexico, the members of the commission met in Santa Fe's historic Palace of the Governors on November 24, 1922, and signed the Colorado River Compact.[14] Addison J. McCune, the state engineer of Colorado, was exultant. A few weeks after the signing of the compact, he wrote: "This move marks a new era in the administration of the rivers of the United States. It substitutes a common sense method of doing business among partners instead of resorting to fruitless and exasperating wrangles in the courts." His rejoicing, however, was somewhat premature. Arizona refused to ratify the compact.[15]

The governor of Arizona, George W. P. Hunt, opposed any limitation of the state's use of the Colorado River and the legislature withheld its endorsement. The southern Californians, however, viewed with increasing impatience the intransigence of their neighbors. Los Angeles wanted potable water and hydroelectric power; the residents of the Imperial Valley, a storage reservoir and an all-American canal. Early in December 1927, Congressman Phil Swing and Senator Hiram Johnson introduced their fourth bill authorizing the construction of both the reservoir and the canal. Under pressure from the upper-basin states, Congress amended the bill in the following manner: the act was not to go into effect until six states had ratified the Colorado River Compact and California had agreed to limit its use of the river to 4.4 million acre-feet, plus half of the unallocated surplus. Moreover, Congress authorized the three lower-basin states to enter into an agreement that would grant Nevada 300,000 acre-feet and Arizona 2.8 million acre-feet of the Colorado River. In addition, the proposed agreement would give Arizona "exclusive beneficial consumptive use of the Gila River and its tributaries within the boundaries" of the state. Congress approved the amended bill and President Calvin Coolidge signed it, December 21, 1928. Six states promptly reratified the compact, the California legislature enacted a self-limitation act, and Herbert Hoover, now president, declared the Boulder Canyon Act effective. Adamant, Arizona resorted to litigation in the U.S. Supreme Court to obtain first a clarification of the provisions of the compact and later, in 1935, a judicial apportionment of the river. The Court rejected both petitions. Finally, in 1944, after a severe drought had revealed the need for both Colorado water and power, Arizona, under the positive leadership of Governor Sidney P. Osborn, ratified the Colorado River Compact.[16]

Part of Arizona's opposition to the compact was due to the provision regarding the sharing of the river's waters with Mexico. The document provided that if in the future the United States recognized the right of Mexico to the use of any of the Colorado River, the amount used should come from the surplus "over and above" that allocated to the basins, and in case that was insufficient the deficiency should be borne equally by each of the basins. Contending that Mexico had no right to the use of the river, Arizona feared that the United States in negotiations with Mexico would give away too much water. Since this fear was shared by the leaders of the other basin states, the Department of State conducted many conferences with them in an effort to reach agreement. Finally, after twenty years of discussion, the department negotiated in 1944 a treaty patterned after that of 1906, by which, in the interest of international comity, Mexico was granted 1.5 million acre-feet of the annual flow of the Colorado River.[17]

With the apportionment of the stream between the basins and with the Mexican grant approved, there remained its division within the basins. The upper basin acted first. After two years of studies and field meetings, representatives of Arizona, Colorado, New Mexico, Utah, and Wyoming met in Vernal, Utah, during the summer of 1948 and divided among the five states the 7.5 million acre-feet apportioned them by the Colorado River Compact. After granting Arizona fifty thousand acre-feet, they granted Colorado 51.75 percent of the apportionment; New Mexico, 11.25 percent; Utah, 23 percent; and Wyoming the remaining 14 percent. These decisions they incorporated into the Upper Colorado River Basin Compact, which they signed in Santa Fe, again in the Palace of the Governors, on October 11, 1948.[18]

To divide the waters of the lower basin, Arizona in 1952 again sought a judicial determination. This time the high court responded affirmatively. In a surprise 1963 decision, it declared that the waters had already been divided, that Congress in passing the amended Boulder Canyon Act had apportioned the waters of the lower basin—4.4 million acre-feet to California, 2.8 million to Arizona, and three hundred thousand to Nevada. Forty-three years had elapsed since Delph Carpenter proposed to a conference of the seven Colorado Basin states, meeting in Denver, that they apportion the river by the negotiation of a contract; forty-three years of controversy, acrimonious feuding, agreement, disagreement, and finally resort to federal dictation.[19]

Nevertheless, the elation of state engineer McCune was not without foundation. By 1963, the western states had concluded fifteen apportionment compacts; by 1973, the number had increased to twenty-one. Of the first fifteen, Colorado had negotiated eight and New Mexico, seven. But negotiations were often prolonged while states tried to obtain as much of the precious resource as possible. Ratification sessions were stormy, and in the case of the Rio Grande Compact of 1939, execution was faulty.[20]

The Rio Grande rises in the San Juan Mountains of southern Colorado, flows across New Mexico, and for twelve hundred miles becomes the boundary between the United States and Mexico. Geographers have divided its watershed into two basins, with Fort Quitman, Texas, as the division point. Within the upper basin irrigators have created three oases, one in the San Luis Valley of southern Colorado, another in central New Mexico, and a third south of Elephant Butte, consisting of the Mesilla and El Paso-Ciudad Juárez valleys. Of these oases, the one in the San Luis Valley was the youngest; the other two were being created by Native Americans in pre-Columbia times. Although the Anglo-Americans augmented the irrigated acreage in the latter two oases, they were largely responsible for irrigation in the San Luis Valley. Following the arrival of the Denver and Rio Grande railroad in 1878, people began to arrive in considerable numbers. To provide them with a livelihood, entrepreneurs like T. C. Henry built a network of large canals, increasing over a decade and a half the number of irrigated acres by nearly 200,000. As a consequence, the waters of the upper basin soon became overappropriated.[21]

Since the San Luis appropriators were located at the head of the river, they filled their ditches first and in the dry years little water flowed down into the ditches of the Mesilla and El Paso-Ciudad Juárez valleys. Faced with this situation, the residents concluded that they needed a storage reservoir, but they disagreed on its location. The El Paso-Ciudad Juárez communities favored a dam in the narrows just north of El Paso, while the Mesilla irrigators preferred a dam 125 miles to the north, at Elephant Butte. The residents of the two valleys feuded over the site for more than a decade, until the Reclamation Service began the construction of a reservoir at Elephant Butte.[22]

Although the reservoir was completed in 1916, its existence did not guarantee a supply of water. The Coloradans continued to fill their ditches. Moreover, they talked of new projects to catch flood waters in upstream reservoirs. The New Mexicans protested, with the result that both states agreed in 1923 to the negotiation of a compact. Before they could draft a document, they were joined by Texas.

The Rio Grande Compact of 1929 sought to maintain the status quo, to freeze existing diversions and to allow no new ones. Colorado agreed not to allow "the water supply at the Interstate Gauging Station to be impaired by new or increased diversions or storage." New Mexico made a similar pledge, agreeing not to impair the water supply of the Elephant Butte reservoir by new diversions or storage. It was a temporary agreement, to last for five years until the commissioners, for whom the compact provided, could negotiate a more lasting agreement.[23]

The commissioners, however, were unable to agree. When it appeared that the compact was not going to be renewed, Texas in October of 1935 sought relief in litigation, complaining that New Mexico had violated the 1929 agreement by allowing new diversions that impaired the water supply of the Elephant Butte reservoir. Texas' action was prompted by the construction of the El Vado reservoir on the Rio Chama by the Middle Rio Grande Conservancy District, organized in 1925 to provide flood protection and improve the efficiency of water use north and south of Albuquerque. With strife imminent, the federal government intervened. President Franklin D. Roosevelt issued an order on September 23, 1935, prohibiting federal agencies from approving "any application for a project involving the use of Rio Grande waters without securing from the National Resources Committee a prompt opinion on it." The committee, a New Deal planning agency, responded by proposing to the Rio Grande commissioners a joint federal-states investigation of the water resources of the upper basin. The commission favored the proposal and, after the completion of the investigation, used its data to write a new compact, the Rio Grande Compact of 1938. Believing that the new agreement would lead to a resolution of its grievances, Texas discontinued its suit.[24]

The compact of 1938 wss a revision of that of 1929. It too was designed to preserve the status quo, but unlike the previous one the revision provided for detailed schedules of water deliveries at the Colorado-New Mexico state line and into the Elephant Butte reservoir. Like the other, the new compact created a commission, but this commission was to serve as an administrative agency with authority to maintain and operate stream gauging stations, to collect data, keep records, and review periodically the provisions of the agreement.[25]

Thereafter, most of the interstate compacts provided for administrative commissions to monitor the division of the waters. The Colorado River Compact did not have such a provision, although it authorized the governors of the signatory states to appoint commissioners to settle controversies, subject to approval by the legislatures. On the other hand, the Upper Colorado River Basin Compact did establish a commission with power to "[l]ocate, establish, construct, abandon, operate and maintain water gauging stations . . . forecast water run-off . . . collect . . . data on stream flows," and conduct studies of the basin's water resources. Another agreement, negotiated in 1958 by Idaho, Utah, and Wyoming to apportion the Bear River, empowered the commissioners, in case of water shortage, to declare an emergency and to enforce water delivery schedules prepared by them, "based on priority of rights . . . without regard to the State boundary line." However useful these agencies proved to be, the Rio Grande Commission did not prevent continued strife over the use of that river.[26]

The Rio Grande Compact was in trouble from the beginning. New Mexico failed to make its contracted deliveries into the Elephant Butte reservoir during the first year that the agreement was in effect, which was 1940. 1941 was a wet year in the Southwest, but after 1942 the state fell behind in its deliveries until in 1951 it was 263,100 acre-feet in arrears. In response, Texas reinstituted its suit, but six years later the U.S. Supreme Court dismissed it. In the meantime, during the drought of the 1950s, Colorado dropped behind in its deliveries and by 1966 its debit was approachng 944,400 acre-feet. This time Texas was joined by New Mexico and together they sued Colorado to enforce compliance with the compact. The high court accepted jurisdiction and in 1968 the three states requested that the case be continued indefinitely, pending Colorado's meeting its delivery obligations. This Colorado was able to do during most of the years of the following decade. The continuance of the case, however, was maintained, hanging like the sword of Damocles over the head of Colorado. Certainly, the Rio Grande has been a river of conflict.[27]

No less controversial has been the Pecos River, which flows through eastern New Mexico, crosses the state line into Texas, and empties into the Rio Grande below Fort Quitman. Irrigation north of that line began on a large scale in 1888 with the organization of the Pecos Irrigation and Investment Company to water lands between Roswell and Eddy, soon to be renamed Carlsbad. As mentioned in Chapter 5, after the disastrous flood of 1904, the Reclamation Service assumed operation and rehabilitation of the southern part of the project. Diversions south of the line in Texas also began in the late 1880s, but the enterprises were smaller and more numerous. By 1920, the normal flow of the Pecos was fully appropriated and water users on both sides of the line were seeking to increase their available supply of water by the construction of storage reservoirs. The Texans sought to build one at Red Bluff astraddle the state line, while the New Mexicans were considering several alternative sites.[28]

Naturally competition arose for the waters of the river and to ward off a lawsuit the legislatures of the two states in 1923 authorized the appointment of commissioners to negotiate a compact. The appointed commissioners lost little time in drafting the Pecos River Compact of 1925. They allotted New Mexico enough water to irrigate seventy-six thousand acres and Texas enough to water forty thousand acres. To offset Texas' disadvantage, they authorized the construction of the Red Bluff Reservoir and denied a similar right to the New Mexicans. "[N]o permit or permits for the construction of any additional storage reservoir or reservoirs," read the compact, "within the Upper Basin, having an aggregate capacity or capacities of more than ten thousand (10,000) acre feet, shall be granted by the State of New Mexico prior to the first day of January, 1940." The legislatures of the two states promptly ratified the document, but at the request of the Carlsbad irrigators, Governor Arthur T. Hannett of New Mexico vetoed his state's approval. And when three successive New Mexican legislatures failed to renew their ratification, the Texas solons in 1931 rescinded theirs. The battle of the reservoirs was underway.

With the inauguration of the New Deal in 1933, Texas sought approval of the Red Bluff project from the Public Works Administration, received it, and began construction the next year. Too late, the New Mexico legislators in 1933 approved the 1925 compact with amendments, but the Lone Star State was no longer interested. In the meantime, the New Mexicans had discovered a reservoir site at the confluence of Alamogordo Creek and the Pecos, and were urging the construction of a dam there. Texas objected and New Mexico countered with an attempt to halt construction of the Red Bluff project. At this point, Secretary of the Interior Harold L. Ickes informed both parties that continued bickering and failure to agree would jeopardize both projects. The response to this threat was the Alamogordo Agreement of 1935.

The agreement was provisional, pending the negotiation of a formal compact. By it, Texas withdrew its opposition to the Alamogordo Reservoir on condition that New Mexico would not "cause or suffer Texas to be deprived in the future of the same proportion of the flood waters originating above Avalon Dam [of the Carlsbad Project] which [had] passed Avalon Dam during the past twenty years." New Mexico further agreed that it would not take from the Pecos more than enough water to irrigate seventy-six thousand acres. Like the Rio Grande Compact of 1929, this agreement was designed to preserve the status quo.

The state of New Mexico, however, made no attempt to translate this accord into a compact. The Texas legislature, on the other hand, in 1939 approved the negotiation of a compact based on the Alamogordo Agreement, but, when New Mexico did not respond, it repealed its action in 1941 and threatened litigation. By this time, the two states, in cooperation with the National Resources Committee (now renamed the National Resources Planning Board), were completing a thorough investigation of the water resources of the Pecos Valley, similar to the one undertaken on the Upper Rio Grande. With the report of the study in hand, Texas and New Mexico in 1942 appointed commissioners to write a compact. Hindered by rivalry and the deaths of the original appointees, it was not until December 3, 1948, that the commission met in Santa Fe for the final approval and signing of the second Pecos River Compact, some twenty-four years after the signing of the first.[29] This document sought to retain the status quo of 1947. Its key provision read: "New Mexico shall not deplete by man's activities the flow of the Pecos River at the New Mexico–Texas state line below an amount which will give to Texas a quantity of water equivalent to that available to Texas under the 1947 condition." Article five created an administrative commission with a mandate to monitor stream gauging stations, collect data, and supervise the execution of the compact.[30]

The first twenty-five years of the agreement were relatively harmonious. The commission conducted an aerial survey of the basin and secured federal assistance in the channelization of the Pecos near Carlsbad, reduction of water-consuming salt cedar growth, and alleviation of the stream's saline content. Only when New Mexico prepared to construct the Brantley Reservoir above Lake Avalon was the harmony shattered. To safeguard Texas' interests, Governor Preston Smith insisted on the inclusion of seven conditions in the authorizing legislation. When the New Mexicans refused, the Texans in 1974 went to court. The battle of the reservoirs resumed.[31]

Bitter rivalry over rivers has not been confined to the desert Southwest. The residents of the Pacific Northwest have tried for more than fifty years to apportion equitably the Columbia River. With the Bureau of Reclamation engaged in a feasibility investigation of the Columbia Basin project, the governor of Washington, in December 1924, proposed to the governors of Idaho, Montana, and Oregon the formation of a commission to allocate the waters of the river. The state executives responded favorably by the appointment of commissioners, who met and quickly disagreed over an allocation between the upstream and downstream states. Unable to bridge their differences, they disbanded without writing a pact.[32]

No further action was taken until President Harry Truman in April of 1949 endorsed the formation of the Columbia Valley Administration, modeled after the Tennessee Valley Authority. Again the governor of Washington took the initiative. Three months after Truman's action, in July of 1949, Governor Arthur B. Langlie invited the governors of Idaho, Montana, Oregon, and Wyoming to send representatives to a conference to consider the negotiation of a compact. The conferees met in Spokane on July 10, 1950, decided to organize a committee, invite Nevada and Utah to join them, and request Congress for authorization to enter into a pact.[33]

Congress gave its permission on July 16, 1952. The governors named their commissioners, who met and organized on October 7, 1952. Meeting frequently during the succeeding two years, they broadened the scope of their negotiations to include not only apportionment of water but also allocation of hydroelectric power, stream pollution, and protection of fish and wildlife. They did not apportion the river among the states, but subordinated downstream nonconsumptive uses of water to consumptive uses in the upstream area. Having come to agreement, they signed the pact in Portland on January 15, 1955, and referred it to the state legislatures. Idaho, Nevada, and Utah ratified it; Montana, Oregon, Washington, and Wyoming did not.[34]

Objections to the negotiated compact quickly emerged. Oregon and Washington objected to its allocation of power, asserting that it favored the upstream states. The federal government did not like the provision that gave upstream users preference over those downstream, and people in the state of Washington wanted greater representation on the pact's commission. The negotiating group discussed these objections and then revised the compact to meet them, adding a provision forbidding the diversion of water from the basin without the unanimous consent of the member states. People in the Pacific Northwest were becoming worried over proposals in Colorado and California to divert some of the Columbia into their states. On December 4, 1956, the commission signed the revised document and submitted it to the states for ratification, but none of the legislatures approved the compact.[35]

At this point in the negotiations a dispute surfaced that had divided the commissioners for some time—the question whether the compact's commission should be a recommendatory agency or an action agency with the power to construct and operate hydroelectric power plants, financed by the issue of revenue bonds. Oregon and Washington favored the latter type, the other states, the former. Because of the difference of opinion, no compact was submitted to the states in 1959. The commission did, however, submit a pact providing for a recommendatory administrative commission to the legislatures in 1961. Five states ratified it; Oregon and Washington did not. With minor alterations, the commissioners resubmitted it in 1963, with the same result. The two downstream states then withdrew their financial support and in 1966 the commission closed its office in Spokane. The commissioners, however, agreed to continue their work, still hoping for a resolution of the states' differences.[36]

There have been other fruitless compact negotiations. In 1948 South Dakota and Wyoming negotiated an agreement to determine rights to the Cheyenne River. Ratified by both legislatures, it was rejected by Congress because it infringed on the rights of Native Americans. When it was revised and resubmitted to the legislatures, the South Dakota solons reapproved it, but those in Wyoming, with second thoughts about its fairness, failed to follow suit. Similarly, the commissioners appointed by the governors of California and Nevada in 1955 to divide the waters of Lake Tahoe and three interstate streams saw fifteen years of hard bargaining come to naught in the early 1970s, when Congress failed to approve their compact because it endangered the rights of the Paiute Indians.[37]

These accounts of conflicts over the use of western waters should not obscure the importance of Delph Carpenter's innovation. Most of the compacts attempted have been consummated, and most of those consummated have been honored without judicial coercion. In other words, compact making has brought comparative peace to the valleys. It has enabled persons who were acquainted with the streams to determine interstate rights in them, rather than judges in Washington, D.C. The negotiating teams have usually been recruited from the valleys and headed by state engineers. To cite one example, the Snake River Compact of 1949 was negotiated by residents of Idaho and Wyoming, each team being headed by its state engineer. These were people familiar with the flow of the river and the diversions of it. Familiar with the hydrography of an entire watershed, negotiators have been able to make a comprehensive basin-wide determination of rights rather than a partial determination of just those in litigation. So comprehensive are the coverages of two relatively recent compacts that they include ground as well as surface water. The Kansas-Nebraska Big Blue River Compact of 1971 provides for the regulation of withdrawals of groundwater, while the Nebraska-Wyoming Upper Niobrara River Compact of 1962 requires inventories of the resource on both sides of the state line. Finally, negotiation rather than resort to federal litigation has enabled the western states to retain considerable control over their waters.[38]

The California
Groundwater Right

The inclusion of groundwater within the jurisdiction of the Upper Niobrara and Big Blue compacts was a reflection of the tremendous increase in the use of that resource for irrigation in this century. Whereas in 1909 the census enumerators recorded only 633,761 acres in the seventeen western states irrigated from wells, by 1929 the number had tripled to 2,117,212. Then, with the advent of deep-well turbine pumps and the availability of low-cost electricity, the acreage within the next three decades increased sixfold. By 1959 western farmers were watering 12,998,250 acres with groundwater, of which one-half were in the Great Plains states.[1]

Rights to groundwater in common law differed from those in surface waters. Whereas the latter were governed by the Doctrine of Riparian Rights, the former were defined by the English rule of absolute ownership, formulated by an English jurist in the mid-nineteenth century. The case was *Acton* v. *Blundell*, a suit that originated in Lancashire between Acton, a textile manufacturer, and Blundell, a coal mine operator. The plaintiff had dug a well 63 feet deep to supply water for the operation of his mill when the defendant excavated a coal pit about three quarters of a mile away. When the mine reached a depth of 105 feet, the mill operator's well dried up. Thereupon he deepened his well first 18 and then 36 feet to gain his needed supply of water, but

Blundell dug a second pit nearer Acton's well, which again went dry. Acton sued, contending that the Doctrine of Riparian Rights, which guaranteed each owner of land along a stream correlative rights to its use, applied also to underground water. Chief Justice Nicholas Tindal disagreed; after citing Roman law precedents, he declared:

> We think the present case . . . is not to be governed by the law which applies to rivers and flowing streams, but that it rather falls within that principle, which gives to the owner of the soil all that lies beneath his surface; that the land immediately below is his property, whether it is solid rock, or porous ground, or venous earth, or part soil, part water; that the person who owns the surface may dig therein, and apply all that is there found to his own purposes at his free will and pleasure; and that if, in the exercise of such right, he intercepts or drains off the water collected from underground springs in this neighbor's well, this inconvenience to his neighbor falls within the description of *damnum absque injuria*, which cannot become the ground of an action.[2]

This individualistic rule quickly crossed the Atlantic to the United States, where it was quoted, paraphrased, and approved by the supreme courts of the humid East and in this manner passed into the body of the American common law. Since land was held in fee simple, so was the water within it. The property right in groundwater was exclusive and absolute, although some courts forbade its exercise with malice, negligence, or waste.

Because groundwater could not be seen and observed like surface water, the eastern courts thought that it could not be regulated and controlled. The Ohio court believed that groundwaters were "so secret, occult and concealed that an attempt to administer any set of legal rules in respect to them would be involved in hopeless uncertainty," while the Vermont court referred to their "secret, changeable and uncontrollable character."

As newly formed territories west of the ninety-eighth meridian adopted the common law, they presumably adopted the English rule of absolute ownership; at least that was the view of the early western courts. The supreme court of California in 1871 abbreviated *Acton* v. *Blundell* in these words: "Water filtrating or percolating in the soil belongs to the owner of the freehold—like the rocks and minerals found there," and the Texas Supreme Court in *Houston & Texas Central Ry.* v. *East* quoted the English decision verbatim as a statement of the law of groundwaters in that state. The Utah court concluded in 1895 that the "doctrine may be said to be settled that the owner of lands has a right to dig thereon, and to appropriate and use percolating waters therein, although by so doing he may dry up the wells or spring of an adjacent proprietor." In similar language most of the other western benches agreed.[3]

As soon as the migrants into the drier region began extensive exploitation of its groundwater resources, they discovered, as settlers had earlier with respect to the riparian doctrine, that this humid-country English rule was ill-adapted to an arid environment. Although it protected the property rights of the well owner, it failed to protect those of his neighbors, for in pumping water from his land he withdrew water from beneath their lands as well. As pressures in their wells diminished and water levels fell, the only protection they had was to drill deeper and deeper. It was no coincidence that the unsuitability of the English rule was first realized in southern California. Here groundwater was first used extensively for irrigation. Here former governor John G. Downey in 1868 bored into an artesian aquifer to irrigate lands near Compton. Soon the climate and the availability of water triggered a real estate boom that attracted thousands of settlers like those who founded Riverside and Ontario, interested in the culture of oranges. To irrigate their orchards, they not only dug canals, but also sank hundreds of wells, so many that by 1890 more than two thousand were supplying water to 38,378 acres. By 1899 the acreage had increased to 152,506, which constituted 89.9 percent of all the land within the United States irrigated from wells. Nonetheless, in that year the Southwest was harassed by a major drought, the same drought that prompted meetings in Phoenix, Arizona, that led to the construction of the Salt River Project. Water levels in southern California dropped, artesian wells ceased to flow, pumps were installed, and tempers flared. Neighborhood feuds ensued and one of them within the city of San Bernardino found its way to the state supreme court, as *Katz* v. *Walkinshaw*.[4]

San Bernardino overlies an artesian basin, which at the turn of the century supplied water to its residents for both irrigation and household purposes. Margaret Walkinshaw, one of these residents, owned nine wells, which she capped when not in use. On July 27, 1899, she uncapped seven of them and allowed the water to flow into a nearby stream for sale beyond the city limits. Within hours the water ceased to flow in the wells of Marcus Katz and several of his neighbors. They responded by applying for an injunction against Mrs. Walkinshaw. The lower court favored the defendant and the plaintiffs appealed to the California Supreme Court. There the defendant argued that, since the English rule was the law of California, she owned the artesian water as "parcel of her premises" and could dispose of it as she wished. The plaintiffs, following the example of Acton, contended that the modified doctrine of riparian rights that governed the utilization of surface waters in the state also governed groundwaters and that consequently they had a right to their use equal to that of the defendant.

The decision was written by Justice Jackson Temple, who had won renown in the California antidebris cases for placing the welfare of the community above private rights. He questioned the validity of the English rule "in an arid country like southern California" and thought that property rights in groundwater should be governed by the doctrine of reasonable use, a doctrine that he found in the New Hampshire case of *Bassett* v. *Salisbury Manufacturing Company.* "Proprietary rights," he asserted, "are limited by the common interests of others." He cautioned, however, that his views were not revolutionary. "It does not require a reversal of the rule laid down in *Acton* v. *Blundell* . . . but only a holding that in certain cases there should be added the element of reasonable use." Since Mrs. Walkinshaw had exercised her property right unreasonably and to the injury of others, he ordered the judgment of the lower court reversed.[5] Thereupon, ten water companies joined with Margaret Walkinshaw in requesting a rehearing, contending that since the English rule was part of the common law of California the court was powerless to change it. The rehearing was granted, but when the time for it arrived Justice Temple had died and Justice Lucien Shaw prepared the second opinion.[6]

In a carefully constructed composition, he supported the decision of his predecessor and then amended it. Rejecting the argument of the water companies, he contended that the English rule had been not merely modified but abrogated by the aridity of the region. The environment, he said, had rendered it inapplicable to conditions in California and had forced the adoption of a different rule, the rule of reasonable use, which better protected enterprises and investments based on the utilization of groundwater. Nonetheless, he closed his opinion with an *obiter dictum* in which he transformed the rule of reasonable use into the rule of correlative rights. Property rights in groundwater must be exercised reasonably, and like riparian rights they were correlative or coequal. When, in times of water scarcity, disputes arose among overlying landowners concerning the use of ground-water, they were "to be settled by giving to each a fair and just proportion." He added that those who, like Margaret Walkin-shaw, sunk wells and transported water from a basin "for use on distant lands" acquired an appropriative right that was junior to the correlative rights of the overlying users. That is, California's aquifers had a mix of rights similar to that in its surface streams.[7]

Although succeeding courts developed and perfected these concepts, no basin-wide adjudication was instituted until 1937, when the city of Pasadena entered a suit in the superior court of Los Angeles County to adjudicate and apportion the groundwaters of the underlying Raymond Basin. Parties to the suit included both overlying users and nonoverlying appropriators, many of them municipalities like the city of Alhambra. In accordance with California law, the court appointed the state Division of Water Resources as referee to investigate the hydrologic situation. After four years of study, it reported a lowering water table caused by an overdraft of 30 percent of the safe yield. Thereupon, the court ordered a reduction in the use of the underground waters of the basin by that percentage, but it did not reduce the use of each appropriator in accordance with his priority, because such a decision would have deprived some cities of their entire water supply. Rather, it assumed that each user, in taking water in excess of the safe yield of the aquifer, had adversely injured every other user and in this manner had acquired a "mutually prescriptive" right. Since these rights had a common origin, the court regarded them as correlative and coequal. Therefore, it reduced the use of each holder by the same percentage, namely 30 percent, and appointed the Division of Water Resources as watermaster to administer the reduction. Dissatisfied with the decision, Pasadena appealed the suit, but the California Supreme Court in the *City of Pasadena* v. *City of Alhambra* affirmed the judgment of the lower court and approved the acquisition of rights bv mutual prescription.[8]

It should be noted that a reduction of 30 percent in groundwater use would not have been tolerated without the availability of Colorado River water. In 1928, Los Angeles, Pasadena, and a number of other southern California cities had organized the Metropolitan Water District, which constructed in the 1930s the Colorado River Aqueduct. As a consequence, when the courts ordered a reduction in the use of groundwater, water from the Colorado was available to take its place.

While the Pasadena case was in trial, residents of the underlying West Coast and Central basins, west of Los Angeles, became concerned about their shrinking supplies of groundwater. The West Coast people acted first. They commenced litigation in 1945, but at the same time took steps to assure themselves of a substitute supply of water. They formed the West Basin Water Association, which sought access to Colorado water from the Metropolitan Water District. Successful, they received their first deliveries in 1949. In the meantime, the superior court appointed the state Division of Water Resources as referee to determine the hydrography of the basin. The division reported in 1952 an annual overdraft of sixty thousand acre-feet and recommended a two-thirds reduction in withdrawals. Since the current use amounted to ninety thousand acre-feet, the proposal represented a cutback to thirty thousand. The principal pumpers balked. Instead they agreed to reduce their use by 30 percent and sought the approval of the court. This they obtained. The court reduced the amount of groundwater to which each user was entitled by 30 percent and appointed the division, now a department, as watermaster to administer the decree.[9]

The Central Basin water producers soon followed suit. They formed the Central Basin Water Association in 1950, gained access to imported water in 1954, and went to court in 1962. To reduce the costs of litigation, they quickly drafted an agreement to curtail their extractions of groundwater and sought the approval of the court. They received tentative permission at first and finally, in 1965, definite approval. As in the previous determinations, a court-appointed watermaster reduced the withdrawals of each pumper proportionately and the Metropolitan Water District replaced them with imported water.[10]

Like the Raymond Basin determination, the West Coast and Central basin adjudications were based on the assumption that both overlying and nonoverlying pumpers had acquired mutually prescriptive rights to the safe yield of the aquifer. Nevertheless, in 1975 the state supreme court, in *Los Angeles* v. *San Fernando*, rejected the mutual prescription solution in controversies involving cities as violating a state statute. Rather, in adjusting existing rights to a safe yield, it favored a "physical solution" in which those rights would be modified so as to "minimize waste and maximize beneficial use of the water in controversy."[11]

Two years later, in the midst of the 1976–77 drought, Governor Jerry Brown appointed the Governor's Commission to Review California Water Rights Law, with a mandate to "review existing California water rights law . . . evaluate proposals for modifications in this law and . . . recommend appropriate Legislation." After a year and a half of study, the commission concluded that the state's groundwater law was "at a point of great uncertainty." "Mutual prescription," it thought, "probably cannot be imposed in most cases. Application of the correlative and appropriation principles is probably impractical since their application would be exceedingly complex. At this time, a groundwater user in a basin which has not previously been adjudicated can have only a very uncertain idea of what his 'right' actually is. To determine what his 'right' is, a ground-water user would have to initiate an adjudication of the entire basin."[12]

The commission decided that the best way to protect these uncertain rights to groundwater was through local administration. It was impressed by the successes that communities had had in southern California in managing ground-water use, either under the supervision of the courts or by the organization of a water district. It cited the Orange County Water District as an example of a jurisdiction that had been able, through the imposition of a tax on pumping, to manage a mix of ground and imported water. Consequently, the commission recommended the designation by the legislature of groundwater management areas within which local people could assume control of their underground water resources.[13]

As the governor's commission implied, the California groundwater right is still evolving. Whatever the outcome, it is apparent that as an adaptation to the arid West, the correlative right has been something less than satisfactory. Rejected as an adjudication principle in California, it has never been popular in most of the other western states. Utah embraced it temporarily, but outside the state of its birth the right exists today only in Hawaii. More popular has been a property right fashioned by the New Mexicans.

13
The New Mexican Groundwater Right

The New Mexican property right originated in the Roswell Artesian Basin of the Pecos Valley. Situated largely in Chaves and Eddy counties, it extends along the river for a distance of one hundred miles, from twenty-four miles north of Roswell to the Seven Rivers Hills, twenty-four miles south of Artesia. With a width varying from four to sixty-six miles, the basin is bounded on the west by the slopes of the Capitan, Sacramento, and Guadalupe mountains. Within it geologists have identified two aquifers, separated by a relatively impermeable layer of gypsum, clay, sand, and other geologic material, known as an aquitard. The lower aquifer is a stratum of limestone called the San Andres Formation, which is exposed along the base of the mountains before it slopes beneath the valley floor. Above the aquitard is a shallow aquifer composed of alluvial debris deposited through the millennia by the Pecos River. The San Andres Formation is an artesian aquifer. Rain and snow falling on the exposed portion fill in the crevices and interstices and create a pressure below the aquitard not unlike the standpipe of a municipal water system. When wells are drilled into it, water gushes forth in considerable volume, and yields of several thousand gallons per minute are not uncommon.[1]

The discovery of the artesian aquifer is attributed to Nathan Jaffa of Roswell in the summer of 1890. Finding that the mineralized water from the shallow wells was detrimental to his health, he employed William Hale to drill a deeper well. At a depth of approximately 250 feet, Hale struck the San Andres aquifer, and a stream of artesian water rose to the surface. Nevertheless, it was not until after 1900 that farmers began to drill wells extensively for irrigation. Then a speculative boom punctured the aquifer with hundreds of wells. The *Albuquerque Journal* reported in May of 1904 that there were "wells everywhere as far as Artesia, thirty-five miles south of Roswell, spouting out streams of water five or six feet above the surface and turning the sand fields into the most productive farming land in the country." By the next year, they numbered 485.[2]

Initially the wells flowed continuously, night and day, winter and summer, without restriction. This wastage of water soon worried the people of Roswell, the seat of Chaves County. Fearing that the supply would quickly be exhausted, they persuaded the 1905 territorial legislature to enact a law forbidding the waste of artesian water and requiring that wells be properly cased and capped when not in use. To enforce these provisions, it authorized the governor to appoint artesian well supervisors, the salaries of whom were to be paid from a license fee of five dollars per annum imposed on each well.[3]

Many farmers objected to the regulations. They refused to pay the fee and failed to case or cap their wells properly. So many expressed their opposition in this manner that other farmers in the vicinity of Roswell organized, in 1907, a water users' protective association to assist the governor-appointed well supervisor in enforcing the law. Early in 1909, its members came to the conclusion that more effective conservation measures were needed and that local enforcement was preferable to that by the territory. Consequently, they drafted a bill that the legislature approved without alteration. In addition to prohibiting waste, it regulated well drilling, weights of casings, and the use of artesian water. Enforcement was placed in the hands of elected county artesian well boards, which were authorized to employ supervisors. Three years later, after New Mexico had been admitted to the Union, the first state legislature revised and strengthened the regulations again.[4]

Although these regulatory laws were placed in the statute books, opposition prevented their effective enforcement. Too many wells remained uncapped and poorly cased. Moreover, new wells continued to be drilled—they totalled 1,082 by 1910—adding to the drain on the aquifer. Consequently, artesian pressures declined, the area of the basin shrank, pumps were installed, and farmers on the western periphery abandoned their farms to the desert, while near the Pecos River, fields became so waterlogged that drainage districts were organized.[5] This was the situation when the Federal Farm Loan Act was passed by Congress in 1916 and when, the following year, the farmers of the artesian basin applied for loans. In February 1918, the Federal Land Bank of Wichita sent an engineer-appraiser and a drainage specialist to determine the feasibility of making loans in the basin. Their report was negative. Noting that "the artesian flow . . . is gradually failing and that a large part of the cultivated land is badly seeped," they warned that it would be "inadvisable at this time to consider long-time loans in this district."[6]

When a second investigation in 1922 produced a similar report, the Roswell Chamber of Commerce on December 13, 1923, created a committee "to go into the whole matter of the artesian wells and water supply and recommend action." The chamber's president appointed Dr. Austin D. Crile as chairman. Dr. Crile—the degree was honorary—was a Lutheran minister who had come West for the health of his wife. He had bought an irrigated farm on the outskirts of Roswell and then became president of the New Mexico Agricultural College in Las Cruces in 1917. He returned to Roswell in 1920 to continue his agricultural interests.[7]

In order to obtain information concerning the character and extent of the artesian supply, Dr. Crile sought the services of the Geological Survey. At that time its Division of Ground Water was under the direction of Oscar E. Meinzer, who was achieving renown for his role in the development of the science of groundwater hydrology. He was willing, but on a cost-sharing basis. After the Chamber of Commerce had secured a five-thousand-dollar matching appropriation from the state legislature, Meinzer sent Albert G. Fiedler to begin the investigation.[8]

An engineer by profession, Fiedler devoted a year to a hydrologic study of the basin. He measured the pressure or head in numerous wells, determined their rate of flow, checked the underground leakage with a specially designed current meter, and observed the surface wastage. The waste from the untended wells was excessive, he noted in a report submitted in August 1926. During the winter of 1925–26 alone, he declared, about twenty-five thousand acre-feet of water had been lost. Although the laws prohibiting such waste had been on the statute books for twenty years, he counted 225 wells without valves to control the flow of water. Such violations, together with unrestricted drilling, had caused well heads to decline and the area of artesian flow to shrink from the original 670 square miles to 430. To check the deterioration of the basin and protect the water supply, Fiedler recommended that new legislation "should be enacted at the earliest possible date to prohibit further irrigation developments with artesian water except as it is shown that such developments will not injure present irrigators."[9]

The civic leaders of Roswell accepted the recommendation, and Crile asked Fiedler and his son, Herman R. Crile—an attorney in Roswell—to draft a bill. This, however, was not an easy task. The English rule of absolute ownership allowed the regulation of the use of groundwater, but not its prohibition. If, on the other hand, the Doctrine of Prior

Appropriation governed the use of groundwater, the state engineer could close an overdrafted aquifer to additional appropriations just as he closed an overappropriated stream. Did the doctrine that applied to surface water in New Mexico also apply to groundwater? *Katz* v. *Walkinshaw* suggested an answer. If in California the laws governing groundwater and surface water were similar, it was reasonable to assume that a parallel situation existed in New Mexico. All that was needed, thought the younger Crile, was a statute that would be declaratory of existing law.[10] He and Fiedler were also confronted by the problem of coverage. Should all the groundwaters of the state be declared public and subject to the appropriation doctrine, or just supplies in those basins critically short of water? If the former approach were taken, it was likely that, because of the general opposition to restrictions, the bill would be rejected by the legislature. And so originated the most distinctive feature of New Mexico's groundwater code.

Using suggestions from the engineer, Herman Crile wrote the bill that was introduced into the legislature as House Bill No. 314 on February 24, 1927. Although it encountered opposition, it passed both houses by large margins.[11] The statute declared basins of groundwater that might "be reasonably ascertained by scientific investigations . . . public waters . . . subject to appropriation for beneficial uses under the existing laws of this State relating to appropriation and beneficial use of waters from surface streams." By means of this language, the act rejected the common-law property right in groundwater and replaced it with the appropriation right in ascertainable basins. The reference to "existing laws . . . relating to appropriation" was from the 1907 surface water legislation, which was patterned after the Bien Code. The state engineer was given supervision of the basins; he was to assume control on the receipt of petitions "signed by not less than ten percent" of the groundwater users within them.[12] Within two months of the passage of the act, the well owners of the Roswell Artesian Basin were circulating petitions, which when signed were forwarded to the state engineer. Finding them in proper order, he placed the area under his administration, effective July 1, 1927, and closed it to further appropriation.[13]

Thinking that the Roswell people had met the objections of the Federal Land Bank of Wichita to loans in the basin, Austin Crile requested another survey, but the bank replied by asking for a test of the constitutionality of the law before consideration of a third survey. Consequently, the Chamber of Commerce, now under the presidency of Dr. Crile, arranged for a friendly suit.[14] John Tweedy, a prominent cotton grower, prepared to drill a well without the consent of the state engineer, Herman W. Yeo. In response, Yeo sought an injunction to restrain him. Judge Granville A. Richardson of the district court granted it and the defendant appealed to the New Mexico Supreme Court. There Tweedy's attorney argued that the 1927 act was unconstitutional because it deprived landowners of property without due process of law, in violation of the constitutions of the United States and New Mexico. Herman Crile, serving as attorney for the state engineer, asserted that property rights as defined by the English rule never existed in New Mexico, that the statute was "merely declaratory of prior existing law upon the subject."

Justice John C. Watson replied for the court. Having lived for thirteen years in the Mimbres Valley of southern New Mexico, where farmers were also having groundwater-depletion problems, he was aware of the need for a change in the property right. He agreed with Herman Crile that the Doctrine of Prior Appropriation had always prevailed in New Mexico, "under Mexican sovereignty" as well as "after the American acquisition," and that the statute under review was declaratory of existing law. Like Lucien Shaw, he thought the climate had nullified the English rule, but unlike the California jurist he found the correlative rule unsatisfactory. Rather, the appropriation doctrine was "the rule best adapted to our condition and circumstances." Nevertheless, Justice Watson declared the statute unconstitutional because in extending to groundwater "the existing laws of this State" governing the appropriation of surface water, it violated the constitution of New Mexico.[15]

Encouraged by the court's approval of the philosophy of the law, the Chamber of Commerce awaited the 1931 session of the legislature. Then state senator John H. Mullis of Roswell introduced Senate Bill No. 112 to replace the voided act, but the new legislation was so controversial that it was twice rewritten before a third version was approved. Even so, the opposition in the senate attached to the third version a crippling amendment that required the approval of a majority of the "free holders" in an affected area before it could be subjected to regulation. Happily, the house refused to concur, and Governor Arthur Seligman signed the bill on March 18, 1931.[16]

The new statute was essentially a restatement of the 1927 law, with provisions governing the method of appropriation added to replace the objectionable references. Like the previous law, it recognized appropriative rights in groundwater, but cautiously restricted them to "waters of underground streams, channels, artesian basins, reservoirs, or lakes, having reasonably ascertainable boundaries." These waters were declared "public waters and to belong to the public and to be subject to appropriation for beneficial use." Borrowing from the surface water code of 1907, the new act provided for the appropriation of groundwater by an application to the state engineer and the issuance of a permit if unappropriated water were available. If there were "no unappropriated waters in the designated source," read the law, "or that the proposed appropriation would impair existing water rights ... the application shall be denied." Existing beneficial uses were protected.[17]

Four months after the approval of the statute, on July 29, 1931, the state engineer, George M. Neel, designated an area within the Mimbres Valley as an underground water basin subject to its provisions. On August 21, 1931, he followed this action, with a declaration of a portion of the Roswell Artesian Basin as an underground water area and forbade within it additional appropriations. Six years later, in 1937, his successor extended the closure to the shallow alluvial aquifer nearer the surface.[18]

Although the water-right statute empowered the state engineer to forbid the drilling of additional wells, it provided no solution to the problem of waste. That was the purpose of a bill introduced in the 1931 session by state representative Clarence E. Hinkle, son of a former governor. A major source of waste was from untended, abandoned wells. Plugging with cement was a remedy, but it was expensive. To provide funds, Hinkle's bill authorized the creation of an artesian conservancy district with the authority to tax both urban and rural properties. Four months after its enactment, the residents of the Roswell Artesian Basin petitioned the district court to organize such a district and Judge Richardson responded by organizing the Pecos Valley Artesian Conservancy District on September 8, 1932. The next day he appointed three commissioners to determine its boundaries, list its taxable properties, establish districts for the election of five directors, and draft an election code. The election was held on February 20, 1932, and three days later the board of directors met and chose Austin Crile as its first president.[19]

At first the board employed contractors to plug the runaway wells, but, since the arrangement proved unsatisfactory, in the fall of 1934 it built its own rig. So satisfactory was this solution that during the spring and early summer of 1935 the board built a second rig. By June 30, 1946, it had plugged

673 wild wells.[20] But, although plugging and strict enforcement of the artesian well laws reduced waste, artesian pressures continued to decrease. This was due to a continued increase in the number of wells, some legal and some illegal. The legal wells were drilled into the San Andres aquifer outside of the declared basin. A succession of state engineers solved the problem by extending the area under their control. By 1959, they had made ten extensions. The illegal wells were drilled by farmers seeking to take advantage of the higher farm prices after 1935. In 1948 state engineer John H. Bliss estimated that almost 10 percent of the acreage in the basin irrigated from groundwater was illegal. When he tried to prevent this illegal use, he was faced with another attack on the constitutionality of the New Mexican groundwater right.[21]

Bliss found a well owner, Bert Troy Dority, using water from the San Andres aquifer and the alluvial fill in excess of his legal appropriation. The state engineer sued him and two other trespassers to enjoin them from the unlawful use of the waters. The district court favored Bliss and the defendants appealed. In their pleadings before the state's supreme court, they contended that they owned the water beneath their farms, that the English rule of absolute ownership governed the use of groundwater in New Mexico, and that the 1931 statute was unconstitutional because it deprived them of property without due process of law. The court responded by upholding the act, declaring that the Desert Land Act of 1877 had recognized the appropriation doctrine as the law of both surface and groundwaters within the state. The constitutionality of the 1931 act upheld, the legislature in 1953 declared that all the groundwaters of the state, not just those in ascertainable basins, were "public waters . . . subject to appropriation for beneficial use."[22]

Bliss's attempt to stop illegal pumping revealed the need for precise definition of rights. State engineer Thomas M.

McClure in the 1930s had conducted a hydrographic survey preparatory to an adjudication, but the war effort thwarted a completion of the process. Now in November, 1952, Bliss resumed the survey and three and a half years later, on April 9, 1956, a successor, Stephen E. Reynolds, joined with the Pecos Valley Artesian Conservancy District in instituting an adjudication suit in the district court of Chaves County. Judge E.T. Hensley appointed a special master who considered and evaluated the claims of nearly 2,000 water users, making the suit the largest in the history of the state. When the procedure was completed in 1965, the court had determined groundwater rights to more than 130,000 acres and prohibited illegal use of water on approximately 12,200 others. Moreover, on January 10, 1966, it ordered the metering of all wells, except those used for household and stock watering purposes; set the annual duty of water at 3 acre-feet; and authorized the appointment of a watermaster to enforce the decree.[23]

The farmers, however, objected to the 3-acre-feet limitation. Many had been using 4 acre-feet and declared they could not farm profitably without that much water. As a consequence, they sought a justification of their position from the Water Resources Research Institute of New Mexico State University in Las Cruces. In response, the institute conducted a study that demonstrated that the use of more than 3 acre-feet was necessary to maximize farm income. Thereupon the farmers demanded an increase of the legal duty to 3.75 acre-feet. The court compromised and in 1970 set the duty at 3.5, allowing 6 acre-inches for carriage losses from the well to the field.[24]

The court continued its jurisdiction over the aquifers. It appointed the watermaster who, with assistants, inspected the meters, read them, and watched for illegal use. Violators who used more than 3.5 acre-feet or altered their meters were brought into court and forced to pay fines in money and reduced water use. With supervision of this nature the over-draft on the two Roswell aquifers was reduced and the water levels stabilized.[25]

In addition to the Roswell and Mimbres basins, the state engineer to date has established 27 other underground water basins and extended his control over the extraction of groundwater within them. One of these was the Rio Grande Underground Water Basin, which state engineer Reynolds created in order to preserve the flow of the river so that New Mexico could fulfill its commitment to Texas under the Rio Grande Compact. Its creation, however, was not without protest. When the city of Albuquerque applied for permits to drill four wells within the basin, Reynolds refused to grant them unless it retired rights to a comparable amount of surface water, since the two flows were interrelated. The city responded by going to court, claiming that "as the successor to the Pueblo de Albuquerque y San Francisco Xavier, founded not later than 1706, it had the absolute right to the use of all the waters [of the Rio Grande], both ground and surface within its limits." The supreme court of New Mexico rejected the claim to a pueblo right and upheld the restrictions on drilling. Although the state engineers have reduced the use of groundwater in this and other basins by restricting withdrawals, they have not reduced it on the basis of priority of appropriation.[26]

14
The Popularity of the New Mexican Right

Impressed by the merits of New Mexico's groundwater right, thirteen of the nineteen western states have followed its leadership in rejecting the absolute ownership right and replacing it with the appropriative one. It should be noted, however, that New Mexico was not the first to take this action. The Nevada legislature took it in 1913, but rescinded it two years later. And Oregon's application of the appropriative right to percolating groundwaters in 1927 preceded by two weeks that of New Mexico. Its legislation received gubernatorial assent on March 3, 1927, while New Mexico's did not receive the approval of Governor Richard C. Dillon until March 16, 1927.[1]

The Oregon act applied the appropriation right to groundwaters, but restricted its jurisdiction to waters "in counties lying east of the summit of the Cascade mountains." Within these counties, the right could be acquired by application to the state engineer and the issuance of a permit if there was sufficient unappropriated water in the aquifer to supply the appropriation. However, the legislature modified the law in 1933, after learning of the New Mexican legislation. Then the Oregon solons further restricted its coverage to "underground streams, channels, artesian basins, reservoirs or lakes, the boundaries of which may reasonably be ascertained," copying nearly verbatim the language of the

New Mexican 1931 statute and declaring those waters to be "public." Nevertheless, the act failed to give the state engineer enforcement powers, was used sparingly, and attracted little attention.[2]

The year following the passage of the act was a year of drought in the majority of the western states. The Association of Western State Engineers, which had been organized in 1928, met in Salt Lake City in December and responded to an increased interest in groundwater by creating a committee of three to draft an "ideal underground law." To this committee the association named Thomas M. McClure, then serving as state engineer of New Mexico. The code that the three members drafted was patterned after that of New Mexico, but it differed from the original in that it gave a state engineer specific authority to "designate administrative underground areas and sub-areas" and in case of scarcity to restrict withdrawals "in order of priority."[3] Within weeks this draft was used in the preparation of a groundwater code for Utah, the second state to be influenced by New Mexico's pioneering. A modest increase in the use of groundwater during the 1920s had been followed during the drought years of the early 1930s by a spurt in drilling and the utilization of the resource. For instance, Salt Lake City, which had relied exclusively on surface water prior to 1931, acquired existing wells and drilled new ones. As in Southern California in the 1890s, water levels dropped, artesian wells ceased to flow, pumps were installed, and aggrieved well owners resorted to the courts.[4]

The state engineers of Utah were not slow to express concern. In 1932 George M. Bacon advised the application of the appropriation right to groundwater and in his biennial report called the attention of the governor "to the new law governing underground waters recently passed by the legislature of New Mexico." With the situation worsening, his successor, T. H. Humphreys, in 1934 repeated the recommendation, urging the "enactment of an underground water law which will recognize and protect the legitimate present user to underground water in the order of his priority and to the extent of actual beneficial use." Two months later the supreme court of Utah agreed. By two decisions issued January 2, and 10, 1935, it rejected the correlative rule that it had approved in 1921 and applied "the doctrine of appropriation and beneficial use to underground percolating waters." One of the justices, William H. Folland, went a step further and, like Humphreys, advised legislative action. "[T]he one thing needed at this time to effect a conservation of this natural resource," he counseled, "is legislation extending a more definite control by the state engineer or other public authority."[5]

Since the state legislature was about to convene, Governor Henry H. Blood immediately acted on Folland's suggestion. He requested the drafting of a bill and in his message to the legislators urged its "prompt consideration." A committee of the Utah Water Storage Commission undertook the assignment and wrote a draft that was patterned after the recently written model code of the western state engineers. However, when this draft was submitted to a public hearing on January 30–31, 1935, those in attendance favored not a separate code as in New Mexico, but the inclusion of groundwater in the 1903 statute regulating the appropriation and use of surface water. Consequently, the 1935 legislature amended the statute to include in one act both sources of water, submitting those under the ground to the same administration as those above it. Since the 1903 act gave the state engineer authority to close streams to additional appropriation, the 1935 statute empowered him to close groundwater basins or to restrict use in them. To date, most of the valleys and basins of central Utah have been closed to new appropriations or have had the number of appropriations restricted.[6]

Before the decade ended, Nevada also imitated New Mexico. The reform originated in the Las Vegas Valley, where an artesian aquifer was tapped as early as 1907. Thereafter the number of wells increased slowly until the construction of the Boulder Dam. Then an influx of people—the population of the city of Las Vegas jumped from 5,165 in 1930 to 8,422 in 1940—brought a similar increase in well drilling. As the number of wells nearly doubled, water pressures declined and many wells stopped flowing. Thinking that the decline was due to underground leakage, the residents of the valley persuaded the state engineer to invite the Geological Survey to investigate. When it did so, it found the decline due not so much to leakage as to uncontrolled flows from uncapped wells. "Much artesian water that is discharged by wells is wasted," observed the investigator. Then he continued, "The people in the Las Vegas area should understand that the artesian water supply is not unlimited and that conservation of the supply is necessary."[7] In response to this advice, the office of the state engineer prepared a bill patterned after the New Mexico institutions and the model code of the Association of Western State Engineers. Introduced into the 1939 legislature, it was promptly enacted.[8]

The 1939 Nevada groundwater code discarded the absolute ownership right by declaring underground waters public and subject to appropriation for beneficial use. Provisions borrowed from New Mexico's 1927 act authorized the state engineer to extend his control over a basin when petitioned by at least ten percent of its well owners. Thereafter no wells were to be drilled in that basin without a permit from that officer who in time of shortage could restrict extractions in conformity with prior rights, a provision copied from the western state engineers' model code. To conserve water, the statute prohibited waste and authorized the employment of artesian well supervisors in controlled areas. Two years after its passage, on January 10, 1941, the state engineer, on receipt of the required petition, extended his control over the Las Vegas Artesian Basin and approved the appointment of a well supervisor.[9]

Groundwater-right reform accelerated during the next two decades, 1940–60. Encouraged by drought, perfection of the deep turbine pump, and the appearance of cheap electric power, farmers in the seventeen contiguous western states increased the acres that they irrigated entirely from groundwater more than fivefold. By 1959, in seven of these states they were irrigating more than half of their acres from wells, in Kansas and Texas more than 80 percent.[10]

As acreages supplied with groundwater increased, so did controversies and an awareness that the English rule of absolute ownership provided inadequate protection for property rights in this resource. Consequently, each odd-numbered year after 1943 saw the enactment by biennial legislatures of laws applying the appropriation doctrine to groundwater.

Kansas and Washington took legislative action in 1945. A state supreme court decision triggered the legislation in Kansas, where the dual system of surface rights still prevailed. When the court in 1944 gave preference to the riparian right, the governor appointed a water-right reform committee, which recommended the abrogation of common law rights in both surface and groundwaters and their subjection in one statute to the appropriation right. This, it contended, would be a recognition that both were interconnected, part of the same hydrologic cycle. The 1945 legislature acted on this recommendation by declaring "all waters within the state" subject to appropriation under the permit system. In Washington the state government also assumed the initiative. Urged by cities dependent on wells for their water supplies, the state Department of Conservation and Development asked the Geological Survey for assistance. Arthur M. Piper, a hydrologist of the agency, responded by drafting a code, which, with some revision, was enacted by the 1945 legislature with little controversy. Like the Nevada code, it authorized the state engineer, known in Washington as the supervisor of hydraulics, to designate groundwater areas and in case the supply was "inadequate for the current needs of all holders of valid rights" to restrict withdrawals in conformity with their priorities.[11]

Neighboring Oregon waited until 1955 to replace its 1927 statute and extend the appropriation right to the groundwaters of the entire state. With one hundred thousand wells in Oregon, increasing at the rate of five thousand a year (many of them west of the Cascade Mountains), the 1953 legislature authorized the governor to appoint a committee to study the state's water resources. After fifteen public meetings, held throughout the state, it concluded that a new law was needed and with the assistance of Arthur Piper drafted one. Introduced into the 1955 legislature, it too was enacted with few revisions and little controversy. It provided for the appropriation of groundwater by the permit system and authorized the state engineer in case of overdraft to restrict withdrawals within designated "critical" groundwater areas.[12]

In the third Pacific Northwest state, Idaho, judicial action preceded legislative. In *Hinton* v. *Little*, decided in 1931, the state's supreme court rejected the English rule and applied the appropriation right to all groundwater. Consequently, when the legislature acted in 1951, it only implemented the court's decision. Applying the provisions of the state's 1903 surface water code to groundwater, the statute declared it "the property of the state," and applied the permit system to its appropriation. Although a similar measure had been rejected in 1945, the new one passed with surprisingly little opposition. Amendments in 1953 and 1963 strengthened the regulatory powers of the state reclamation engineer and authorized him to designate critical groundwater areas.[13]

The acceptance of adaptive change in the Pacific North-west was in marked contrast to the attitude in Wyoming, Montana, Colorado, and Arizona. In these states landowners regarded the ability to drill a well without restrictions as one of the American freedoms. They had experienced no such restrictions in the humid East; they wanted none in the arid West. In spite of the fact that the enacted codes recognized vested rights and exempted from their provisions wells supplying water for domestic and livestock uses, they opposed the annulment of the English right as deprivation of property without due process of law, in violation of both their state and national constitutions. If they needed controls, they wanted local control, by landowners organized into ground-water districts rather than by state bureaucracies. So they battled the reformers.

In Wyoming, landowners battled the state engineer, Loren C. Bishop. He drafted a bill, incorporating the New Mexican institutions, for introduction into the 1941 legislative assembly, but no member would introduce it. The solons did consider as a compromise a statement of policy, which they enacted in 1945 after rejecting it in 1941 and 1943. Regarding it as inadequate, Bishop drafted a new bill, patterned after Washington's recently enacted code, but the lawmakers reduced it to a well registration measure. Disappointed, the state engineer declared it inadequate to protect the rights of appropriators and awaited the emergence of grassroots interest in a more effective code. This occurred following a severe drought in 1954, which was accompanied by an increased use of groundwater. As a consequence, the legislators in 1955 created an interim study committee. In meetings around the state, it found people wary of "unnecessary regulation" and desirous of "a voice in the regulation of water underlying their lands." In response to this sentiment, the committee drafted a bill embodying the New

Mexico institutions, but provided for advisory boards to assist in their administration. With these checks on bureaucratic dictation, the 1957 Wyoming legislature passed the bill, sixteen years after Bishop's original proposal.[14]

Similar opposition to change occurred in Montana. Here the Montana Reclamation Association assumed the role of change agent and in 1951 sponsored a bill to alter the property right in groundwater. Introduced into the legislature, it was opposed by ranching interests and the Anaconda Mining Company because they contended that it confiscated property without compensation. "Never in the history of Montana," declared Dr. Henry C. Gardiner of the Mt. Haggin Land and Livestock Company, "has there been such a flagrant and ruthless proposal . . . made for the taking of vested property." Defeated in 1951, the reclamation association reintroduced the measure into the next legislature, only to have it again rejected.[15]

Undaunted, the association in 1955 tried a third time to effect property-right change. Although industry continued to object, the most determined opposition came from the ranchers in the Gallatin Valley, where a number of them relied on subirrigation. They opposed the 1955 bill because it gave too much authority to the state engineer. They favored local control and the protection of rights by the courts and rancher-organized districts similar to soil conservation districts. It seemed to them, said a spokesman, "that persons residing in a groundwater area should . . . have more interest in, and more knowledge of, their local problems and needs concerning groundwater use in their area than a person residing elsewhere." With these convictions, they killed the measure, but were responsible for the enactment of a well registration statute by the 1957 legislature.[16] Now the leadership of the reform movement passed to the Montana Association of Soil Conservation Districts. It submitted a bill

to the 1959 legislature that would have altered the groundwater property right, but, encountering the same industrial
and agricultural adversaries, the measure suffered the same
fate as its predecessors.

Among the legislative measures sponsored by the Gallatin Valley ranchers in 1957 was an appropriation to conduct
a study of the state's groundwater problems by the Montana
Bureau of Mines and Geology in Butte. The bureau used the
money to employ Sidney L. Groff to conduct the study. Groff
was a young geologist, a native Montanan, fresh from
graduate studies at the University of Utah. When the fourth
attempt at water-right reform failed, he began preparations
for a fifth. Convinced that if the proponents and opponents of
reform could meet and talk together they could reach
agreement, he held a conference in Butte, followed by one in
Bozeman. Agreements were reached and a representative
committee drafted two bills, one of which was enacted by the
1961 legislature. Nevertheless, because the statute omitted
reference to groundwater as public property, it was not until
the adoption of the 1972 constitution declaring "underground . . . waters . . . the property of the state" that Montana
annulled the English right and followed the leadership of
New Mexico in applying the appropriation right to groundwaters.[17]

In Colorado a state agricultural planning committee
assumed leadership of the reform movement. When the
drought of the middle fifties reduced the stream flows and
surface appropriators blamed the reduction on irrigation
from wells, it prepared a groundwater-control bill that
several state senators introduced in the 1955 legislative
session as Senate Bill No. 206. Partially patterned after the
New Mexican code, it applied the doctrine of prior appropriation to underground water, established a permit system
for the acquisition of rights, and gave the state engineer

authority to allocate the resource among appropriators according to priorities. The bill immediately encountered opposition, especially from the residents of the Bijou Basin in the South Platte Valley.[18]

Extensive drilling in this area, as in much of the Central Plains, began in the late 1930s and increased rapidly during the following decade, until more than 250 wells were irrigating thirty-seven thousand acres. As elsewhere, a decline in the water table accompanied this development.[19] This situation, however, did not alarm most of the pumpers; not having been restrained in their well drilling, they opposed regulation. When a research team from Colorado State University interviewed seventy-four of them in the summer of 1956, 59 percent favored unrestricted use of groundwater. If controls were inescapable, 66 percent desired control by local people.[20] Consequently, their state senator, Frank L. Gill, opposed the proposed code and championed local administration. In seeking this objective, he was joined by the representatives from the San Luis Valley in the southern part of the state.[21]

There were, however, other objections aside from statewide administration. Some, like a prominent Greeley lawyer, objected to any change in the laws governing the use of groundwater. Senator Gill feared that neighboring states would claim it under provisions of interstate compacts if it were declared public property. Well drillers objected to the bill because of the regulations that it would impose on them —objections enough to defeat it in the committee of the whole on March 24, 1955.[22]

Two years later the reformers, with the support of the Colorado Farm Bureau, reintroduced a modified version of the bill. It provided for a groundwater commission with authority to designate as "tentatively critical groundwater districts" any areas where withdrawals appeared "to have approached, reached or exceeded the normal annual rate of replenishment" and to close them to additional drilling. It also authorized the formation in each district of an advisory board to assist with its administration. The measure passed the senate easily, but the house amended it to give advisory boards the power to annul designations and to reopen areas to drilling.[23]

The amended bill having passed, the Ground Water Commission held a hearing in the Bijou Basin on November 16, 1957, followed by a meeting in Denver on January 10, 1958, to consider designation. It listened to a description of the groundwater depletion in the area by a geologist from the Geological Survey and then designated it as the Bijou Creek Tentatively Critical Ground Water District. This action polarized the residents. Some favored acceptance of the designation, at least until its effects could be studied; others wished to reject it. Consequently, in the ensuing election for members of the advisory board, the voters were presented with two slates of candidates. With voting restricted to well owners, those who went to the polls favored the rejectors by a better than three to one margin. Thereupon, the new board in a meeting on March 31, 1958, voted to request that "the Ground Water Commission . . . remove the Critical Designation from the Bijou Alluvial Basin immediately." The commission complied, reopening the basin to unrestricted drilling.[24]

Opposition to controls did not remove the need for them. In fact, as drilling accelerated that need increased. Consequently, in 1964 Governor John A. Love requested advice from the Colorado Water Conservation Board concerning the improvement of the situation. The board responded by drafting a bill for submission to the legislature. This time Senator Gill was one of its principal supporters. Amended, it passed the house by a vote of sixty to three; the senate, by a vote of thirty-three to two.[25]

The Colorado Ground Water Management Act of 1965 applied the appropriation right to groundwater and authorized the groundwater commission to protect it within designated groundwater basins by limiting or prohibiting withdrawals of water when such withdrawals "would cause unreasonable injury to prior appropriators." To assist the commission in the administration of a designated basin, the statute authorized the taxpayers within it to organize a groundwater management district, but did not give the board of directors the power to annul the designation.[26]

In central Arizona, the drought began in 1942 and continued with few interruptions until 1957. It was accompanied, however, by a spectacular increase in population—the number of inhabitants of Maricopa County, in which Phoenix, Scottsdale, and Tempe are located, tripled. Just as spectacular was the increase in cotton production and the pumpage of groundwater, with a consequent drop in water tables. When the Salt River Valley water users, now partially dependent on water from wells, became aware of the situation, they drafted a water-right reform bill for submission to the 1945 legislature. Although they obtained the support of Governor Sidney P. Osborn, opponents of change killed it in committee.[27]

Rebuffed, the reformers soon found an ally in the Bureau of Reclamation. This occurred a few weeks after the adjournment of the legislature, when the Bureau announced that it would not approve the Central Arizona Project unless Arizona enacted a groundwater code. The agency believed that Arizonans faced eventual disaster unless they curbed their use of the resource. Since Osborn's principal goal as governor was to obtain Colorado River water for central Arizona, he immediately called the legislators into special session to enact a code. They refused.[28]

Groundwater-right reform split the agricultural community. Landowners like the Salt River Valley irrigators who had been using groundwater for some time wanted to protect their prior rights to it, whereas those who had recently undertaken cotton growing wanted no restraints on their use of the resource. They were supported by the agricultural implement dealers, together with members of the legal profession who viewed reform as taking property without due process of law. These men provided determined opposition to adaptive change.[29]

The governor, however, remained hopeful. In November 1946 he wrote the acting commissioner of the Bureau of Reclamation, William E. Warne, that he "confidently expected that ... an adequate, workable and satisfactory underground water code [would] be adopted," and when two months later the solons met in regular session he renewed his appeal. Again the opposition killed the code bill in committee. Then, impatient and ill with a fatal disease, he called the legislature into six special sessions, three of them specifically to enact a code. The foes of regulation fought hard. Finally, in March of 1948, they consented to the passage of a compromise measure. It authorized the designation of critical groundwater areas within which the state land commissioner could halt the expansion of irrigated acreage, but not the flow of existing wells.[30]

As the economic boom continued, the drought worsened. Amid continuing decline in water levels, J. Howard Pyle was elected governor in 1950. Responding to the demands of distressed farmers in the summer of 1951, he appointed a committee under the chairmanship of Paul S. Burgess of the University of Arizona to prepare a more effective code. A few weeks before its introduction into the legislature, the supreme court of Arizona tossed a bomb into the controversy. In *Bristor* v. *Cheatham*, it declared that the English rule of absolute ownership had been voided by the Desert Land Act of 1877 and that groundwater belonged to the state, subject to appropriation for beneficial use. The supporters of groundwater control were jubilant; the way was now open for effective regulation. On the other hand, the opponents were frantic. Believing that their investments were threatened, they petitioned the court for a rehearing, side-tracked the Burgess bill for the creation of a study committee, and waited for the court's second decision. They were not disappointed. The court reversed itself, declaring that the rule of absolute ownership was still the law of Arizona, limited only by the rule of reasonable use. Although a majority of the judges thought that it was difficult sometimes to determine what is reasonable, they considered unreasonable the transportation of groundwater away from the land on which it is pumped if the overlying owners are injured.[31]

During the succeeding years, as the legislation of 1948 failed to reduce pumpage and an annual overdraft of approximately 1.8 million acre-feet continued, the alignment of forces supporting and opposing control changed. The farmers tended to close ranks and oppose control while the city dwellers favored it. This was especially true of residents of Tucson, where the population increased eightfold from 1940 to 1970. To assure itself of an adequate supply of water, the city drilled wells during the late 1960s in the Avra Valley sixteen miles distant and prepared to transport the water into the city limits. The overlying farmers objected and sought an injunction. Faced with urban needs, the Arizona Supreme Court vacillated. In *Jarvis* v. *State Land Department* it upheld the second Bristor decision and forbade Tucson to obtain water beyond its city limits, but eighteen months later, in a second Jarvis decision, it changed its mind and gave the city the green light. Six years later, in *Farmers Investment Company v. Bettwy* (FICO), it changed its mind again and returned to its first Jarvis position. Since FICO involved mining companies as well as the city of Tucson, the 1977 legislature acted. It authorized the appointment of a groundwater management study commission with the task of studying the situation and drafting a code.[32]

The Commission began its deliberations on November 16, 1977. Since its members included representatives of agriculture, industry, and the cities as well as legislators, they were able to view groundwater problems from many different angles. Just as they were having difficulty reconciling their divergent points of view, Secretary of the Interior Cecil Andrus visited Phoenix on October 5, 1979, and reminded them that Congress in approving the Central Arizona Project had made allocation of water from it dependent on control of the expansion of irrigated acreage. Consequently he warned that unless a code were enacted by the following spring, project allocations would be delayed. Meeting that deadline, the commission completed its draft on June 7, 1980. Governor Bruce Babbitt promptly convoked a special session of the legislature, which in one day approved the measure. The governor signed it and it became law on June 12, 1980.[33]

The Arizona Groundwater Management Code of 1980 retains the reasonable use right, but subjects it to regulation. The code creates four active management areas (AMAS) and places them under state control. The commission considered local control, but decided to follow the example of Wyoming and Colorado and limit the local people to advisory roles. Within the AMAS a department of water resources may reduce groundwater use over a period of forty-five years by conservation measures and retirement of rights. Rights may be purchased and water transported, but new ones may be acquired only with the permission of the department.[34]

Although Arizona rejected local control, it has been popular on the Great Plains, that borderland between the humid East and the arid West, semihumid, semiarid. Here

Texas was the first to provide for the control of groundwater by local users organized into districts.

Texas still retains the English absolute ownership property right, although attempts have been made to replace it. The Texas board of water engineers advocated the application of the appropriation right to groundwater, the same right that the legislature had applied to surface water. Bills to effect this change were introduced in the legislature in 1937, 1941, and 1947, but each one was rejected. Texans preferred to retain their freedom to drill or not to drill. Nonetheless, by the late 1940s water tables were declining as the number of wells increased dramatically on the Texas High Plains —11,000 of them between 1943 and 1951. When the reformers prepared to enact a state-control measure patterned after the Arizona code of 1948, the conservatives countered in 1949 with a bill to provide for local control through the creation of underground water conservation districts. Like the Bijou pumpers, if controls were inescapable, the Texans preferred control by the local people.[35]

The statute allows local residents to petition the board of water engineers, now reconstituted as the water rights commission, to create a district operated by their elected officials to make and enforce rules for the conservation of subsurface water. The district may require permits for the drilling of wells, spaced at certain intervals, and prohibit waste. Under the provisions of the statute, six districts have been created, but only three are operational. Since the efforts of these three have been restricted to conservation rather than to reduction of withdrawals, they have done little to check the continuing drop in the water table beneath the High Plains.[36]

Nebraska and Kansas have also authorized the formation of groundwater management districts similar to those of Texas. In 1959, Nebraska, which like Arizona has modified the common-law property right by the rule of reasonable use,

empowered local residents to form groundwater conservation districts. Ten years later the legislature gave residents
the authority to form larger, multipurpose natural resource
districts (NRDS). With groundwater use increasing and well
levels dropping, in 1975 these districts, with the permission
of the state department of water resources, were authorized
to establish control areas, resembling New Mexico's underground water basins. Within them, as in New Mexico's
basins, drilling and water use can be restricted. As of the
summer of 1978, two control areas had been designated, one
of them the Upper Republican Ground Water Control Area,
located in that valley where the interests of Nebraska and
Colorado have collided. Within it, an NRD has ordered the
installation of meters and reduction in use so as to achieve a
less-than-one-percent drop each year in the water table. The
Kansas authorization of locally organized groundwater management districts came in 1972. The five districts that have
been formed under this statute have regulated well spacing
and the drilling of new wells.[37]

With two-thirds of its area in the humid region east of the
ninety-eighth meridian, Oklahoma has vacillated in its allegiance to groundwater-control institutions. In 1936 its
judiciary approved the reasonable use rule, but thirteen years
later its legislature followed the leadership of New Mexico
and applied the appropriation rule to the use of groundwater.
The executive department, however, administered the
statute as if it had provided for the correlative right! Finally,
in 1972, in an effort to reconcile the law with practice, the
legislators entitled each well owner to a proportionate share
of the available supply.[38]

On the northern Great Plains, with sprinkler irrigation
accelerating, both North and South Dakota applied the appropriation right to groundwater in 1955 and provided for its
acquisition by the permit system. The constitutionality of

the South Dakota statute was challenged in *Knight* v. *Grimes* in 1964, but it was upheld by the state's supreme court.[39]

Of the two noncontiguous states, Alaska applied the appropriation doctrine to subsurface waters in its constitution and subjected the right to regulation by its Water Use Act of 1966. On the other hand, Hawaii, influenced by both California and New Mexico, chose the correlative right to govern the utilization of artesian waters, but authorized its protection by the exercise of bureaucratic controls in designated groundwater areas.[40]

As most of the western states applied the appropriation doctrine to groundwater, water users and hydraulic engineers discovered that it did not fit the utilization of groundwaters as well as those on the surface. The latter can be seen, their course observed, and the flow easily diverted. Groundwater, on the other hand, cannot be seen, nor can the character of the aquifers be easily determined. They will vary in thickness and texture. Moreover, pumping is likely to be from the top of an aquifer, at least initially, rather than from its bottom, so that a well may run dry even though there is still an abundance of water in the source of supply. Since groundwater moves so slowly, reduction of production of junior wells in an area where they are scattered may not affect senior ones for some time. Consequently, administrators have been reluctant to reduce withdrawals in conformity to prior rights as the earlier codes directed. They have also been hesitant to require the maintenance of senior well levels. The newer codes have provisions like the one in the Colorado Ground Water Management Act of 1965 that reads, "Prior appropriations of groundwater should be protected and reasonable groundwater pumping levels maintained, but not to include the maintenance of historical water levels." A similar provision in the 1957 Wyoming code reads, "It shall be an express condition of each permit and of each appropriation of underground water acquired thereunder that the right of the appropriator does not include the right to have the water level or artesian pressure at the appropriator's point of diversion maintained at any level higher than that required for maximum beneficial use of the water in the source of supply." In this manner, prior appropriation has been modified to give rights to junior appropriators in respect to senior ones if their uses result in greater utilization of the aquifer. And when well withdrawals are rotated, a prior appropriation right becomes something akin to a correlative right. The view of Justice Lucien Shaw may still prevail.[41]

15
Federal Assertions, States' Fears

One of the most persistent controversies in the western states regarding water rights has been one concerning the relationship of the appropriation right to the federal government. At the core of the dispute lay the meaning of the congressional legislation of 1866, 1870, and 1877. Westerners believed that by these acts Congress relinquished federal control of their nonnavigable streams, enabling them to claim ownership. There was no dispute over navigable streams; federal attorneys agreed that they were owned by the states, subject to the paramount authority of the United States to maintain their navigability. It was the proprietorship of nonnavigable streams that was contested. Since most of western streams are of this nature, the dispute was of vital concern to the residents of the region.

The first skirmish occurred on the Rio Grande, where in the late 1890s the Rio Grande Dam and Irrigation Company prepared to build a dam across the river at Elephant Butte. Contending that it would impede the navigability of the stream, the federal government sought an injunction from the territorial courts. The New Mexicans countered with the argument that the Rio Grande was not navigable as it flowed through the territory and consequently, under the legislation of 1866, 1870, and 1877, it was under territorial control. When the case came to the U.S. Supreme Court, Justice

David J. Brewer granted the contention of the New Mexicans, but he said that control was limited in two respects: "First, that in the absence of specific authority from Congress a state cannot by its legislation destroy the right of the United States, as the owner of lands bordering on a stream, to the continued flow of its waters; so far at least as may be necessary for the beneficial uses of the government property. Second, that it is limited by the superior power of the general government to secure the uninterrupted navigability of all navigable streams within the limits of the United States." In other words, the federal government retained or *reserved* the right to use as much water as it needed to develop its lands, a right that was superior to those sanctioned by the states and territories. The federal government also retained control of nonnavigable portions of a river system when it became necessary to maintain the navigability of the lower flows.[1]

The Supreme Court announced the Rio Grande decision on May 22, 1899. By that time the national reclamation movement was gaining momentum. Hiram Chittenden had made his recommendation, Senator Francis Warren had proposed congressional funding of two irrigation reservoirs, and George Maxwell was about to launch the National Irrigation Association. When westerners sought federal financial aid for reclamation projects, they had mixed emotions. On the one hand, they wanted the assistance; on the other, they were fearful of the controls that might come with it. During the debate over Warren's proposal, which took the form of an amendment to the river and harbor bill, the veteran legislator and author of the Act of 1866, Senator William Stewart of Nevada, emphasized that federal funding was "under no circumstances" to interfere with "State law." His colleague, Senator Joseph L. Rawlins of Utah, was even more explicit. "If these moneys are expended by the Government," he declared, "it must be with the distinct understanding that the reservoirs are to be created, first subject to all the rights of the use of the water already accrued, and secondly, to the control of the States themselves in respect to the management and disposition of the waters that may be thus impounded."[2]

The fear of federal encroachment surfaced while the Newlands bills were under consideration. Congressman Newlands introduced the first of them into the lame-duck session of the Fifty-sixth Congress during the winter of 1901, but it adjourned before taking action. Fearful that federal construction would be accompanied by federal control, the state engineers of Wyoming, Colorado, Idaho, Utah, and Nebraska assembled in Cheyenne in June to draft a bill to safeguard state-granted rights by having the states construct the projects. According to Senator Warren, it provided "[t]hat construction, supervision, control or sale of irrigation works[,] and storage, diversion, disposal and distribution of stored water, shall be in the engineer's office of each state or territory accepting the benefits of Government aid." The bill, however, was never introduced. Favoring federal construction, Congressman Newlands opposed it, but included in his measure a section protecting state water rights. This became section eight of the Reclamation Act of 1902. It read, "Nothing in this Act shall be construed as affecting or intended to affect or to in any way interfere with the laws of any State . . . relating to the control, appropriation, use, or distribution of water used in irrigation . . . the Secretary of the Interior, in carrying out the provisions of this Act, shall proceed in conformity with such laws.[3]

In the debate over the final Newlands bill, western legislators defended it by emphasizing that according to its provisions, the secretary of the interior, in acquiring rights to water, had to follow state procedures. "The bill," declared Congressman Frank Mondell of Wyoming, "provides explicitly that even an appropriation of water can not be made except under state law." These legislators also noted that the secretary, in distributing the waters of a federally constructed reservoir, was subordinate to state law. Senator Clarence D. Clark of Wyoming pointed out, "The control of waters after leaving the reservoirs shall be vested in the States and Territories through which such waters flow."[4]

If section eight was a gain for the states, the Winters decision of the U.S. Supreme Court in 1908 was a triumph for the federal government. The dispute that led to the decision originated in the Milk River Valley of northern Montana, where Congress had established the Fort Belknap Indian Reservation on May 1, 1888, for the Gros Ventre and Assiniboine tribes. Since the object of the reservation was to transform a pastoral people into farmers, the Indian Service constructed, beginning in 1898, a large diversion from the Milk River, capable of irrigating thirty thousand acres. It was not, however, the first diversion of the stream, for settlers situated upstream had constructed others. As a consequence, they were in a position during the drought of 1904–05 to deplete the stream and leave no water to flow into the reservation ditch. With the Indian farmers desperate, the Indian Service sought a court order restraining the settlers from diverting the needed water. The Ninth Federal Circuit Court complied and the settlers, among them Henry Winter, appealed the case to the U.S. Supreme Court.

Before that tribunal the settlers argued that they were qualified entrymen on the public domain, that they had diverted the waters of the stream before the Indian Service did, and consequently according to the laws of Montana they had a prior right to their use. The Court disagreed. It ruled that when the federal government created the reservation it reserved water for the use of the Indian farmers, a use that took precedence over the settlers' use. Citing the Rio Grande decision, the Court declared: "The power of the government to reserve the waters and exempt them from appropriation under the state laws is not denied, and could not be. That the government did reserve them we have decided, and for a use which would be necessarily continued through years." In other words, the federal government's reserved right was superior to the state's prior appropriation right. How much water was reserved? The Court did not say. Was the use restricted to agricultural purposes? Several months later, the Ninth Federal Circuit Court, in *Conrad Investment Company* v. *United States*, answered that question. In a controversy involving the use of the waters of Birch Creek by the Indians of the Blackfeet Indian Reservation it declared that they had a "paramount right" to use those waters "to the extent reasonably necessary for the purposes of irrigation and stock raising, and domestic and other useful purposes." In contrast to the appropriation right, the reserved right was to an unspecified, unquantified amount of water. It was open-ended.[5]

Winters v. *United States* was followed by a federal assault, formulated by Morris Bien and his colleagues in the Department of Justice, on the states' position. Taking a concept from the California Doctrine, they struck at the foundations of the Colorado Doctrine. They asserted that the United States owned all the unappropriated waters of the nonnavigable streams in the western states, that the nation had acquired that ownership through cession of the area from France, Mexico, and the United Kingdom. Having acquired rights to water with the land, the United States never surrendered those rights to the states. By the acts of 1866, 1870, and 1877, it granted water users the right to appropriate water and only gave the states the authority to devise methods of acquiring and enforcing those rights. Consequently, western waters never became the property of the states. Rephrasing the language of *Lux* v. *Haggin*, Bien declared: "The water being part of the land, it is difficult to see any ground for the theory of State control. Where the United States has disposed of the land it has either transferred the water with it to the new owner or has retained its right to it." Nonetheless, when the Department of Justice presented this argument to the U.S. Supreme Court in *Wyoming* v. *Colorado,* Justice Van Devanter ignored it. Instead, he granted that the statutes of 1866, 1870, and 1877 sanctioned the appropriation right and that Section 8 of the Reclamation Act of 1902 protected it.[6]

Wyoming v. *Colorado* was decided in 1922. During the succeeding years, the tension between the states and the national government continued. In 1927, when the Bureau of Indian Affairs attempted to usurp appropriation rights in South Dakota, the state engineers organized the Association of Western State Engineers to protect water rights from federal infringement. Eight years later the U.S. Supreme Court came again to the defense of the states' position in *California-Oregon Power Co.* v. *Beaver Portland Cement Co.,* a case involving an interpretation of the Desert Land Act of 1877. Justice George Sutherland wrote the opinion. He had grown to manhood in Utah, where he was admitted to the bar in 1883. He had also been a member of the Fifty-seventh Congress, which had enacted the Reclamation Act of 1902. Familiar with the rights philosophy of the arid West, he held "that following the act of 1877, if not before, all nonnavigable waters then a part of the public domain became *publici juris,* subject to the plenary control of the designated States . . . with the right of each to determine for itself to what extent the rule of appropriation or the common-law rule in respect to riparian rights should obtain."[7]

Sutherland's decision notwithstanding, the Department of Justice renewed its assault in a suit brought by the state of Nebraska against the state of Wyoming for the equitable apportionment of the North Platte River. Again the department claimed federal title to the unappropriated waters of the western nonnaviable streams. This time it encountered the opposition of the National Reclamation Association. Organized in 1932 by representatives of thirteen western states to promote federal reclamation, the association soon became

the watchdog of state-created water rights. Following inter-
vention in the case by the Department of Justice in May of
1938, the association met in Reno, Nevada, in October 1938,
and approved the following resolution:

> WHEREAS, the ownership and control of the non-navi-
> gable streams within the states . . . is in the states and not
> in the federal government; . . .
>
> THEREFORE BE IT RESOLVED, that this association formally
> asserts the principle of state ownership and control of both
> navigable and non-navigable streams, save to the extent
> that the congress shall intervene in good faith in the
> preservation of navigation on navigable streams; and
>
> BE IT FURTHER RESOLVED, that the attorney generals of the
> states of this association are hereby requested to file briefs
> as friends of the court in any case in which the department
> of justice should assert the contrary principle of federal
> ownership and control.

The attorney generals of eleven western states responded to
this appeal. When the court issued its decision in 1945, it
again ignored the federal claim. In writing the decision,
Justice William O. Douglas declared, "The question of the
ownership by the United States of unappropriated water is
largely academic so far as the narrow issues of this case are
concerned."[8]

Although the leadership of the National Reclamation
Association remained apprehensive, the integrity of state
water codes seemed fairly secure. The Bureau of Reclamation
observed section eight of the reclamation statute and appropriated western waters according to state law. The navy, in
drilling six wells within the naval ammunition depot at
Hawthorne, Nevada, filed applications for permits with the
state engineer. In 1952, Congress, in passing the McCarran
Amendment, subordinated the federal government to state

courts in stream adjudication suits. It was, in the language of Justice William H. Rehnquist, an era of "cooperative federalism," an era that was shattered by the Pelton Dam decision.[9]

The Federal Power Commission issued in 1951 a license to a private power company to construct a dam across the Deschutes River in Oregon. The state of Oregon objected because the structure would prevent salmon and steelhead trout from ascending the river for spawning. It declared that the commission, in granting a license to the use of the nonnavigable Deschutes River, was subject to state authority because Congress had relinquished control of nonnavigable western streams to the states in the legislation of 1866, 1870, and 1877. When the dispute was adjudicated by the U.S. Supreme Court, Justice Harold H. Burton ruled in favor of the Federal Power Commission. He pointed out that the project, known as Pelton Project No. 2030, was to be constructed on reserved lands of the United States, one wing of the dam to abut on an Indian reservation and the other on federal land reserved for power puposes in 1909. The congressional legislation to which the state referred applied only to public lands, not to those reserved. "The lands before us in this case," he stated, "are not 'public lands' but 'reservations'." The project could be built and the water impounded without the consent of the state of Oregon, without compliance with its laws.[10]

A tremor of fear passed through the western states. Heretofore their residents had assumed that federal reserved water rights pertained only to Indian reservations; now it seemed that they adhered to other types of reservations, such as power sites and national forests. With more than 50 percent of the water supply of the eleven contiguous western states either originating in or flowing through these forest reserves and national parks, the assertion of paramount rights in that water by the federal government was indeed threatening. The decision jeopardized state-enforced water rights, upon which the livelihood of much of the West depended. Justice William O. Douglas in his dissent expressed the danger well. "If by mere Executive action the federal lands may be reserved and all the water rights appurtenant to them returned to the United States," he warned, "vast dislocations in the economies of the Western States may follow."[11]

That there was a substantial basis to western fears was revealed within six weeks of the Pelton Dam decision. On July 25, 1955, the commanding officer at the Hawthorne naval ammunition depot notified the Nevada state engineer that the navy was discontinuing its application for water rights under the state's laws because it was no longer necessary under a "recent rule of the United States Supreme Court." When the state engineer sought a reversal of the navy's decision in a federal circuit court, he was rebuffed.[12]

After the Pelton Dam decision, what was the status of section eight? The Interior Department continued to acquire rights to water through state procedures, but the high court, in *Ivanhoe Irrigation District* v. *McCracken*, announced that the department could extinguish state rights by condemnation, that is, by exercising the power of eminent domain. More disturbing to the West was that aspect of the decision which nullified the portion of section eight requiring the secretary of the interior to distribute project water in accordance with state law. The Ivanhoe Irrigation District case was a dispute over the distribution of the waters of the Central Valley Project. The plaintiffs requested the approval of contracts limiting the delivery of irrigation water to 160 acres under one ownership. The defendants objected, contending that such limitation was contrary to California law. The Court favored the plaintiffs and ruled that the congressional limitation overrode state law. "We read nothing in § 8," it stated, "that compels the United States to deliver water on conditions imposed by the State."[13]

Following the Pelton Dam decision, the Department of Justice continued to assert that the federal government owned the unappropriated waters of the western streams. When the city of Fresno sued the California Water Rights Board for a greater allocation of the San Joaquin River, the department intervened with the argument that the board did not have any water to allocate, that whatever unappropriated water remained in California's streams belonged to the United States. These assertions alarmed Californians, particularly southern Californians, because they raised questions about the availability of water for the recently approved state water plan. According to a statement by U.S. Senator Thomas H. Kuchel on the floor of the Senate, May 26, 1960, they "caused the deepest concern in California, threatening the future of nearly 16 million American citizens resident in the Golden State."[14]

The post-Pelton federal encroachment on states' water rights culminated in 1963 in the Supreme Court's *Arizona* v. *California* decision. The suit was initiated by Arizona to determine the allocation of the waters of the Colorado River. The Court decided that Congress had made an allocation in the Boulder Canyon Project Act that gave the secretary of the interior authority to apportion and distribute "the water among users within each State" without regard to priorities established under state law. "[W]e cannot," the Court declared, "hold that the Secretary must be bound by state law in disposing of water under the Project Act"; rather, the secretary was granted "full power to control, manage, and operate the Government's Colorado River works and to make contracts for the sale and delivery of water on such terms as are not prohibited by the . . . Act." As Professor Frank Trelease of the University of Wyoming observed, "[t]he worst fears of the westerners had come true; federal administrative control of water is substituted for the appropriation system of property rights."[15]

In its decision the court recognized the reserved rights of five Indian reservations to the waters of the Colorado.

Moreover, in addition to recognizing them, it quantified them, allocating to each reservation enough water to irrigate its "irrigable portion." Nor did it restrict its consideration of reserved rights to Indian reservations. The Supreme Court extended the rights to other types of federal reserves. "We agree," it stated, "that the United States intended to reserve water sufficient for the future requirements of the Lake Mead National Recreation Area, the Havasu Lake National Wildlife Refuge, the Imperial National Wildlife Refuge and the Gila National Forest."[16]

The West responded to these encroachments on state-created water rights by denunciations, resolutions, and the introduction of prohibitory legislation. Shortly after the receipt of news of the navy's termination of its application for groundwater rights in Nevada, Senator Frank Barrett of Wyoming revised a bill that he had earlier introduced, apparently at the request of the National Reclamation Association. The senator was well known in his state for his opposition to the reservation of land for the creation of the Jackson Hole National Monument. His amended bill, co-sponsored by seven other western senators, was designed to protect state-sanctioned water rights from federal infringement. The key provision read, "Subject to existing rights under State law, all navigable and nonnavigable waters are hereby reserved for appropriation and use of the public pursuant to State Law, and rights to the use of such waters for beneficial purposes shall be acquired under State laws relating to the appropriation, control, use, and distribution of such waters." Then, to emphasize the subservience of the federal government to state law in the acquisition of water rights, the bill provided, "Federal agencies and permittees, licensees, and employees, of the Government, in the use of water for any purpose in connection with Federal programs . . . shall, as a condition precedent to the use of any such water, acquire rights to the use thereof in conformity with State laws and procedures relating to the control, appropriation, use, or distribution of such water."[17]

The Barrett bill with these provisions was never enacted. Although the secretary of the interior approved it, the Departments of Justice and Defense did not. Rather, in cooperation with the Interior Department, they drafted a competing bill, which was introduced in 1959 into the Eighty-sixth Congress. Seeking to compromise, but avoiding any suggestion of state ownership of western waters, the opening paragraph of the agency bill provided, "The withdrawal or reservation of surveyed or unsurveyed public lands, heretofore or hereafter established, shall not affect any right to the use of water acquired pursuant to State law either before or after the establishment of such withdrawal or reservation." Nonetheless, as soon as the bill appeared in the Senate, Senator Joseph C. O'Mahoney of Wyoming, long an opponent of the centralization of political power, amended it to confirm state ownership: "Nor shall [withdrawals or reservations] affect the right of any State to exercise jurisdiction over water rights conferred by the Act admitting such State into the Union or such State's constitution, as accepted and ratified by such Act of admission." The departments objected and the bill did not pass.[18]

Within a decade some fifty water rights settlement bills were introduced into Congress. They included several bills, sponsored in 1961 and 1964 by Senator Thomas Kuchel, that incorporated the original first paragraph of the agencies' bill. None were enacted. The agencies reversed their position, and even the secretary of the interior, Stewart L. Udall, opposed the Kuchel bills as too restrictive of federal authority. Federal opponents were joined by some within the states such as members of the Izaak Walton League and officials of state fish and game departments. Sportsmen wanted recognition of rights to the maintenance of instream flows, which state governments did not favor.[19]

Congressional protection of appropriative rights failing, the federal courts continued to define and delineate the new water right that they were forging to western waters. In two controversies that came to it from Colorado, the U.S Supreme Court in the 1971 Eagle River cases recognized the existence of federal reserved rights in four national forests as well as in properties administered by the Departments of the Interior and the Navy. Although it ruled that the McCarran Amendment subjected those rights to adjudication in state courts, it ominously declared that they represented rights to an indeterminate amount of water in case the federal government decided to extract oil from shale. The Court said, "The Department of the Navy administers certain naval petroleum and oil shale reserves which, if ever developed, would require water to accomplish the federal purpose for which the reservations were made." The justices reaffirmed the conclusion reached in the Winters and Conrad Investment Company decisions that the reserved right was open-ended.[20]

Five years later, in *Cappaert* v. *United States*, the Supreme Court extended the reserved right to groundwater. Like the Hawthorne dispute, this case originated in Nevada, where President Truman in 1952 had reserved, as part of a national monument, a forty-acre tract of land containing a deep limestone cavern known as Devil's Hole. Since the purpose of the reservation was to preserve a rare species of desert fish in a pool at the bottom of the cavern, it was necessary to maintain a certain water level in it. The pool, however, was connected hydrologically with the surrounding groundwater aquifer. Consequently, when the Cappaerts, nearby ranchers, drilled wells into the aquifer and in 1968 began pumping, the water level in Devil's Hole fell, endangering the survival of the fish. The United States responded by seeking an injunction to limit the ranchers' pumping, contending that in creating the reservation it had reserved enough unappropriated ground and surface water to maintain the purpose for which it was created. The Cappaerts countered with the argument that they had rights superior to those of the government because they had appropriated water according to the laws of Nevada, but the United States had not. The justices disagreed. Reserved rights, they said, are not determined by the priorities of state law; rather they are created with the establishment of a reservation by the federal government and are senior to "subsequent diversion, whether the diversion is of surface or ground water." States' rights to underground waters as well as surface waters were imperiled.[21]

The Cappaert decision was the high-water mark of the federal assault on state-granted water rights. In fact, the tide was already ebbing. Having ruled in the Eagle River cases that the McCarran Amendment had authorized the adjudication of reserved rights in state courts, the United States Supreme Court ruled in *Colorado River Conservation District* v. *United States* (decided three months before Cappaert) that those rights included water rights reserved for Indians under the Winters doctrine. In fact, it contended in this decision— usually referred to as "Akin"—that they should be litigated in state courts if such action promoted the comprehensive adjudication of water rights in a river system.[22]

These favorable decisions were followed by a confrontation with the federal government, from which the states came away victorious. On May 23, 1977, President Jimmy Carter notified Congress and the nation that he was directing "the Office of Management and Budget, the Council on Environmental Quality, and the Water Resources Council to conduct . . . a review of the present federal water resource policy" in order to establish a comprehensive national management program. He further requested that the review be conducted within six months. His announcement, which came without warning, alarmed the West, already alienated by the president's recommendation to Congress that it eliminate six western water projects and reduce the funding of three others, including the Central Arizona Project. Alarm turned into panic as the agencies published, in mid-July, four position papers, one of which attacked western "water rights systems" as inflexible, conducive "to inefficiencies and inequities" in the "allocation and use of water," and suggested the need "to develop a national perspective . . . to ensure that Federal policies promote the recognition of realistic goals through changes in existing institutions at all levels of government." The region's leaders feared that the administration had "a new water policy in its hip pocket," which it was about to impose upon them. As a consequence, when the agencies announced a hearing in Denver for July 28–29, many of those leaders came to protest. Governor Ed Herschler of Wyoming spoke for the West when he declared that the proposals of the administration could result in the "complete strangulation" of the western states. Then he added: "Since the founding of our country it has been the sole responsibility of state governments to allocate their waters. By and large state water law has done an excellent job." Faced with protests of this nature, President Carter hastened to Denver in October to assure westerners "that there absolutely [would] be no federal preemption of state or private prerogatives in the use or management of water," a pledge that he repeated in his water policy message on June 6, 1978. "States," he conceded in that message, "must be the focal point for water resource management."[23]

In two decisions a month later, the United States Supreme Court marched to the same tune. Both were written by Justice William Rehnquist, a resident of arid Arizona for sixteen years; both reduced federal encroachment on states' control of their water resources. In a dispute arising out of the adjudication of rights to the use of the Rio Mimbres in southwestern New Mexico, federal attorneys argued that in creating the Gila National Forest within the watershed of the river the United States had reserved rights to "minimum instream flows for aesthetic, recreational, and fish-preservation purposes" as well as for the watering of livestock. Justice Rehnquist did not agree. Federal reserved rights in the national forests, he said, were limited to the purposes for which those forests were created; namely, for the preservation of the timber and the maintenance of satisfactory flows of water. The West breathed a sigh of relief. If reserved rights were limited, they were much less a threat to state-sanctioned water rights. In a twin case, *California* v. *United States*, the justice reversed the dictum in Ivanhoe and ruled that section eight of the reclamation act allows a state to impose conditions on the use of project water.[24]

So definite was the states' victory that political scientist Helen Ingram and two colleagues on the staff of Resources for the Future would write in the September 1979 issue of the *Western Political Quarterly*, "Decisions made within states will determine future allocations of water resources in the West. . . . They have successfully asserted their independence in determining water allocation." But conflicts have not disappeared. Within a year following the Rehnquist decisions, the federal government declared that it had "unreserved" rights in the waters of the West. In addition, open-ended Indian reserved rights remain a thorny problem. Most parties agree on the need for quantification, but disagree as to the appropriate forum. The Indians prefer the federal courts, but, encouraged by the Akin decision, several states, including New Mexico, South Dakota, and Washington, have instituted the adjudication of Indian water rights in state courts. The Department of Justice sought to have the reserved rights of the Montana tribes quantified by federal courts, but the judges of two of those courts cited Akin and dismissed the suits in favor of water rights determination by the state of Montana. Indeed, sources of conflict still remain, but it appears that for the time being the appropriative right that the states have forged in western waters is safe and secure.[25]

16
The Appropriation Right
and Its Critics

When the Carter administration attacked the appropriation right as inflexible and inefficient, it touched a tender nerve of the West. For a number of years sportsmen and other urban-based environment preservation groups had been critical of the right, suggesting that it either be modified or discarded. The West, however, remained loyal to it because of at least two major strengths.

First, the appropriation right provides the security that is desirable in a property right. It is attached to a definite quantity of divertible water during a certain flow of a stream. The earlier the date of appropriation, the better the right, according to the first in time, first in right principle. When the stream is at flood stage in the spring from the melting snows, the rights of all users may be satisfied, but as the stream flow decreases rights to use the water are suspended in reverse order of the dates of appropriation. Whatever the priority, the use must be beneficial. The Reclamation Act of 1902 declares that "beneficial use shall be the basis, the measure, and the limit of the right." When beneficial use ceases, the right ceases. The nature of the appropriation right may be illustrated by reference to the situation in Colorado's Cache la Poudre River valley. Among the many diversions of that stream, the John G. Coy Ditch, dating from 1865, has the thirteenth priority right to 31 cubic feet per second of its flow during the irrigating season. The Union Colony's Canal No. 2, commenced in the fall of 1870, has the thirty-seventh priority to 110 cubic feet per second, while the larger Larimer and Weld Canal, dating from 1878, carries the eighty-eighth priority to 571 cubic feet per second. When the Cache la Poudre is at flood stage in the spring, all three of these canals will receive their full allotments of water, but when in early July the flow is not sufficient to supply all three canals, the water commissioner will order closed the headgate of the upstream Larimer and Weld Canal so that the other two can receive their full appropriations. Similarly, when the river's flow drops so low that the appropriations of both the Coy and the Colony No. 2 ditches cannot be satisfied, the Coy ditch, which heads above the No. 2 canal, will receive its full entitlement before the colony canal receives any of its allotment. Irrigators under these ditches are aware of the situation and have constructed reservoirs to store water for late season irrigation.[1]

To give increased security to appropriative rights, legislatures around the turn of the century followed the advice of John Wesley Powell, Isaac Bond, and Elwood Mead and tied the water to the land. However, in most states either the legislatures or the courts have permitted, under certain conditions, the sale and transfer of water rights. This gives the appropriative right a second strength, a desirable flexibility, which allows for change in economic use and permits expanding cities to acquire augmented sources of water supply.

Perhaps the most spectacular development in the West in the twentieth century has been the growth of cities, creating what Professor Gerald D. Nash of the University of New Mexico has called an "urban oasis." This growth can be illustrated by noting the increase in size of several western cities. In a span of seventy years, from 1910 to 1980, the population of Los Angeles jumped from 319,000 to 3,122,000, while Phoenix during the same period grew from a little city of 11,000 to a metropolis of 772,400. Although the rate of growth was less, the population of Denver more than doubled during these years.[2]

As western cities grew, so did their need for water. They have sought to satisfy those needs either by purchasing appropriation rights from farmers or by developing new sources. In 1891 a Colorado farmer, protesting the purchase of water rights by the city of Colorado Springs, triggered the landmark decision, allowing the transfer of agricultural rights to urban communities. He owned rights to the use of waters of Fountain Creek for irrigation purposes, which he claimed the sale jeopardized. He contended that in Colorado, water rights could not be sold separately from the land. The court concluded that a water right was a property right that could be bought and sold if the rights of others were not "injuriously affected." Many other cities have followed the example of Colorado Springs in acquiring water for their burgeoning populations.[3]

The acquisition of new sources of water in the mountains touched off the West's biggest water fights. San Francisco provoked one of them when it applied to the secretary of the interior in the Theodore Roosevelt administration, James R. Garfield, for permission to build a municipal reservoir in the Hetch Hetchy Valley of the Yosemite National Park. When the secretary granted it, John Muir and members of his Sierra Club launched a nation-wide campaign to save the sanctity of the park. So effective was the protest that President William Howard Taft's secretary of the interior revoked the action of his predecessor, but the Woodrow Wilson administration gave the project its blessing. San Francisco dammed the Tuolumne River in the Yosemite National Park and carried its waters through a 155-mile aqueduct to its residents.[4]

Los Angeles' search for water led to a noisy confrontation with the farmers of Owens Valley, located on the eastern side of the Sierra Nevada, 250 miles north of the city. Settlers began to occupy the valley in the 1860s and to divert the waters of the Owens River. By 1899 they were irrigating more than forty-one thousand acres, some of them by relatively large canals. Since there was still considerable unappropriated water in the stream, those farmers were pleased to learn in 1903 that the Reclamation Service was investigating the feasibility of a project in the valley. The investigation was under the supervision of Joseph B. Lippincott, who had lived in Los Angeles since 1891, serving as a part-time employee of the Geological Survey and as a part-time private consulting engineer. He was, therefore, well acquainted with William Mulholland, the engineer in charge of the Los Angeles Water Department, and with Fred Eaton, an engineer who had recently served as the city's mayor. During the mid-summer of 1904, Lippincott decided to visit the Owens Valley, and he invited Eaton to join him. They visited the valley and noted its water resources. On their return, Eaton shared the richness of those resources with Mulholland, who was worried about Los Angeles' existing supplies of water. The current drought was demonstrating that they were insufficient for a city growing at the rate of twenty-five thousand residents a year. Consequently, he was interested in the possibility of obtaining water from the Owens River and lost no time in visiting the valley with Eaton and in examining a possible route for an aqueduct. When the two men returned to Los Angeles, they studied the Geological Survey stream flow records furnished to them by Lippincott and concluded that Owens River water was the answer to the city's water problem. While Mulholland shared their plans with the Los Angeles Board of Water Commissioners, Eaton, early in 1905, went back to the Owens Valley and purchased options on land and water rights. Thinking that he was in the employ of the Reclamation Service, the farmers willingly cooperated, only to learn four or five months later that they had sold to the city of Los Angeles.

Angry and frustrated by the theft of their water, the farmers fought back. They urged the Reclamation Service to remain in the valley, but instead it withdrew. They tried to prevent the construction of the aqueduct by dissuading Congress from granting a right-of-way for it across public lands, but again they were not successful. Mulholland commenced its construction in 1907 and completed it in 1913. When, ten years later, in the midst of another drought, the city sought to increase its use of Owens Valley water by the purchase of additional land and water rights, the residents responded by dynamiting the aqueduct, first in 1924 and again in 1926 and 1927. Although no one was killed, the repair costs were considerable. Moreover, the protest was in vain. Los Angeles succeeded in expanding its water supply. Defeated, many farmers departed, abandoning their farms to the desert.[5]

The drought of the mid-twenties revealed to Mulholland that not even an increased share of the Owens River would satisfy the needs of Los Angeles. So in 1923 he visited the Colorado River and the next year appeared before a congressional committee as an advocate of the Boulder Canyon Project. Already interested in the hydroelectric power to be generated by the project, the city now joined the Imperial Valley in demanding a share of the Colorado water. Soon, in association with twelve other southern California cities, it organized the Metropolitan Water District and in 1933 began the construction of the three-hundred mile long Colorado Aqueduct. As the district reached for a share of the big river, Arizona reacted by instituting in succession three interstate lawsuits and a military expedition. When in 1934 the district and the Bureau of Reclamation began construction of Parker Dam to divert the waters of the river into the aqueduct, Governor Benjamin B. Moeur of Arizona sent a contingent of the Natonal Guard to halt it. A violent confrontation was avoided when Secretary of the Interior Harold

Ickes suspended operations until Congress could authorize the construction. Indeed, Los Angeles' search for water has been turbulent.[6]

Struggles of lesser intensity occurred within Arizona and Colorado, although Phoenix was able to avoid them by purchasing water from the well-managed Salt River Project. As related in Chapter 14, Tucson has been in court several times to obtain a municipal supply of groundwater claimed by agricultural interests. In Colorado, Denver's search for water precipitated a contest. After exhausting the available supplies in the South Platte Valley, the city sought to divert a portion of the headwaters of the Colorado through transmountain tunnels. To do this it constructed three projects—the Fraser River, the Williams Fork, and the Blue River. The Fraser River Project was commenced in 1929, using the pioneer bore of the Moffat Railroad tunnel as a transmountain diversion aqueduct. It was completed in 1936. Shortly thereafter Denver undertook the construction of the Williams Fork Project, which was followed by the commencement in 1946 of the Blue River Project, with its twenty-three-mile Harold D. Roberts Tunnel. As Denver reached for the waters of the Colorado, it encountered opposition on the Western Slope from other users of the river. In a series of legal battles in state and federal courts, the city's claim of 1914 as the priority date of its Blue River Project was reduced to 1946, junior to the 1935 priority of the Colorado–Big Thompson Project, and its transmountain diversions restricted to municipal uses. A federal court forbade their use for irrigation.[7]

Cities in their search for adequate supplies of water have had relatively little impact on water rights, less so on surface rights than on rights to groundwater. The legal profession had fairly well formulated the appropriation right governing the use of surface waters when sizable cities appeared on the western scene. The cities simply accepted it as the paramount right to the streams. They have, however, increased the flexibility of the right. Los Angeles developed the pueblo right, but the courts have granted it to only two other western cities—namely, San Diego, California, and Las Vegas, New Mexico.[8] Rights to groundwater were younger and more malleable when cities appeared and consequently more affected by them. Residents of Roswell played a major role in the formulation of the New Mexican right. The cities of Washington played a similar role in changing the groundwater right in that state. In California, the mutual prescription right was molded by a conflict among the cities extracting water from the Raymond Basin, while in Arizona Tucson's thirst has increased the flexibility of the state's reasonable use right.

The impact of cities on the appropriative right may be greater in the future than it has been in the past, for urban residents have been increasingly critical of it in recent decades. They have attacked it as wasteful, inflexible, and exhaustive of stream flows, reducing opportunities for recreational activities, particularly fishing. They declare it wasteful because beneficial use is loosely defined. They contend that farmers, who use approximately 83 percent of the western flows, apply too much water to their fields. The question of the proper duty of water has concerned western irrigators from the beginning. The Mormons grappled with it. Elwood Mead as territorial engineer of Wyoming conducted tests and as chief of irrigation investigations in the United States Department of Agriculture devoted a large share of his budget to determine the duty of water in the irrigated valleys of the West. After he concluded that a constant flow of one cubic foot per second or less was sufficient to irrigate seventy acres, the Wyoming legislature incorporated the figure into its statute of December 22, 1890. Some states have followed the example of Wyoming and quantified the duty in legislation; others have given the courts a freer role. It is a difficult problem, for the efficient use of water varies with the character of the soil, the crops, the rate of evaporation, and the method of application. Inasmuch as the legislatures and the courts have defined beneficial use in the past, so they can in the future as the public demands a more precise definition.[9]

In spite of the relaxation of transfer restrictions, critics of the appropriation right maintain that it is still too inflexible. They urge the removal of additional restrictions and regulations so that the right can be transferred, bought, and sold, as freely as any other resource commodity in response to the demands of the marketplace. It is to be remembered that the appurtenancy rule, the chief target of these critics, was formulated during the conflict between the farmers and the canal corporations. The companies were gaining monopolistic control of the farmers' water. To prevent it, Isaac Bond and Elwood Mead advocated the tying of the water right to the irrigated land. Since the fear had a substantial basis, most legislatures and Congress responded affirmatively, as did a district court in Arizona under the judgeship of Joseph H. Kibbey. Nonetheless, if the danger no longer exists, legislatures and the courts can modify or discard the restrictions, provided they remember that water rights, whatever their character, are correlative, interconnected with other rights in the same stream or aquifer. In allowing the transfer of one right, they must take care to protect the others from injury.[10]

The most articulate critics of the appropriation right have been the sportsmen. They have objected to the exhaustion of streams by appropriators and the destruction of recreational fishing. Consequently, they have demanded that recreation be declared a beneficial use and that minimum flows be preserved. In response to these demands, the right is being modified.

One of the requirements in perfecting an appropriative right has always been the diversion of water from a stream.

This is no longer the case in several states. The Colorado and Idaho legislatures have waived that requirement and allow public agencies to appropriate water for instream use, especially for the preservation of minimum flows. A 1973 Colorado statute authorizes the state water conservation board to appropriate "such waters of natural streams and lakes as may be required to preserve the natural environment to a reasonable degree." The courts in both states have approved legislation of this nature. Similarly, the Arizona Supreme Court construed acts allowing the appropriation of streams for recreation and the maintenance of "wild life, including fish," as waiving diversion. Using a somewhat different legal approach, Washington, Montana, and Oregon have authorized the "reservation" of minimum flows to preserve fish and other aquatic life. The Montana Water Use Act of 1973 empowers the board of natural resources and conservation "to reserve waters for existing or future beneficial uses, or to maintain a minimum flow, level, or quality of water throughout the year ... or for such length of time as the board designates." In 1978 the agency implemented the statute by reserving minimum flows of the Yellowstone River. It required, for instance, a flow in the river of at least 5,492,310 acre-feet per year at Sidney near the Montana-North Dakota border. It is of interest to note that this modification of the appropriative right represents a reappearance in several states of the dual system of water rights, where part of the stream is required to flow in its accustomed channel and another part is subject to diversion.[11] The appropriation right is not a static institution. Forged as an adaption to the arid West, it continues to be shaped by western needs and pressures.

Notes

Chapter 1

1. U.S. Department of Commerce, Environmental Science Services Administration, *Climatological Data: National Summary*, vol. 20, no. 13 (Annual 1969): 43–49; Charles W. Stockton and David M. Meko, "A Long-Term History of Drought Occurrence in Western United States as Inferred from Tree Rings," *Weatherwise* 28 (1975): 244–49.

2. Emil W. Haury, *The Hohokam: Desert Farmers & Craftsmen. Excavations at Snaketown. 1964–65* (Tucson: University of Arizona Press, 1976); Emil W. Haury, "Arizona's Ancient Irrigation Builders," *Natural History* 54 (1945): 300–303; Emil W. Haury, "The Hohokam: First Masters of the American Desert," *National Geographic Magazine* 131 (May 1967): 670–95.

3. Omar A. Turney, "Prehistoric Irrigation," *Arizona Historical Review* 2 (1929): 11–52; Richard B. Woodbury, "The Hohokam Canals at Pueblo Grande, Arizona," *American Antiquity* 26 (1960): 267–70.

4. Juan Matheo Mange, *Lux de Tierra Incógnita en la América Septentrional: Diario de las Exploraciones en Sonora* in *Publicaciones del Archivo General de la Nación*, 30 vols. (Mexico City: Talleres Graficos de la Nacion, 1910–1936), 10:256.

5. Herbert E. Bolton, *Kino's Historical Memoir of Pimeria Alta . . . 1683–1711*, 2 vols. (Cleveland: Arthur H. Clark, 1919), 1:205, 235–36; Herbert E. Bolton, *Rim of Christendom: A Biography of Eusebio Francisco Kino, Pacific Coast Pioneer* (New York: Macmillan, 1936), pp. 502–7.

6. Herbert E. Bolton, *Anza's California Expeditions*, 4 vols. (Berkeley: University of California Press, 1930), 2:303.

7. Herbert E. Bolton, *Spanish Exploration in the Southwest, 1542–1706* (New York: Scribners, 1916), pp. 182–83; Marc Simmons, "Spanish Irrigation Practices in New Mexico," *New Mexico Historical Review* 47 (1972): 137.

8. Thomas F. Glick, *Irrigation and Society in Medieval Valencia* (Cambridge: Harvard University Press, Belknap Press, 1970).

9. Bolton, *Spanish Exploration in the Southwest*, p. 203; Simmons, "Spanish Irrigation Practices," pp. 138–39; Charles W. Hackett, *Historical Documents Relating to New Mexico, Nueva Vizcaya, and Approaches Thereto, to 1773*, 3 vols. (Washington, D.C.: Carnegie Institution of Washington, 1923–37), 3:379.

10. R. Louis Gentilcore, "Mission and Mission Lands of Alta California," *Annals of the Association of American Geographers* 51 (1961): 54–55; Frank Adams, "The Historical Background of California Agriculture," in Claude B. Hutchinson, ed., *California Agriculture* (Berkeley and Los Angeles: University of California Press, 1946), p. 16.

11. Maynard Geiger, *Mission Santa Barbara, 1782–1965* (Santa Barbara: Serra Shop, Old Mission, 1965), pp. 52–53; Francis Rand Smith, *The Mission of San Antonio de Padua California* (Stanford: Stanford University Press, 1932), pp. 58–81; J. B. Lippincott, "Water Supply of San Bernardino Valley," *Nineteenth Annual Report of the United States Geological Survey*, pt. 4 (Washington, D.C.: GPO, 1899), p. 542; Edith P. Hinckley, *On the Banks of the Zanja: The Story of Redlands* (Claremont, California: Saunders Press, 1951), pp. 24–27.

12. Edwin A. Beilharz, *Felipe de Neve, First Governor of California* (San Francisco: California Historical Society, 1971), pp. 101–4; John W. Caughey, *California* (New York: Prentice-Hall, 1940), pp. 164–65.

13. Lynn Bowman, *Los Angeles: Epic of a City* (Berkeley: Howell-North 1974), pp. 30–33; Vincent Ostrom, *Water and Politics: A Study of Water Policies and Administration in the Development of Los Angeles* (Los Angeles: Haynes Foundation, 1953), pp. 27–30; Beilharz, *Felipe de Neve*, pp. 107–8; *Feliz v. Los Angeles*, 58 Cal. 73 (1881); *Vernon Irrigation Co. v. City of Los Angeles*, 106 Cal. 237, 39 Pac. 762 (1895).

14. Betty E. Dobkins, *The Spanish Element in Texas Water Law* (Austin: University of Texas Press, 1959), p. 104; Edwin P. Arneson,

"Early Irrigation in Texas," *Southwestern Historical Quarterly* 25 (1921): 121–23.

15. Dobkins, *Spanish Element in Texas Water Law*, pp. 108–12; Arneson, "Early Irrigation in Texas," pp. 123–29; Thomas F. Glick, *The Old World Background of the Irrigation System of San Antonio, Texas*, University of Texas at El Paso, Southwestern Studies, Monograph no. 35 (El Paso, 1972), pp. 26–31; William F. Hutson, *Irrigation Systems in Texas*, United States Department of the Interior, United States Geological Survey (hereafter cited as USGS), Water Supply and Irrigation Paper 13 (Washington, D.C.: GPO, 1898), pp. 43–45.

16. Wells A. Hutchins, "The Community Acequia: Its Origin and Development," *Southwestern Historical Quarterly* 31 (1928): 261–84; Ostrom, *Water and Politics*, p. 30; Glick, *Old World Background of the Irrigation System of San Antonio*, pp. 31–49; Simmons, "Spanish Irrigation Practices," pp. 139–46.

Chapter 2

1. *The Latter-Day Saints' Millennial Star* 12 (June 15, 1850): 178; Charles W. Stockton and David M. Meko, "A Long-Term History of Drought Occurrence in Western United States as Inferred from Tree Rings," *Weatherwise* 28 (1975): 248; Ray A. Billington and James B. Hedges, *Westward Expansion: A History of the American Frontier* (New York: Macmillan, 1949), p. 538.

2. *The Latter-Day Saints' Millennial Star*, 12: 178–79; William Clayton, *William Clayton's Journal: A Daily Record of the Journey of the Original Company of "Mormon" Pioneers from Nauvoo, Illinois, to the Valley of the Great Salt Lake* (Salt Lake City: Deseret News, 1921), pp. 312–14, 340–43; Clesson S. Kinney, *A Treatise on the Law of Irrigation and Water Rights and the Arid Region Doctrine of Appropriation of Waters*, 4 vols. (San Francisco: Bender-Moss, 1912), 1:403; Dale L. Morgan, *The Great Salt Lake* (Indianapolis: Bobbs-Merrill, 1947), pp. 198–99.

3. Orson F. Whitney, *History of Utah*, 4 vols. (Salt Lake City: G. Q. Cannon and Sons, 1892–1904), 1:339–40, 347–65; George D. Clyde, "History of Irrigation in Utah," *Utah Historical Quarterly* 27 (1959): 28–29; Dale L. Morgan, "The Changing Face of Salt Lake City," *Utah Historical Quarterly* 27 (July 1959): 210–24; Samuel L. Clemens, [Mark Twain], *Roughing It*, 2 vols. (New York: Harper

and Brothers, 1903), 1:114; Clayton, *Journal*, pp. 340–43; LeRoy W. Hooten, Jr., "The Early History and Investigation into Salt Lake City's Water Rights in City Creek," MS in the Department of Water Supply and Water-Works, Salt Lake City, no pagination.

4. Leonard J. Arrington, *Great Basin Kingdom: An Economic History of the Latter-day Saints, 1830–1900*, (Cambridge, Mass.: Harvard University Press, 1958), pp. 50–52; Orson W. Israelsen, J. Howard Maughan, and George P. South, *Irrigation Companies in Utah: Their Activities and Needs*, Utah State Agricultural College Agricultural Experiment Station, Bulletin 322 (Logan, Utah, 1946), p. 10; George L. Strebel, "Irrigation as a Factor in Western History, 1847–1890," Ph.D. diss., University of California, Berkeley, 1965, pp. 86–89; R.C. Gemmell, *Duty of Water on Big Cottonwood Creek*, United States Department of Agriculture (hereafter cited as USDA), Office of Experiment Stations, Bulletin 86 (Washington, D.C.: GPO, 1900) pl. 45; Whitney, *History of Utah*, pp. 357, 384–86; E.R. Morgan, "Irrigation in Mountain Water District, Salt Lake County, Utah," in *Report of Irrigation Investigations, 1902, under the Direction of Elwood Mead*, USDA, Office of Experiment Stations, Bulletin 133 (Washington, D.C.: GPO, 1903), pp. 20–27.

5. Milton Hunter, *Brigham Young the Colonizer* (Independence, Mo.: Zion's Printing and Publishing Co., 1945), pp. 195–210; Emily M. Carlisle, "Early Irrigation along the Big Cottonwood Creek," MS, Utah Division of State History, Salt Lake City, pp. 2–3; Appellants' Abstract of Record, *Progress Company and Rudolph Knudsen* v. *Salt Lake City*, Case No. 2831, Utah Supreme Court Library, Capitol, Salt Lake City, pp. 481–86, 512.

6. Hunter, *Brigham Young*, pp. 212–13, 361–62.

7. Ibid., pp. 55–61; Leonard J. Arrington, "Economic History of a Mormon Village," *Pacific Northwest Quarterly* 46 (1955): 97–99; Charles H. Brough, *Irrigation in Utah* (Baltimore: Johns Hopkins Press, 1898), pp. 9–13; Leonard J. Arrington and Dean May, "'A Different Mode of Life': Irrigation and Society in Nineteenth-Century Utah," *Agricultural History* 49 (1975): 8–9; Arrington, *Great Basin Kingdom*, pp. 88–94.

8. Arrington, *Great Basin Kingdom*, pp. 87–88, 177–78; Charles S. Peterson, *Take Up Your Mission: Mormon Colonizing Along the Little Colorado River, 1870–1900* (Tucson: University of Arizona Press, 1973), pp. 154–91; James H. McClintock, *Mormon Settlement in Arizona: A Record of Peaceful Conquest of the Desert* (Phoenix: By the author, 1921), pp. 182–83, 212–14,

244–65; Kate B. Carter, ed., *Pioneer Irrigation: Upper Snake River Valley* (n.p.: Daughters of Utah Pioneers, 1955); Eliza R. Lythegoe, "Colonization of the Big Horn Basin by the Mormons," *Annals of Wyoming* 14 (1942): 39–50; Charles Lindsay, *The Big Horn Basin* (Lincoln: University of Nebraska, 1932), pp. 163–205.

9. Leonard J. Arrington, Feramorz Y. Fox, and Dean L. May, *Building the City of God: Community & Cooperation Among the Mormons* (Salt Lake City: Deseret Book Co., 1976), pp. 1–40; Leonard J. Arrington, "Early Mormon Communitarianism: The Law of Consecration and Stewardship," *Western Humanities Review* 7 (1953): 341–69; Arrington, *Great Basin Kingdom*, pp. 3–12, 52–53.

10. Dale L. Morgan, "The State of Deseret," *Utah Historical Quarterly* 8 (1940): 197–200; George Thomas, *The Development of Institutions under Irrigation with Special Reference to Early Utah Conditions* (New York: Macmillan Co., 1920), pp. 44–51.

11. *Acts, Resolutions and Memorials Passed at the Several Annual Sessions of the Legislative Assembly of the Territory of Utah* (Great Salt Lake City: 1855), p. 127; Thomas, *Development of Institutions*, pp. 60–74.

12. Arrington, *Great Basin Kingdom*, p. 53; Whitney, *History of Utah*, 1:356.

13. William R. Palmer, "Utah's 'Water Courts'," *Reclamation Era* 33 (1947): 232, 240.

14. Hooten, Jr., "The Early History and Investigation into Salt Lake City's Water Rights in City Creek"; Thomas, *Development of Institutions*, pp. 92–110; *Levy v. Salt Lake City*, 3 Utah 63, 1 Pac. 160 (1884).

15. Thomas, *Development of Institutions*, pp. 58–60.

16. Ibid., p. 58; George L. Strebel, "Irrigation as a Factor in Western History, 1847–1890," pp. 142–45.

17. Gemmell, *Duty of Water on Big Cottonwood Creek*, pp. 198–99; Carlisle, "Early Irrigation along the Big Cottonwood Creek," pp. 4–6; Arthur P. Stover, "Irrigation in Utah Lake Drainage System," in *Report of Irrigation Investigations in Utah*, USDA, Office of Experiment Stations, Bulletin 124 (Washington, D.C.: GPO, 1903), pp. 136–37.

18. Utah, *Session Laws, 1880*, pp. 36–41; Gustive O. Larson, *The 'Americanization' of Utah for Statehood* (San Marino, Calif.: Huntington Library, 1971), pp. 301–2; Charles S. Peterson, "The 'Americanization' of Utah's Agriculture," *Utah Historical Quarterly* 42 (1974): 109–11; Elwood Mead, *Irrigation Institutions* (New

York: Macmillan, 1903), pp. 222–23; Ray P. Teele, "General Discussion of Irrigation in Utah," USDA, Office of Experiment Stations, in *Report of Irrigation Investigations in Utah*, Bulletin 124, pp. 22–27; Utah State Engineer, *First Biennial Report, 1897–1898* (Salt Lake City, 1899), pp. 14–22.

Chapter 3

1. Rose M. Boening, "History of Irrigation in the State of Washington," *Washington Historical Quarterly* 9 (1918): 261–62; Donald W. Meinig, *The Great Columbia Plain: A Historical Geography, 1805–1910* (Seattle: University of Washington Press, 1968), pp. 66–91, 125–45; Clifford M. Drury, ed., *The Diaries and Letters of Henry H. Spalding and Asa Bowen Smith relating to the Nez Perce Mission, 1838–1842* (Glendale, Calif.: A. H. Clark, 1958), pp. 87–88, 277, 293, 361; Thomas J. Farnham, *Travels in the Great Western Prairies, the Anahuac and Rocky Mountains, and in the Oregon Territory*, 2 vols. (London, 1843), reprinted in Reuben Gold Thwaites, ed., *Early Western Travels, 1748–1846*, 32 vols. (Cleveland: A. H. Clark, 1904–7), 28:334–37; John Winchell, to R. G. Dunbar, Dec. 15, 1972, Folder, Dunbar—Water-Right History Papers, Special Collections, Roland R. Renne Library, Montana State University, Bozeman.

2. *Wilderness Kingdom: Indian Life in the Rocky Mountains, 1840–1847, The Journals & Paintings of Nicolas Point, S.J.*, trans. and introduced by Joseph P. Donnelly, S.J. (New York: Holt, Rinehart and Winston, 1967), pp. 39, 45 (see map of St. Mary's Mission, p. 57); L. B. Palladino, *Indian and White in the Northwest: A History of Catholicity in Montana, 1831 to 1891* (Lancaster, Pa.: Wickersham Publishing, 1922), pp. 41–42, 60–61; Pierre-Jean DeSmet, *Letter and Sketches: with a Narrative of a Year's Residence among the Indian Tribes of the Rocky Mountains* (Philadelphia, 1843) reprinted in Thwaites, *Early Western Travels*, 27: 281–82; Pierre-Jean DeSmet, *Oregon Missions and Travels over the Rocky Mountains in 1845–46* (New York, 1847), reprinted in Thwaites, *Early Western Travels*, 29:321–22; Albert J. Partoll, ed., *Mengarini's Narative of the Rockies: Memoirs of Old Oregon, 1841–1850, and St. Mary's Mission*, Sources of Northwest History no. 25 (Missoula: Montana State University, 1938), p. 8; *The Journals and Letters of Major John Owen*, ed. Seymour Dunbar and Paul C. Phillips, 2 vols.

(Helena: Montana Historical Society, 1927), 1:125, 127; William N. Bischoff, S.J., *The Jesuits in Old Oregon, 1840–1940* (Caldwell, Idaho: Caxton Printers, 1945), pp. 29–30, 66.

3. *Proceedings of First Conference of Engineers of the Reclamation Service with Accompanying Papers,* USGS, Water-Supply and Irrigation Paper 93 (Washington, D.C.: GPO, 1904), p. 176; E. S. Nettleton, *The Reservoir System of the Cache La Poudre Valley,* USDA, Office of Experiment Stations, Bulletin 92 (Washington, D.C.: GPO, 1902), p. 11; Calvin B. Coulter, "The Victory of National Irrigation in the Yakima Valley, 1902–1906," *Pacific Northwest Quarterly 42* (1951): 100.

4. Alvin T. Steinel, *History of Agriculture in Colorado* (Fort Collins: State Agricultural College, 1926), pp. 180–82; *Rocky Mountain News,* Feb. 22, 1860; Everett Dick, *Conquering the Great American Desert,* Nebraska State Historical Society Publication, Vol. 27 (Lincoln: Nebraska State Historical Society, 1975), p. 383; Deposition of Oscar E. Penwell, filed March 5, 1890, *Nelson Story* v. *Bozeman Water Works Co. et al.,* File Box 86, Office of the Clerk of the 18th Judicial District Court, Gallatin County Law and Justice Center, Bozeman, Mont.; Arthur Jerome Dickson, ed., *Covered Wagon Days* (Cleveland: Arthur H. Clark, 1929), p. 229.

5. U.S. Department of Commerce, Bureau of the Census, *Fourteenth Census of the United States, 1920,* Vol. 7, *Irrigation and Drainage* (Washington, D.C.: GPO, 1922), pp. 200, 203, 332, 336.

6. Hallock F. Raup, *The German Colonization of Anaheim, California,* University of California Publications in Geography, no. 6 (Berkeley: University of California, 1932), pp. 123–32; Erwin G. Gudde, "Anaheim—the Mother Colony of Southern California," *American-German Review* 7 (1941): 4–5; George L. Strebel, "Irrigation as a Factor in Western History, 1847–1890," Ph.D. dissertation, University of California-Berkeley, 1965, pp. 305–8; William H. Hall, *Irrigation in California* (Sacramento: State Printing, 1888), pp. 612, 616–21; William H. Hall, *Report of the State Engineer to the Legislature of the State of California— session of 1880,* pt. 4, App. A; *Report on Irrigation Works and Practice in Los Angeles and San Bernardino Counties* (Sacramento, 1880), pp. 28–29.

7. James F. Willard, ed., *The Union Colony at Greeley, Colorado, 1869–1871* (Boulder: University of Colorado, 1918),

pp. xix–xxiv, 1–17, 229–55; David Boyd, *A History: Greeley and the Union Colony of Colorado* (Greeley: Tribune Press, 1890), pp. 11–44.

8. Richard J. Hinton, *A Report on Irrigation and the Cultivation of the Soil thereby, with Physical Data, Conditions, and Progress within the United States for 1891*, U.S. Congress, *Senate Exec. Doc.* 41, 52nd Cong., 1st sess., 1892, pt. 1:138–46; Willard, *Union Colony*, pp. 27–35; Boyd, *History*, pp. 431–32.

9. David Boyd, *Irrigation near Greeley, Colorado*, USGS, Water-Supply and Irrigation Paper 9 (Washington, D.C.: GPO, 1897), pp. 27–30; James Maxwell Clark, *Colonial Days* (Denver: Smith-Brooks, [1902]), pp. 68–70; John H. Tice, *Over the Plains and the Mountains, or Kansas and Colorado, Agriculturally, Mineralogically, and Aesthetically* (Chicago: Western News Co., 1872), pp. 80–81; *Dictionary of American Biography*, s.v. "Nettleton, Edwin S."; Hinton, *Report on Irrigation*. pp. 138–40; Boyd, *History*, pp. 59–63, 381–426; Willard, *Union Colony*, pp. xxx, 21, 40, 55, 76, 103, 298, 344–45.

10. James F. Willard and Colin B. Goodykoontz, eds., *Experiments in Colorado Colonization 1869–1872*, University of Colorado Historical Collections, vol. 3 (Boulder, 1926), pp. 137–330; Boyd, *History*, p. 184; Steinel, *History of Agriculture in Colorado*, pp. 392–94; Articles of Incorporation of the Highland Ditch Company, Certificates of Domestic Incorporation, Book D, pp. 469–70, Department of Archives and Public Records, Denver.

11. Roger V. Clements, "British-Controlled Enterprise in the West between 1870 and 1900, and Some Agrarian Reactions," *Agricultural History* 27 (1953): 137; U.S. Department of the Interior, Census Office, *Report on Agriculture by Irrigation in the Western Part of the United States at the Eleventh Census; 1890* (Washington, D.C.: GPO, 1894), p. 101; Herbert M. Wilson, "American Irrigation Engineering," American Society of Civil Engineers, *Transactions* 25 (1891): 177–79, 185–86, 191–92; Anne Carolyn Hansen, "The Congressional Career of Senator Francis E. Warren from 1890 to 1902," *Annals of Wyoming* 20 (1948): 37–38; *Report of the Special Committee of the United States Senate on the Irrigation and Reclamation of Arid Lands*, U.S. Congress, *Senate Report* 928, 51st Cong., 1st sess., 1890, 6 pts., pt. 2:328–29, pt. 4:100, map facing p. 100, 410–11; Vernon L. Sullivan, *Irrigation in New Mexico*, USDA, Office of Experiment Stations, Bulletin 215 (Washington, D.C.: GPO, 1909), p. 22; Mary H. Foote, *A Victorian Gentlewoman in the Far West: The Reminiscenses of Mary Hallock Foote*, ed.

Rodman W. Paul (San Marino, Calif.: Huntington Library, 1972), pp. 264–330.

12. Ray P. Teele, *Irrigation in the United States* (New York: D. Appleton and Company, 1915), pp. 203–6.

13. Richard J. Hinton, *Irrigation in the United States* in *Report of the Special Committee of the United States Senate, Senate Report* 928, 51st Cong., 1st sess., pt. 6:74, 153–62; Boyd, *History*, p. 184; *Constitution of Colorado*, art. 16, sec. 8; Colorado, *Session Laws, 1879*. pp. 94–96.

14. *Rocky Mountain News*, Jan. 7, 30, March 3, 1887; *Wheeler* v. *Northern Colorado Irrigation Co.*, 10 Colo. 582, 17 Pac 487 (1888); Clements, "British-Controlled Enterprise in the West," pp. 136–41.

15. *Rocky Mountain News*, Jan. 28, Feb. 14, 1887; Leonard P. Fox, "State Regulation of the Canal Corporation in Colorado," *Michigan Law Review* 16 (1917–18): 165–67; Colorado, *Session Laws, 1887*, pp. 308–10; Earl L. Mosley, "History of the Denver Water System," 2 vols., typewritten ms., Denver Public Library, 2:155.

16. *Boise City Irrigation and Land Co.* v. *Clark et al*, County Com'rs, 131 Fed. 415 (1904); *Report of Irrigation Investigations for 1901*, USDA, Office of Experiment Stations, Bulletin 119 (Washington, D.C.: GPO, 1902), pp. 199–203; Idaho State Engineer, *Sixth Biennial Report, 1905–1906* (Nampa: n.d.), pp. 171–72.

17. Wells A. Hutchins, *Commercial Irrigation Companies*, USDA, Technical Bulletin 177 (Washington, D.C.: GPO, 1930), pp. 7–8, 15; George Thomas, *The Development of Institutions under Irrigation* (New York: Macmillan, 1920), pp. 203–18; Elwood Mead, *Irrigation Institutions* (New York: Macmillan, 1903), pp. 20, 244–45; Leonard J. Arrington, *Beet Sugar in the West: A History of the Utah-Idaho Sugar Company, 1891–1966* (Seattle: University of Washington Press, 1966), pp. 42–46; C.A. Hundertmark, "Reclamation in Chaves and Eddy Counties, 1887–1912," *New Mexico Historical Review* 47 (1972): 304–6; Paul L. Murphy, "Early Irrigation in the Boise Valley," *Pacific Northwest Quarterly* 44 (1953): 179–81; U.S. Reclamation Service, *Fourth Annual Report, 1904–5* (Washington, D.C.: GPO, 1906), pp. 268–69; *Report of Irrigation Investigations for 1901*, pp. 269–70.

18. Paul W. Gates, *History of Public Land Development* (Washington, D.C.: GPO, 1968), p. 651; *Fourteenth Census of the United States: 1920*, vol. 7, *Irrigation and Drainage*, p. 166; U.S. Department of Commerce Bureau of the Census, *Census of Agriculture, 1969*, vol. 4, *Irrigation* (Washington D.C.: GPO, 1973), pp. 142–43.

19. *Acts, Resolutions and Memorials passed at the Several Annual Sessions of the Legislative Assembly of the Territory of Utah* (Great Salt Lake City, 1866), pp. 185–97; Wells A. Hutchins, *Mutual Irrigation Companies in Utah*, Utah Agricultural Experiment Station, Bulletin 199 (Logan, Utah, 1927), pp. 20–24; Colorado, *Session Laws, 1872*, p. 143; *Constitution of Colorado*, art. 10, sec. 3; Raphael J. Moses, "Irrigation Corporations," *Rocky Mountain Law Review* 32 (1960): 527.

20. Wells A. Hutchins, *Organization and Operation of Cooperative Irrigation Companies*, U.S. Farm Credit Administration, Circular no. C 102 (Washington, D.C.: GPO, 1936); Wells A. Hutchins, *Mutual Irrigation Companies*, USDA, Technical Bulletin 82 (Washington, D.C.: GPO, 1929).

21. Christine Lewis, "The Early History of the Tempe Canal Company," *Arizona and the West* 7 (1965): 229–35; Alfred J. McClatchie, *Utilizing Our Water Supply*, University of Arizona Agricultural Experiment Station, Bulletin 43 (Tucson, 1902), 79–80, 91–92.

22. Certificate of Incorporation of the Big Ditch Company, dated May 16, 1900, on file in the Office of the Clerk and Recorder, Yellowstone County Courthouse, Billings, Montana; *Billings Gazette*, July 6, 1897, July 12, 15, 1898, May 18, 1900, Dec. 3, 1944; *State ex rel. Crawford* v. *Minnesota and Montana Land and Improvement Co.*, 20 Mont. 198, 50 Pac. 420 (1897); Robert B. Tootell, *An Inventory of Montana Irrigation Projects*, Montana Extension Service, Bulletin 124 (Bozeman, 1932), p. 88.

23. *Census of Agriculture, 1969*, vol. 4, *Irrigation*, pp. xxv, 142–45.

24. Hutchins, *Commercial Irrigation Companies*, p. 5; Wells A. Hutchins, H.E. Selby, and Stanley W. Voelker, *Irrigation Enterprise Organizations*, USDA Circular 934 (Washington, D.C.: GPO, 1953), p. 14.

25. Merlin Stonehouse, *John Wesley North and the Reform Frontier* (Minneapolis: University of Minnesota Press, 1965), pp. 80–232; Robert Hornbeck, *Roubidoux's Ranch in the 70s* (Riverside, Calif.: Riverside Press, 1913), pp. 106–18; Tom Patterson, *A Colony for California: Riverside's First Hundred Years* (Riverside: Press-Enterprise, 1971), pp. 29–44; Hall, *Irrigation in California*, pp. 222–41.

26. Joseph A. Alexander, *The Life of George Chaffey: A Story of Irrigation Beginnings in California and Australia* (Melbourne:

Macmillan, 1928), 30–37; Hall, *Irrigation in California*, pp. 172, 332–38; Frederick D. Kershner, Jr., "George Chaffey and the Irrigation Frontier," *Agricultural History* 27 (1953): 115–26; Hinton, *Report on Irrigation*, p. 109.

27. Hinton, *Report on Irrigation*, pp. 95–96; Thomas E. Malone, "The California Irrigation Crisis of 1886; Origins of the Wright Act," Ph.D. diss., Stanford University, 1965, pp. 77–205.

28. Wells A. Hutchins, *Irrigation District Operation and Finance*, USDA, Bulletin 1177 (Washington, D.C.: GPO, 1923); Wells A. Hutchins, *Irrigation Districts, Their Organization, Operation and Financing*, USDA, Technical Bulletin 254 (Washington, D.C.: GPO, 1931); Wells A. Hutchins, *Summary of Irrigation District Statutes of Western States*, USDA, Miscellaneous Publication 103 (Washington, D.C.: GPO, 1931); Malone, "California Irrigation Crisis of 1886," pp. 205–17; *Census of Agriculture, 1969*, vol. 4; *Irrigation*, p. 142.

29. Frank Adams, "The Distribution and Use of Water in Modesto and Turlock Irrigation Districts, California," in *Annual Report of Irrigation and Drainage Investigations, 1904*, USDA, Office of Experiment Stations, Bulletin 158 (Washington, D.C.: GPO, 1905), pp. 94–107; Tootell, *Inventory of Montana Irrigation Projects*, pp. 13–15; Hutchins, *Irrigation Districts, Their Organization, Operation and Financing*, p. 81; Idaho State Engineer, *Sixth Biennial Report, 1905–1906*, pp. 171–72; E. Courtland Eaton and Frank Adams, "Irrigation Development through Irrigation Districts," American Society of Civil Engineers, *Transactions* 90 (1927): 774–82; *Encyclopedia Americana*, 1969, s.v. "Imperial Valley."

30. Robert G. Dunbar, "Pioneering Groundwater Legislation in the United States; Mortgages, Land Banks, and Institution-Building in New Mexico," *Pacific Historical Review* 47 (1978): 579–81; Oliver Knight, "Correcting Nature's Error: The Colorado Big Thompson Project," *Agricultural History* 30 (1956): 161–62; Moses, "Irrigation Corporations," pp. 531–33; William R. Kelly, "Water Conservancy Districts," *Rocky Mountain Law Review* 22 (1950): 432–52.

Chapter 4

1. Leonard J. Arrington and Thomas C. Anderson, "The 'First' Irrigation Reservoir in the United States: The Newton, Utah,

Project," *Utah Historical Quarterly* 39 (1971): 210–12; "Utah—
Cradle of American Irrigation," *Reclamation Era* 32 (1946): 198;
Edwin S. Nettleton, *The Reservoir System of Cache la Poudre*,
USDA, Office of Experiment Stations, Bulletin 92 (Washington,
D.C.: GPO, 1901), pp. 1–48; C.E. Tait, *Storage of Water on Cache la
Poudre and Big Thompson Rivers*, USDA, Office of Experiment
Stations, Bulletin 134 (Washington, D.C.: GPO, 1903), pp. 18–37.

2. Herbert M. Wilson, "American Irrigation Engineering,"
American Society of Civil Engineers, *Transactions* 25 (1891): 213–
14; Edith Parker Hinckley, *On the Banks of the Zanja: The Story of
Redlands* (Claremont, Calif.: Saunders Press, 1951), pp. 59–67;
William H. Hall, *Irrigation in California* (Sacramento: State Print-
ing, 1888), pp. 179–88; James Dix Schuyler, *Reservoirs for Irriga-
tion, Water-Power and Domestic Water-Supply* (New York: John
Wiley and Sons, 1901), pp. 126–52, 163–74; U.S. Congress, Senate,
*Report of the Special Committee of the United States Senate on the
Irrigation and Reclamation of Arid Lands*, 51st Cong., 1st sess.,
1890, *Senate Report* 928, 6 pts., pt. 4:386.

3. Thomas E. Malone, "The California Irrigation Crisis of
1886: Origins of the Wright Act," Ph.D. diss., Stanford University,
1965, pp. 71–76.

4. Alvin Steinel, *History of Agriculture in Colorado* (Fort
Collins: State Agricultural College, 1926), p. 208; James E. Wright,
The Politics of Populism: Dissent in Colorado (New Haven: Yale
University Press, 1974), pp. 117–18; Donald A. MacKendrick, "Be-
fore the Newlands Act: State-Sponsored Reclamation Projects in
Colorado, 1888–1903," *Colorado Magazine* 52 (1975): 1–21.

5. *Report of the Special Committee of the United States Sen-
ate*, 1:51, 84–85, 3:143, 4:484; Lawrence B. Lee, "William Ellsworth
Smythe and the Irrigation Movement: A Reconsideration," *Pacific
Historical Review* 41 (1972): 293–97; Thomas G. Alexander, "John
Wesley Powell, the Irrigation Survey, and the Inauguration of the
Second Phase of Irrigation Development in Utah," *Utah Historical
Quarterly* 37 (1969): 200–202; Anne Carolyn Hansen, "The Con-
gressional Career of Senator Francis E. Warren from 1890 to 1902,"
Annals of Wyoming 20 (1948): 39–40; U.S. Congress, Senate, *Con-
gressional Record*, 52d Cong., 1st sess., 1892, 23, pt. 2:1862, pt.
7:6485–86; George W. Paulson, "The Congressional Career of
Joseph Maull Carey," *Annals of Wyoming*, 35 (1963): 71–73; John
W. Hakola, "The Development of a Policy towards Irrigation in
Montana in 1908," M.A. thesis, Montana State University, 1951,
pp. 80–87.

6. Mikel H. Williams, "The History of Development and Current Status of the Carey Act in Idaho," published by the Idaho Department of Reclamation, March 1970, pp. 1–5; Ray P. Teele, *Irrigation in the United States* (New York: D. Appleton, 1915), pp. 60–67.

7. U.S. Department of the Interior, Bureau of Land Management, "Report of the Director, 1957, Statistical Appendix" (Washington, D.C.: [1957]), p. 135; Williams, "History of Development . . . of the Carey Act in Idaho," pp. 10–15, 79–81; Hakola, "Development of a Policy towards Irrigation in Montana," pp. 100–109.

8. Lindsay, *The Big Horn Basin*, pp. 185–91; T. Alfred Larson, *History of Wyoming* (Lincoln: University of Nebraska Press, 1965), pp. 349–50; Wyoming Commissioner of Public Lands and Farm Loans, *Seventeenth Biennial Report, 1936–1938*, (Cheyenne, n.d.), pp. 22–27.

9. Williams, "History of Development . . . of the Carey Act in Idaho," pp. 71–72; James Stephenson, *Irrigation in Idaho*, USDA, Office of Experiment Stations, Bulletin 216 (Washington, D.C.: GPO, 1909), pp. 42–44.

10. Hugh T. Lovin, "A 'New West' Reclamation Tragedy: The Twin Falls Oakley Project in Idaho," *Arizona and the West* 20 (1978): 5–24; Williams "History of Development . . . of the Carey Act in Idaho," pp. 69, 75.

11. Williams, "History of Development . . . of the Carey Act in Idaho," pp. 15–82.

12. George Thomas, *The Development of Institutions under Irrigation* (New York: Macmillan, 1920), pp. 219–30; Orson W. Israelsen, J. Howard Maughan, and George P. South, *Irrigation Companies in Utah: Their Activities and Needs*, Utah State Agricultural College Agricultural Experiment Station, Bulletin 322 (Logan, Utah, 1946), p. 29; *Report of Irrigation Investigations for 1901*, USDA, Office of Experiment Stations, Bulletin 119 (Washington, D.C.: GPO, 1902), pp. 38–39; Paul W. Gates, *History of Public Land Law Development* (Washington, D.C.: GPO, 1968), p. 316.

13. Montana, *Session Laws, Extraordinary Session of the Twenty-third Legislative Assembly, 1933–1934*, pp. 2, 92–109; Montana State Water Conservation Board, *First Biennial Report, 1964–1966* (Helena, 1967), pp. 2–3; D. P. Fabrick, "The Role of the State Water Conservation Board in the Development of Montana's Water Resources," in "Water Use in Montana: The Role of Three Governmental Agencies," Montana University Joint Water Re-

sources Research Center, Report 85 (Bozeman: 1976), pp. 3–18; Montana State Engineer, *Water Resources Survey, Musselshell County, Montana,* 2 pts (Helena, 1949), 1:13–15 *Roundup Record-Tribune,* May 8, 1958.

14. Erwin Cooper, *Aqueduct Empire: A Guide to Water in California, Its Turbulent History and Its Management Today* (Glendale, Calif.: A. H. Clark, 1968), pp. 50–53; *Reclamation Era* 36 (1950): 7, 20.

15. California Department of Water Resources, *The California Water Plan,* Bulletin no. 3, May 1957; *California State Water Project,* Bulletin no. 200, 5 vols., November 1974, 1:1–165; Johannes Humlum, *Water Development and Water Planning in Southwestern United States* (Aarhus, Netherlands: Aarhus Universitet, 1969), pp. 53–95; H. E. Thomas, *The Meteorologic Phenomenon of Drought in the Southwest,* USGS, Professional Paper 372–A (Washington, D.C.: GPO, 1962), pp. 21–24; Vincent Ostrum, "State Administration of Natural Resources in the West," *American Political Science Review* 47 (1953): 481–84; Cooper, *Aqueduct Empire,* pp. 52–53, 149, 199–242; Harvey P. Grody, "From North to South: the Feather River Project and other Legislative Water Struggles in the 1950s," *Historical Society of Southern California Quarterly* 60 (1978): 287–326.

Chapter 5

1. Daryl V. Gease, "William N. Byers and the Case for Federal Aid to Irrigation in the Arid West," *Colorado Magazine* 45 (1968): 340–45; Malone, "The California Irrigation Crisis of 1886: Origins of the Wright Act,'" pp. 60–63. For a comprehensive review of the literature of the national reclamation movement, see Lawrence B. Lee, *Reclaiming the American West: An Historiography and Guide* (Santa Barbara, Calif.: American Bibliographical Center-Clio Press, 1980).

2. U.S. *Statutes at Large,* vol. 19. p. 377.

3. U.S. Department of the Interior, General Land Office, *Annual Report,* 1888 (Washington, D.C.: GPO, 1888), pp. 48–49, 73, 77; Paul W. Gates, *History of Public Land Law Development* (Washington, D.C.: GPO, 1968), pp. 638–43; Benjamin H. Hibbard, *A History of the Public Land Policies* (New York: Peter Smith,

1939), pp. 426–34; John T. Ganoe, "The Desert Land Act in Operation, 1877–1891," *Agricultural History* 11 (1937): 142–57; Alfred J. McClatchie, *Utilizing Our Water Supply*, University of Arizona Agricultural Experiment Station, Bulletin 43 (Tucson, 1902), p. 81.

4. Department of the Interior, USGS, *Tenth Annual Report, 1888–1889*, pt. 2, *Irrigation* (Washington, D.C.: GPO, 1890), pp. 1–16; U.S. Congress, Senate, *Congressional Record*, 50th Cong., 1st sess., 1888, 19, pt. 2:1137, 1766, pt. 3:2428–29.

5. John Wesley Powell, *Report on the Lands of the Arid Region of the United States*, ed. Wallace Stegner (Cambridge: Harvard University Press, Belknap Press, 1962). Quotation appears on p. 22.

6. USGS, *Tenth Annual Report, 1888–1889*, pt. 2, pp. 16–108; Everett E. Sterling, "The Powell Irrigation Survey, 1888–1893," *Mississippi Valley Historical Review* 27 (1940): 421–34; John G. Rabbitt and Mary C. Rabbitt, "The U.S. Geological Survey: 75 Years of Service to the Nation, 1879–1954," *Science* 119 (1954): 749–51.

7. Donald A. MacKendrick, "Before the Newlands Act: State-Sponsored Reclamation Projects in Colorado, 1888–1903," *Colorado Magazine* 52 (1975): 2–3; U.S. Congress, House, *Congressional Record*, 50th Cong., 1st sess., 1888, 19, pt. 1:236, Senate, 19, pt. 1:826, House, *Congressional Record*, 51st Cong., 1st sess., 1889, 21, pt. 1:261; Rose M. Boening, "History of Irrigation in the State of Washington," *Washington Historical Quarterly* 9 (1918): 266; *Bozeman Chronicle*, Jan. 20, 1892; Montana, *House Journal, 1893*, pp. 24–25; Everett N. Dick, *The Lure of the Land; A Social History of the Public Lands from the Articles of Confederation to the New Deal* (Lincoln: University of Nebraska Press, 1970), p. 313; U.S. Congress, Senate, *Report of the Special Committee of the United States Senate on the Irrigation and Reclamation of Arid Lands*, 51st Cong., 1st sess., 1890, *Senate Report 928*, 6 pts., 3:507.

8. U.S. Congress, House, Committee on Irrigation of Arid Lands, *Preliminary Examination of Reservoir Sites in Wyoming and Colorado*, 55th Cong., 2d sess., 1897, *House Document 141*; Gordon B. Dodds, *Hiram Martin Chittenden: His Public Career* (Lexington: University Press of Kentucky, 1973), pp. 24–41.

9. William E. Smythe, *The Conquest of Arid America*, with introduction by Lawrence B. Lee (Seattle: University of Washington Press, 1969), pp. 271–93; George W. James, *Reclaiming the Arid West: The Story of the United States Reclamation Service* (New York: Dodd, Mead and Co., 1917), pp. 13–20; John T. Ganoe, "The

Origin of a National Reclamation Policy," *Mississippi Valley Historical Review* 18 (1931): 39–51; Samuel P. Hays, *Conservation and the Gospel of Efficiency: The Progressive Conservation Movement, 1890–1920* (Cambridge: Harvard University Press, 1959), pp. 9–19; Andrew Hudanick, Jr., "George Hebard Maxwell: Reclamation's Militant Evangelist," *Journal of the West* 14 (July, 1975): 108–21.

10. U.S. *Statutes at Large*, vol. 32, pp. 388–90; Gates, *History of Public Land Law Development*, pp. 654–56.

11. USGS, *First Annual Report of the Reclamation Service from June 17 to December 1, 1902*, 57th Cong., 2nd sess., 1903, *House Document 79*, p. 15.

12. U.S. Department of the Interior, Bureau of Reclamation, *Reclamation Project Data* (Washington, D.C.: GPO, 1961), pp. 343, 535, 550, 664, 762; Dorothy Lampen, *Economic and Social Aspects of Federal Reclamation* (Baltimore: Johns Hopkins University, 1930), p. 53.

13. *Reclamation Project Data*, pp. 534–42, 662–69, 708–17, 728–33; R. L. Meredith, "Reclamation in the Salt River Valley, 1902–1917," *Journal of the West* 7 (1968): 76–78; Karen L. Smith, "The Campaign for Water in Central Arizona, 1890–1903," *Arizona and the West* 23 (1981): 127–48; H. H. Johnson, "Forty-Three Years on the Shoshone Project," *Reclamation Era* 33 (1947): 124–27; Beryl Gail Churchill, *Dams, Ditches and Water; A History of the Shoshone Reclamation Project* (Cody, Wyo.: Rustler Printing, 1979); Thomas G. Alexander, "An Investment in Progress: Utah's First Federal Reclamation Project, the Strawberry Valley Project," *Utah Historical Quarterly* 39 (1971): 286–304; John M. Townley, *Turn This Water into Gold: The Story of the Newlands Project* (Reno: Nevada Historical Society, 1977), pp. 31–52; Donald J. Pisani, "Federal Reclamation and Water Rights in Nevada," *Agricultural History* 51 (1977): 540–46; *New York Times*, March 19, 1911.

14. Arthur P. Davis, *Irrigation Works Constructed by the United States Government* (New York: J. Wiley and Sons, 1917), pp. 113–18, 225–30, 325–76; *Reclamation Project Data*, pp. 33–48, 81–88, 761–67, 819–36; MacKendrick, "Before the Newlands Act," pp. 18–19; G. J. Van Gieson, "Holing through in 1909: The Story of the Gunnison—Reclamation's First Major Tunnel," *Reclamation Era* 33 (1947): 173–74, 182; Calvin B. Coulter, "The Victory of National Irrigation in the Yakima Valley, 1902–1906," *Pacific Northwest Quarterly* 42 (1951): 99–122; Calvin B.

Coulter, "Building the Tieton Irrigation Canal," *Pacific Northwest Quarterly* 49 (1958): 11–18; Roscoe Sheller, *Courage and Water: A Story of Yakima Valley's Sunnyside* (Portland, Oreg.: Binford and Mort, 1952), pp. 11–13, 117–18.

15. Lampen, *Economic and Social Aspects of Federal Reclamation*, pp. 59–74; Gates, *History of Public Land Law Development*, pp. 661–72; U.S. Reclamation Service, *Fourteenth Annual Report, 1914–1915* (Washington, D.C.: GPO, 1915), pp. 3–8; Alfred R. Golze, *Reclamation in the United States* (Caldwell, Idaho: Caxton Printers, 1961), p. 315; Michael C. Robinson, *Water for the West: The Bureau of Reclamation, 1902–1977* (Chicago: Public Works Historical Society, 1979), pp. 37–42; William E. Warne, "Land Speculation," *Reclamation Era* 33 (1947): 176–180, 186.

16. Gates, *History of Public Land Law Development*, pp. 672–78; Lampen, *Economic and Social Aspects of Federal Reclamation*, pp. 61–62.

17. Paul K. Conkin, "The Vision of Elwood Mead," *Agricultural History* 34 (1960): 88–95; Lampen, *Economic and Social Aspects of Federal Reclamation*, pp. 74, 114–18; Gates, *History of Public Land Law Development*, pp. 678–88.

18. U.S. Reclamation Service, *Fourteenth Annual Report*, pp. 29, 41; Robinson, *Water for the West*, pp. 25–29; Gates, *History of Public Land Law Development*, pp. 659–60.

19. Remi A. Nadeau, *The Water Seekers* (Garden City, N.Y.: Doubleday, 1950), pp. 171–244; Beverley B. Moeller, *Phil Swing and Boulder Dam*(Berkeley: University of California Press, 1971), pp. 1–122; William E. Warne,*The Bureau of Reclamation* (New York: Praeger, 1973), pp. 104–122; Golze, *Reclamation in the United States*, pp. 68–76; *Reclamation Project Data*, pp. 1–7, 49–56, 599–605.

20. *Reclamation Project Data*, pp. 92–112, 121–53, 171–88; Golze, *Reclamation in the United States*, pp. 176–97; Robinson, *Water for the West*, pp. 63–69; George Sundborg, *Hail Columbia: The Thirty-Year Struggle for Grand Coulee Dam* (New York: Macmillan, 1954); Bruce Mitchell, "Rufus Woods and Columbia River Development," *Pacific Northwest Quarterly* 52 (1961): 139–44; Earl Clark, "Rufus Woods: Grand Coulee Promoter," *Montana: The Magazine of Western History* 29 (1979): 38–51; Robert De Roos, *The Thirsty Land: The Story of the Central Valley Project* (New York: Greenwood Press, 1968); Oliver Knight, "Correcting Nature's Error: The Colorado-Big Thompson Project," *Agricultural History*

30 (1956): 157–69; William R. Kelly, "Colorado-Big Thompson Initiation, 1933–1938," *Colorado Magazine* 34 (1957): 66–74.

21. *Reclamation Project Data,* pp. 161–70, 374–527; Golze, *Reclamation in the United States,* pp. 198–217; Robinson, *Water for the West,* pp. 83–94, 105–6; Rich Johnson, *The Central Arizona Project, 1918–1968* (Tucson: University of Arizona Press, 1977), pp. 149–231; Elmo Richardson, *Dams, Parks, & Politics: Resource Development & Preservation in the Truman-Eisenhower Era* (Lexington: University Press of Kentucky, 1973), pp. 39–152.

22. U.S. Bureau of Reclamation, *Summary Report of the Commissioner, 1970, Statistical & Financial Appendix, Parts I, II & III* (Washington, D.C.: GPO, 1970), pp. xv, 103; U.S. Department of the Interior, *River of Life, Water: The Environmental Challenge Conservation Yearbook Series,* vol. 6 (Washington, D.C.: GPO, 1970), p. 83; U.S. Department of Commerce, Bureau of Census, *1969, Census of Agriculture,* vol. 4, *Irrigation* (Washington, D.C.: GPO, 1973), p. 82.

Chapter 6

1. Gordon M. Bakken, "The English Common Law in the Rocky Mountain West," *Arizona and the West* 11 (1979): 109–12.

2. James Kent, *Commentaries on American Law,* ed. Charles M. Barnes, 13th ed., 4 vols. (Boston: Little, Brown, and Co., 1884), 3:439; Charles J. Meyers and A. Dan Tarlock, *Water Resource Management: A Coursebook in Law and Public Policy* (Mineola, N.Y.: Foundation Press, 1971), pp. 52–53, 117–19.

3. Earl F. Murphy, "English Water Law Doctrines before 1400," *American Journal of Legal History* 1 (1957): 108–10; Henri de Bracton, *De Legibus et Consuetudinibus Angliae,* ed. Sir Travers Twiss, 3 vols. (London: Longman, 1880), 3:577.

4. Wells A. Hutchins, *Water Right Laws in the Nineteen Western States,* USDA, Miscellaneous Publication 1206, 3 vols., (Washington, D.C.: GPO, 1971–1977), 1:164–67; Charles H. Shinn, *Mining Camps: A Study in American Frontier Government,* ed. Rodman W. Paul (New York: Harper and Row, 1965) pp. 105–258: U.S. Census Office, *The United States Mining Laws and Regulations Thereunder, and State and Territorial Mining Laws, to Which Are Appended Local Mining Rules and Regulations,* vol. 14 of the *Tenth Census of the United States: 1880* (Washington, D.C.: GPO,

1885) pp. 271–345; *Jennison* v. *Kirk*, 98 U.S. 453 (1879).

5. Samuel C. Wiel, *Water Rights in the Western States*, 3d ed., 2 vols. (San Francisco: Bancroft-Whitney, 1911), 1:72–75: Gordon R. Miller, "Shaping California Water Law, 1781 to 1928," *Historical Society of Southern California Quarterly* 55 (1973): 13–15.

6. Hutchins, *Water Right Laws in the Nineteen Western States*, 1:164, n. 24.

7. *Eddy* v. *Simpson*, 3 Cal. 249 (1853); *Irwin* v. *Phillips*, 5 Cal. 140 (1855); Wiel, *Water Rights*, 1:77–80.

8. *Civil Code of the State of California*, 2 vols. (San Francisco, 1874), 1:402.

9. Ibid., 1:403–4.

10. Ibid., 1:405; *Ferrea* v. *Knipe*, 28 Cal. 341 (1865).

11. Malone, "The California Irrigation Crisis of 1886," pp. 118–32; *Pope* v. *Kinman*, 54 Cal. 3 (1879).

12. Malone, "California Irrigation Crisis of 1886," pp. 122–24.

13. Ibid., pp. 124–26; *Proceedings of the State Irrigation Convention Held at Riverside, California, May 14, 15, and 16, 1884* (Riverside: 1884); Winfield J. Davis, *History of Political Conventions in California, 1849–1892*, Publications of the California State Library, no. 1 (Sacramento, 1893), p. 473. North was no longer living in Riverside, having joined the Washington Colony near Fresno in 1880. See Merline Stonehouse, *John Wesley North and the Reform Frontier* (Minneapolis: University of Minnesota Press, 1965), pp. 233–38.

14. *Lux* v. *Haggin*, 69 Cal. 255, 4 Pac. 919 (1884), 10 Pac. 674 (1889); Edward F. Treadwell, *The Cattle King: A Dramatized Biography* (Boston: Christopher Publishing House, 1931), pp. 78–91; Miller, "Shaping California Water Law," p. 21.

15. Malone, "California Irrigation Crisis of 1886," pp. 126–31.

16. *Lux* v. *Haggin*, 69 Cal. 255, 10 Pac. 674; Wiel, *Water Rights*, 1:135–36; Norris Hundley, Jr., *Water and the West: The Colorado River Compact and the Politics of Water in the American West* (Berkeley: University of California Press, 1975), pp. 66–72.

17. Edward Hyatt, "Administration of Stream Flow," American Society of Civil Engineers, *Transactions* 94 (1930): 302.

18. Wiel, *Water Rights*, 1:809–26; Meyers and Tarlock, *Water Resource Management*, pp. 54–65; Morton J. Horwitz, *The Transformation of American Law, 1780–1860* (Cambridge: Harvard University Press, 1977), pp. 34–42; Miller, "Shaping California Water Law," pp. 23–26.

19. Miller, "Shaping California Water Law," pp. 24–27; Harry N. Scheiber and Charles W. McCurdy, "Eminent-Domain Law and Western Agriculture, 1849–1900," *Agricultural History* 49 (1975): 126; Lucien Shaw, "The Development of the Law of Waters in the West," *California Law Review* 10 (1922): 455–56; Wells A. Hutchins, *The California Law of Water Rights* (Sacramento, 1956), pp. 256–62, 298–343. For example of a water right gained by prescription, see *Miller and Lux* v. *Madera Canal and Irrigation Co.*, 155 Cal. 59, 99 Pac. 502 (1907).

20. *Herminghaus* v. *Southern California Edison Co.*, 200 Cal. 81, 252 Pac. 607 (1926); J.M.J., "Note," *California Law Review* 15 (1927): 229–34; Samuel C. Wiel, "The Pending Water Amendment to the California Constitution, and Possible Legislation," *California Law Review* 16 (1928): 171–75; California, *Session Laws, 1927*, pp. 2373–74; Hyatt, "Administration of Stream Flow," pp. 307–8; Edward F. Treadwell, "Developing a New Philosophy of Water Rights," *California Law Review* 38 (1950): 572–87; Miller, "Shaping California Water Law," pp. 29–33; *United States* v. *Gerlach Live Stock Co.*, 339 U.S. 725 (1950).

21. *Low* v. *Schaffer*, 24 Ore. 239, 33 Pac. 678 (1893); *Benton* v. *Johncox*, 17 Wash. 277, 49 Pac. 495 (1897); *Lone Tree Ditch Co.* v. *Cyclone Ditch Co.*, 15 S. Dak. 519, 91 N.W. 352 (1902); *Crawford Co.* v. *Hathaway*, 67 Nebr. 325, 93 N.W. 781 (1903); *Clark* v. *Allaman*, 71 Kans. 206, 80 Pac. 571 (1905); *Watkins Land Co.* v. *Clements*, 98 Tex. 578, 86 S.W. 733 (1905): Wells A. Hutchins, *Selected Problems in the Law of Water Rights in the West*, USDA, Miscellaneous Publication 418 (Washington, D.C.: GPO, 1942), pp. 48–64.

22. *Vansickle* v. *Haines*, 7 Nev. 249 (1872); *Thorp* v. *Freed*, 1 Mont. 651 (1872).

Chapter 7

1. Rodman W. Paul, *Mining Frontiers of the Far West 1848–1880* (New York: Holt, Rinehart and Winston, 1963), pp. 37–160; LeRoy R. Hafen, *Colorado and Its People*, 4 vols. (New York: Lewis Historical Publishing Co., 1948), 1:141–48, 177–78; Percy S. Fritz, *Colorado: The Centennial State* (New York: Prentice-Hall, 1941), pp. 105, 115–18; Russell R. Elliott, *History of Nevada* (Lincoln: University of Nebraska Press, 1973), pp. 51, 61–62; Merle W. Wells,

Rush to Idaho, Idaho Bureau of Mines and Geology, Bulletin 19 (Moscow, Idaho. n.d.), pp. 1–16; Merle W. Wells, *Gold Camps and Silver Cities*, Idaho Bureau of Mines and Geology, Bulletin 22 (Moscow, Idaho, n.d.), pp. 1–86; Merrill G. Burlingame, *The Montana Frontier* (Helena: State Publishing, 1942), pp. 79–91; Joseph Gaston, *The Centennial History of Oregon, 1811–1912*, 4 vols. (Chicago: S. J. Clarke, 1912), 1:494–97; Odie B. Falk, *Arizona: A Short History* (Norman: University of Oklahoma Press, 1970), pp. 143–44.

2. U.S. Census Office, *The United States Mining Laws and Regulations Thereunder*, pp. 247–685; Thomas M. Marshall, "The Miners' Law of Colorado," *American Historical Review* 25 (1920): 426–39; Percy S. Fritz, "The Constitutions and Laws of Early Mining Districts—in Boulder County, Colorado," *University of Colorado Studies* 21 (1934): 127–48; *Bailey* v. *Tintinger*, 45 Mont. 154, 122 Pac. 575 (1912), *Maynard* v. *Watkins*, 55 Mont. 54, 173 Pac. 551 (1918).

3. Hafen, *Colorado and Its People*, 1:199–221; *Provisional Laws and Joint Resolutions passed at the first and called sessions of the General Assembly of Jefferson Territory* (Omaha, 1869), p. 214.

4. *General Laws, joint resolutions, memorials, and private acts, passed at the first session of the Legislative Assembly of the Territory of Colorado, begun and held at Denver, Colorado Ter., September 9th 1861* (Denver, 1861), pp. 67–69; *Coffin* v. *Left Hand Ditch Co.*, 6 Colo. 443)1882).

5. Robert W. Swenson, "Legal Aspects of Mineral Resources Exploitation," in Paul W. Gates, *History of Public Land Law Development* (Washington, D.C.: GPO, 1968), pp. 714–21; Paul, *Mining Frontiers of the Far West*, pp. 171–73.

6. U.S. *Statutes at Large*, vol. 14, pp. 251–53, vol. 16, p. 218, vol. 19, p. 327; Wells A. Hutchins, *Selected Problems in the Law of Water Rights in the West*, USDA, Miscellaneous Publication 418 (Washington, D.C.: GPO, 1942), pp. 71–72.

7. *Atchinson* v. *Peterson*, 87 U.S. 507 (1874); *Kansas* v. *Colorado*, 206 U.S. 46 (1907).

8. Colo. 551 (1872); Ralph H. Hess, "The Colorado Water Right," *Columbia Law Review* 16 (1916): 649–51; John D. W. Guice, *The Rocky Mountain Bench* (New Haven: Yale University Press, 1972), p. 124.

9. *Proceedings of the Constitutional Convention held in Denver, December 20, 1875 to Frame a Constitution for the State of Colorado* (Denver, 1907), pp. 296, 393–94.

10. Clesson S. Kinney, *A Treatise on the Law of Irrigation and Water Rights, and the Arid Region Doctrine of Appropriation of Water*, 2d ed., 4 vols. (San Francisco: Bender-Moss, 1912), 1:466–67, 560, 961–65, 2:1105–6; William H. Hall, *Irrigation Development* (Sacramento: State Printing, 1886), pp. 38–41; Charles F. Davis, *The Law of Irrigation* (Fort Collins: Private Printing, 1915), pp. 71–72.

11. *Coffin* v. *Left Hand Ditch Co.*, 6 Colo. 443 (1882).

12. *Jones* v. *Adams*, 19 Nev. 78, 6 Pac. 442 (1885); *Drake* v. *Earhart*, 2 Idaho 750, 23 Pac. 541 (1890); *Stowell* v. *Johnson*, 7 Utah 215, 26 Pac. 290 (1891); *Moyer* v. *Preston*, 6 Wyo. 308, 44 Pac. 845 (1896); Samuel C. Wiel, *Water Rights in the Western States*, 3d ed., 2 vols. (San Francisco: Bancroft-Whitney, 1911), 1:94–96, 143.

13. Ray P. Teele, "General Discussion of Irrigation in Utah," in *Report of Irrigation Investigations in Utah*, USDA, Office of Experiment Stations, Bulletin 124 (Washington, D.C: GPO, 1903), pp. 23–24, 32; U.S. Congress, Senate, *Report of the Special Committee of the United States Senate on the Irrigation and Reclamation of Arid Lands*, 51st Cong., 1st sess., 1890, Senate Report 928, 6 pts., pt. 3:59; Arthur Maass and Raymond L. Anderson, . . . *and the Desert Shall Rejoice: Conflict, Growth, and Justice in Arid Environments* (Cambridge: MIT Press, 1978), pp. 325, 337–44: Elwood Mead, *Irrigation Institutions* (New York: Macmillan, 1903), pp. 228–32.

14. *Clough* v. *Wing*, 2 Ariz. 371, 17 Pac 453 (1888); *Snow* v. *Abalos*, 18 N. Mex. 681, 140 Pac 1044 (1914); *State ex rel State Game Commission* v. *Red River Valley Co.*, 51 N. Mex. 207, 182 Pac. 2d, 421 (1945); G.E.P. Smith, *Groundwater Law in Arizona and Neighboring States*, University of Arizona Agricultural Experiment Station, Technical Bulletin 65 (Tucson: 1936), pp. 54–55; Wells A. Hutchins, *Water Right Laws in the Nineteen Western States*, 3 vols. (Washington, D.C.: GPO, 1971–77), 3:163, 389–91.

15. *Mettler* v. *Ames Realty Co.*, 61 Mont. 152, 201 Pac. 702 (1921).

16. Frank J. Trelease, "Alaska's New Water Use Act," *Land and Water Review* 2 (1967): 8–18; Robert Emmet Clark, ed., *Water and Water Rights*, 7 vols. (Indianapolis: Allen Smith, 1967–76), 5:9–10: Hutchins, *Water Right Laws in the Nineteen Western States*, 3:150–51.

17. Hutchins, *Water Right Laws in the Nineteen Western States*, 3:286–30, 333–58, 408–18, 423–35, 441–67, 478–98, 504–27, 571–601; Otis W. Templer, "Institutional Constraints and Water Resources: Water Rights Adjudication in Texas," *Rocky Mountain Social Science Journal* 10 (1973): 37–45.

Chapter 8

1. Wells A. Hutchins, *Water Right Laws in the Nineteen Western States*, 3 vols. (Washington, D.C.: GPO, 1971–77), 1: 284–95; Samuel C. Wiel, *Water Rights in the Western States* 3d ed., 2 vols. (San Francisco: Bancroft-Whitney Co., 1911), 1:386–434.

2. Robert G. Dunbar, "The Origins of the Colorado System of Water-Right Control," *Colorado Magazine* 27 (1951): 242–43.

3. Ibid., pp. 243–44; Robert G. Dunbar, "Water Conflicts and Controls in Colorado," *Agricultural History* 22 (1948): 181–83; *Greeley Tribune*, July 22, 1874; *Fort Collins Standard*, July 22, 1874.

4. Dunbar, "Origins of the Colorado System," pp. 244–45.

5. Ibid., pp. 245–46; *Greeley Tribune*, Oct. 9, 23, 1878; *Colorado Sun*, Oct. 5, 26, 1878.

6. Dunbar, "Origins of the Colorado System," pp. 246–49; *Denver Weekly Times*, Dec.11, 1878; *Rocky Mountain News*, Dec. 6, 1878.

7. Dunbar, "Origins of the Colorado System," pp. 250–51.

8. *Greeley Tribune*, Dec. 11, 1878.

9. House Bill No. 22, A bill for an act entitled an act concerning irrigation, 2d sess., General Assembly of the State of Colorado, 1879, Division of Archives and Public Records, Denver.

10. Henry L. McClintock, "The Administrative Determination of Public Land Controversies," *Minnesota Law Review* 9 (1925): 420–41, 542–54, 638–56; David Boyd, *A History; Greeley and The Union Colony* (Greeley, Colo.: Greeley Tribune Press, 1890), pp. 122–23, 184.

11. Colorado, *Session Laws*, 1879, pp. 99–105.

12. Ibid., pp. 94–99.

13. Dunbar, "Origins of the Colorado System," pp. 255–56; Boyd, *Greeley and the Union Colony*, p. 124; *Colorado Sun*, Aug. 30, 1879.

14. Report of H. N. Haynes, Esq., Referee of Water Dist. No. 3, filed in District Court this 9th day of April A.D. 1880, Case no. 320,

Larimer County Courthouse, Fort Collins, Colo.; *Colorado Sun,* June 19, 1880.

15. Boyd, *Greeley and the Union Colony,* pp. 128–34.

16. Robert G. Dunbar, "The Significance of the Colorado Agricultural Frontier," *Agricultural History* 34 (1960): 124.

17. Frank Hall, *History of the State of Colorado* 4 vols. (Chicago: Blakely Printing Co., 1889–95), 4:512; Colorado, *Senate Journal,* 1881, pp. 171, 225–26.

18. Senate Bill No. 93, A bill for an act to make further provisions for settling the priority of rights to the use of water for irrigation, 3d sess., General Assembly of the State of Colorado, 1881, Division of Archives; Colorado *Session Laws, 1881,* pp. 142–46; Colorado, *Senate Journal, 1881,* pp. 171, 369; *House Journal, 1881,* pp. 553, 669–70.

19. *Proceedings Concerning Adjudication of Priorities under Irrigation Act of 1881, in Water District No. 3, Cache la Poudre District* (Denver, n.d.), pp. 1–9; *Colorado Sun,* Jan. 22, 1881; Boyd, *Greeley and the Union Colony,* p. 135.

20. Colorado State Engineer, *Biennial Report, 1881–1882,* (Denver, 1882), pp. 9–13; California, *Session Laws, 1877–1878,* 634; Charles P. Korr, "William Hammond Hall: The Failure of Attempts at State Water Planning in California, 1878–1888," *Historical Society of Southern California Quarterly,* 45 (1963), 307–8; Malone, "The California Irrigation Crisis of 1886," pp. 63–68; *Rocky Mountain News,* Jan. 23, 1881.

21. Colorado State Engineer, *Biennial Report, 1881–1882,* pp. 9–13.

22. Colorado, *Session Laws, 1881,* pp. 119–21; Colorado State Engineer, *Second Biennial Report, 1883–1884* (Denver, 1885), 30–45; Colorado, *Senate Journal, 1881,* pp. 317, 333–36.

23. Colorado, *Session Laws, 1881,* pp. 119; *Session Laws, 1887,* pp. 295–300.

24. Colorado, *Session Laws, 1881,* 161–62; *Session Laws, 1887,* pp. 314–15.

25. Elwood Mead, *Irrigation Institutions* (New York: Macmillan, 1903), pp. 147–59.

Chapter 9

1. James R. Kluger, "Elwood Mead: Irrigation Engineer and Social Planner," Ph.D. diss., University of Arizona, 1970, pp. 3–14;

"Elwood Mead," American Society of Civil Engineers, *Transactions* 102 (1937): 1611–12; *Dictionary of American Biography*, s.v. "Mead, Elwood"; James E. Hanson II, *Democracy's College in the Centennial State: A History of Colorado State University* (Fort Collins: Colorado State University, 1977), pp. 67–70.

2. *Portrait and Biographical Record of Denver and Vicinity, Colorado* (Chicago, 1898), p. 983; Boyd, *Greeley and the Union Colony*, pp. 398–99, 435; Colorado State Engineer, *Second Biennial Report, 1883–1884* (Denver, 1885), p. 28.

3. Colorado State Engineer, *Second Biennial Report*, pp. 121–32.

4. Ibid., pp. 86–87.

5. Colorado State Engineer, *Third Biennial Report, 1885–1886* (Denver, 1887), pp. 9–18.

6. Roger V. Clements, "British-Controlled Enterprise in the West between 1870 and 1900 and Some Agrarian Reactions," *Agricultural History* 27 (1953): 137–41; U.S. Department of the Interior, Census Office, *Report on Agriculture by Irrigation in the Western Part of the United States at the Eleventh Census: 1890* (Washington, D.C.: GPO, 1894), pp. 91, 101, 119; Leonard P. Fox, "State Regulation of the Canal Corporation in Colorado," *Michigan Law Review* 16 (1917–18): 159.

7. *Rocky Mountain News*, Jan. 13, 1881; see chap. 3.

8. *Rocky Mountain News*, Jan. 7, 1887; *Field and Farm*, Jan. 15, 1887.

9. Kluger, "Elwood Mead," 14–15; Hansen, *Democracy's College*, p. 70.

10. William H. Hall, *Irrigation Development* (Sacramento: State Printing, 1886).

11. House Bill No. 294, Bill for an act to provide regulations for the diversion and appropriation of water from the public streams, 6th sess., General Assembly of the State of Colorado, 1887, Division of Archives and Public Records, Denver.

12. House Bill No. 271, Bill for an act to establish rights to the use of water for irrigation arising from priorities of appropriation among persons using water from the same ditch or reservoir, 6th sess., General Assembly of the State of Colorado, 1887, Division of Archives.

13. *Rocky Mountain News*, Jan. 30, 1887.

14. Wyoming State Engineer, *Twenty-sixth Biennial Report, 1941–42* (Cheyenne, [1942]), pp. 81–89; John Wesley Powell,

Report on the Lands of the Arid Region of the United States, ed. Wallace Stegner (Cambridge: Harvard University Press, Belknap Press, 1962), p. 54.

15. Colorado, *Session Laws, 1887*, pp. 308–10, *House Journal, 1887*, pp. 1178, 1458, 2056.

16. Wyoming Territorial Engineer, "First Annual Report, 1888," (typescript), p. 1; T. A. Larson, *History of Wyoming* (Lincoln: University of Nebraska Press, 1965), p. 162; Kluger, "Elwood Mead," pp. 20–22.

17. Wyoming Territorial Engineer, "First Annual Report, 1888," pp. 2–11, *Second Annual Report, 1889* (Cheyenne, 1890), pp. 3–21; Elwood Mead, *Irrigation Institutions* (New York: Macmillan, 1903) pp. 248–52; Elwood Mead to Wm. M. Stewart, May 9, 1889, Official Letter Book of the Territorial Engineer's Office, April 23, 1888–Aug. 16, 1890, Wyoming State Archives Museums and Historical Department, Cheyenne.

18. W. E. Chaplin, "Reminiscences of a Member of the Wyoming Constitutional Convention," *Annals of Wyoming* 12 (1940): 191–92; "A Memorial to the Members of the Constitutional Convention of Wyoming," *Annals of Wyoming* 13 (1940): 176–77, 183–84; E. S. Nettleton to Elwood Mead, Jan. 21, March 6, 1887, Folder, Incoming Correspondence from Federal Government Officials, 1888–90, in Correspondence of Elwood Mead, Territorial and State Engineer, 1888–99, Wyoming State Archives.

19. Charles H. Burritt to Elwood Mead, Sept. 6, 1889, Correspondence of Elwood Mead, 1888–90, Wyoming State Archives; Kluger, "Elwood Mead," p. 27. The drafts with revisions may be found in folder entitled "Elwood Mead, State Engineer, Correspondence: Observations of River Heights; Various Reports, 1889–1897," in Correspondence of Elwood Mead, 1888–99, Wyoming State Archives.

20. *Journal and Debates of the Constitutional Convention of the State of Wyoming* (Cheyenne, 1893), pp. 23, 227 296–97; Letter to Irrigation Committee of the Constitutional Convention, reproduced in the *Cheyenne Daily Leader*, Sept. 13, 1889. A copy of the original document may be found in the folder entitled, Dunbar—Water-Rights History Papers, Special Collections, Roland R. Renne Library, Montana State University.

21. *Journal and Debates of the Constitutional Convention*, pp. 291, 497–512; Larson, *History of Wyoming*, pp. 253–55.

22. Constitution of the State of Wyoming, pp. 35–36, in appendix of the *Journal and Debates of the Constitutional Convention*.

23. Wyoming, *Session Laws, 1890–1891*, pp. 91–106; Elwood Mead to F. H. Newell, Dec. 9, 1890, Official Letters, Engineer's Office, from August 18, 1890 to May 27, 1891, Wyoming State Archives.

24. Elwood Mead, *Irrigation Institutions*, pp. 253–60.

25. 9 Wyo. 110, 61 Pac. 258 (1900).

26. Ibid.; "Memorial to Members of The Constitutional Convention," pp. 185–86; *National Cyclopedia of American Biography*, s.v. "Potter, Charles Nelson."

Chapter 10

1. Dick, *Conquering the Great American Desert*, pp. 331–53, 384–97; Nebraska State Board of Irrigation, *First Biennial Report, 1895–1896* (Lincoln, 1897), pp. 11–22, 51–56, 71–73, 309; *Engineering News and American Railway Journal* 25 (Feb. 7, 1891): 121.

2. Nebraska, *Session Laws, 1895*, pp. 244–69; *Crawford Company v. Hathaway*, 67 Neb. 325, 93 N. W. 781 (1903); Elwood Mead, *Water Rights on the Missouri River and Its Tributaries*, USDA, Office of Experiment Stations, Bulletin 58 (Washington, D.C.: GPO, 1899), pp. 58–64.

3. *Statutes at Large*, 32: 390.

4. U.S. Reclamation Service, *Second Annual Report, 1902–3* (Washington, D.C.: GPO, 1904), p. 33; H. L. Holgate, "The Legal Status of Irrigation," in *Proceedings of First Conference of Engineers of the Reclamation Service*, USGS, Water-Supply and Irrigation Paper 93 (Washington, D.C.: GPO, 1904), p. 297; Townley, *Turn This Water Into Gold*, p. 26; Donald J. Pisani, "Federal Reclamation and Water Rights in Nevada," *Agricultural History* 51 (1977): 547; Henry Thurtell and Gordon H. True, *A Report on Irrigation Laws and Litigation in Nevada*, University of Nevada Agricultural Experiment Station, Bulletin 69 (Reno, 1909), p. 45.

5. Arthur B. Darling, ed., *The Public Papers of Francis G. Newlands*, 2 vols. (Boston: Houghton Mifflin, 1932), 1:77; Townley, *Turn This Water into Gold*, p. 27; *Official Proceedings of the Eleventh National Irrigation Congress, September 15–18, 1903* (Ogden, Utah, 1904), p. 145; A. E. Chandler to R. G. Dunbar, Nov. 4,

Dec. 15, 1948, Folder, Dunbar—Water-Right History Papers, Special Collections, Roland R. Renne Library, Montana State University, Bozeman.

6. Nevada, *Session Laws, 1903*, pp. 24–30, *1905*, pp. 66–69 Nevada State Engineer, *First Biennial Report of the State Engineer, 1903–1904* (Carson City, 1905), pp. 23–24.

7. Nevada, *Session Laws, 1903*, pp. 26–28.

8. Thurtell and True, *Report on Irrigation Laws*, pp. 46–48, 56–57; Nevada, *Session Laws, 1913*, pp. 192–220; John Bird, "A History of Water Rights in Nevada—Part II," *Nevada Historical Society Quarterly* 20 (1976): 28–29; *Ormsby County* v. *Kearney*, 37 Nev. 314, 142 Pac. 803 (1914).

9. Utah, *Session Laws, 1897*, pp. 76–80; Utah, *House Journal, 1901*, p. 409, *Senate Journal, 1901*, p. 382; Utah State Engineer, *First Biennial Report, 1897–1898* (Salt Lake City, 1899), pp. 16, 23.

10. *Message of the Governor of Utah to the Fifth Session of the State Legislature of Utah, January 13, 1903* (Salt Lake City, 1903), p. 11; *Salt Lake Tribune*, Oct. 2, 3, 4, 1902.

11. Utah, *Session Laws, 1903*, pp. 88–107.

12. Utah State Engineer, *Ninth Biennial Report, 1913–1914* (Salt Lake City, 1915), p. 17. See also *Tenth Biennial Report, 1915–1916* (Salt Lake City, 1917), p. 34.

13. Ray P. Teele, "General Discussion of Irrigation in Utah," in USDA, Office of Experiment Stations, *Report of Irrigation Investigations in Utah*, Bulletin 124 (Washington, D.C.: GPO, 1903), pp. 14–26; Utah State Engineer, *Second Biennial Report, 1899–1900* (Salt Lake City, 1901), pp. 30–31, 49–52; Clesson S. Kinney, *A Treatise on the Law of Irrigation and Water Rights*, 2d ed., 4 vols. (San Francisco: Bender-Moss, 1911), 4:3605.

14. Idaho, *Session Laws, 1903*, pp. 223–52; Idaho State Engineer, *Sixth Biennial Report, 1905–1906* (Nampa, Idaho, n.d.), pp. 12–44.

15. *Statutes at Large*, 32:388.

16. Morris Bien, "Proposed State Code of Water Laws," in *Proceedings of Second Conference of Engineers of the Reclamation Service*, USGS, Water-Supply and Irrigation Paper 146 (Washington, D.C.: GPO, 1905), p. 30; Calvin B. Coulter, "The Victory of National Irrigation in the Yakima Valley, 1902–1906," *Pacific Northwest Quarterly* 42 (1951): 110–11.

17. Morris Bien, *Draft of a State Irrigation Code: Prepared for Comment and Criticism* (Washington, D.C.: U.S. Reclamation

Service, 1904), pp. 1–53.

18. *Report of Irrigation Commission of Washington* (Seattle, 1904), pp. 10–46; Coulter, "Victory of National Irrigation," pp. 11–12; Emmett K. Vandevere, "History of Irrigation in Washington," Ph.D. diss., University of Washington, 1948, pp. 195–207.

19. Oregon, *Session Laws, 1905*, pp. 401–6.

20. North Dakota, *Session Laws, 1905*, pp. 44–60; South Dakota, *Session Laws, 1905*, pp. 201–15; Oklahoma, *Session Laws, 1905*, pp. 274–301; South Dakota State Engineer, *Twenty-Third Report, 1950–1952* (Pierre, S. Dak., [1953]), p. 29; Dean W. Loucks to R. G. Dunbar, Nov. 25, 1950, Vernon Fahy to Dunbar, April 20, 1981, Folder, Dunbar—Water-Rights History Papers.

21. New Mexico, *Session Laws, 1899*, p. 166, *1905*, pp. 270–83; New Mexico Commission of Irrigation, minutes of meetings, June 6, 1901, and Feb. 20, 1905, Minute Book, 1901–1906, Records of the Territorial Engineer, State of New Mexico Records Center and Archives, Santa Fe; Proceedings of the House of Representatives, Territory of New Mexico, 36th sess., Ms. in State of New Mexico Records Center, pp. 232–34.

22. New Mexico, *Session Laws, 1907*, pp. 71–95; *Snow v. Abalos*, 18 N.M. 681, 140 Pac. 1044 (1914); U.S. Department of Commerce, Bureau of the Census, *Fifteenth Census of the United States: 1930, Irrigation of Agricultural Lands* (Washington, D.C., 1932), p. 27.

23. Oregon State Engineer, *First Biennial Report, 1905–1906* (Salem, Oreg., 1906), p. 92; Will R. King, "Law of Water Conservation and Use," *Proceedings of the Oregon Bar Association, 18th and 19th Sessions, 1908 and 1909* (Portland, Oreg., n.d.), pp. 42–50.

24. Oregon State Engineer, *Second Biennial Report, 1907–1908* (Salem, Oreg., 1908), pp. 7–8.

25. *Report of the Oregon Conservation Commission to the Governor, November 1908* (Portland, 1908), pp. 5–9; Samuel P. Hays, *Conservation and the Gospel of Efficiency: The Progressive Conservation Movement, 1890–1920* (Cambridge: Harvard University Press, 1959), pp. 127–33.

26. *Report of the Oregon Conservation Commission to the Governor*, pp. 66–77, 84–86; Oregon State Engineer, *Second Biennial Report, 1907–1908*, pp. 15–18; *Message of George E. Chamberlain, Governor of Oregon, to the Twenty-fifth Legislative Assembly, 1909* (Salem, Oreg., 1909), pp. 21–22.

27. *Portland Oregonian*, Dec. 15, 1908, Feb. 12, 13, 19, 1909.

28. Oregon, *Session Laws, 1909*, pp. 319–43.

29. John H. Lewis, "Water Rights and Appropriations," in F. F. Henshaw, John H. Lewis, and E. J. McCaustland, *Deschutes River, Oregon and Its Utilization*, USGS, Water-Supply Paper 344 (Washington, D.C.: GPO, 1914), p. 132; Nevada, *Session Laws, 1915*, pp. 378–86; Utah, *Session Laws, 1919*, pp. 177–203.

30. Robert H. Forbes, *Irrigation and Agricultural Practice in Arizona*, University of Arizona Agricultural Experiment Station, Bulletin 63 (Tucson, 1911), pp. 59–61; Arthur Powell Davis, *Irrigation Near Phoenix*, USGS, Water-Supply and Irrigation Paper 2 (Washington, D.C.: GPO, 1897), pp. 55–62; Elwood Mead, *Irrigation Institutions* (New York: Macmillan, 1903), pp. 279–82; A. J. McClatchie, *Utilizing Our Water Supply*, University of Arizona Agricultural Experiment Station, Bulletin 43 (Tucson, 1902), pp. 82–87.

31. Arizona Territory, *Journals of the Twenty-first Legislative Assembly, 1901*, (Phoenix, 1901), pp. 6, 359, 453; *Report of Irrigation Investigations for 1901 under the Direction of Elwood Mead*, USDA, Office of Experiment Stations, Bulletin 119 (Washington, D.C.: GPO, 1902), pp. 83–84; Gordon M. Bakken, "The Arizona Constitutional Convention of 1910," *Arizona State Law Journal* 1978, p. 21.

32. Arizona, *Session Laws, 1919*, pp. 278–300; G. E. P. Smith, *The Proposed Water Code*, University of Arizona College of Agricultural Extension Service, Circular 11 (Tucson, 1916); G. E. P. Smith, *Water Storage and Water Code*, University of Arizona College of Agriculture Extension Service, Circular 26 (Tucson, 1918); G. E. P. Smith, "Arizona Has A New Water Code," *Engineering News-Record* 82 (1919): 1027; University of Arizona Agricultural Experiment Station, *Twenty-sixth Annual Report, 1915* (Tucson, 1915), p. 577; Arizona, *Journals of the Second Legislature, Regular Session, 1915*, pp. 216–74; G. E. P. Smith to R.G. Dunbar, March 7, 1974, Folder, Dunbar—Water-Rights History Papers; *Arizona Republican*, March 1, 1919.

33. *Report of the State Engineer to the Legislature of the State of California, Session of 1881*, pt. 4, *Irrigation* (Sacramento, 1880), pp. 7–30; *Proceedings of the State Irrigation Convention held at Riverside, California, May 14, 15, and 16, 1884* (Riverside, Calif., 1884), pp. 51–59; Charles P. Korr, "William Hammond Hall: The Failure of Attempts at State Water Planning in California, 1878–1888," *Historical Society of Southern California Quarterly* 45 (1963): 307–14.

34. *Report of Irrigation Investigations in California Under the Direction of Elwood Mead* (Washington, D.C.: GPO, 1901); *Regulation of Water Rights*, Transactions of the Commonweath Club of California, vol. 1 (Dec. 1905), p. 29; Donald J. Pisani, "Water Law Reform in California, 1900–1913," *Agricultural History* 54 (1980): 300–302; USDA, *Yearbook, 1899* (Washington, D.C.: GPO, 1900), pp. 36–39.

35. *Regulation of Water Rights*, pp. 29–101; Pisani, "Water Law Reform," pp. 302–8.

36. Gordon R. Miller, "Shaping California Water Law, 1781 to 1928," *Historical Society of Southern California Quarterly* 55 (1973): 27–28; Pisani, "Water Law Reform" pp. 310–14; Frank Adams to R. G. Dunbar, Oct. 19, 1948, Folder, Dunbar—Water-Rights History Papers.

37. California, *Session Laws, 1913*, pp. 1012–33.

38. Texas, *Session Laws, 1913*, pp. 358–79, *Session Laws, 1917*, pp. 211–43, *Session Laws, 1967*, pp. 86–94; *Official Proceedings of the 21st International Irrigation Congress held at Calgary, Alberta, Canada, October 5–9, 1914* (Ottawa, 1915), pp. 238–39; Otis W. Templer, "Institutional Constraints and Water Resources: Water Rights Adjudication in Texas," *Rocky Mountain Social Science Journal* 10 (Oct. 1973): 40–41; *Board of Water Engineers* v. *McKnight*, 111 Tex 82, 229 S.W. 301 (1921).

39. Washington State Irrigation and Arid Lands Commission, *Water Code Submitted by the Code Commission Appointed by Governor M. E. Hay* (Olympia, 1912); Washington State Water Code Commission, *Report . . . Including Copy of the Proposed Code* (n.p., n.d.); Vandevere, "History of Irrigation," pp. 108–10; Washington, *Session Laws, 1917*, pp. 454–58; Washington Irrigation Institute, *Proceedings of the Second Annual Meeting, Dec. 16–18, 1914*, (North Yakima, Wash., 1915), pp. 1, 67–83; *Proceedings of the Third Annual Meeting, Jan. 10–12, 1916*, (North Yakima, Wash., 1916), pp. 67–69, 72–73, 193–96, 209; *Proceedings of the Fifth Annual Meeting, Dec. 4–5, 1917*, (Yakima, Wash., [1918]), p. 32.

40. Robert G. Dunbar, "The Search for a Stable Water Right in Montana," *Agricultural History* 28 (1954): 145–47.

41. Ibid., pp. 148–49; Montana, *Session Laws, 1939*, p. 475, *Session Laws, 1953*, pp. 174–75; Montana State Engineer, *Water Resources Survey: Lewis and Clark County, Montana* (Helena, Mont., 1957); Montana State Water Conservation Board, *First Biennial Report, 1964–1966* ([Helena], n.d.), p. 14.

42. U.S. Congress, House, Committee on Interior and Insular Affairs, *Colorado River Basin Project: Report 1849,* 89th Cong., 2nd sess., 1966, pp. 1–4; Wesley A. D'Ewart, "Proposed Ways to Solve Our Water Problem," *Montana Farmer-Stockman* 54 (Jan. 5, 1967): 32–33; Rich Johnson, *The Central Arizona Project, 1918–1968* (Tucson: University of Arizona Press, 1977), pp. 162–63, 175–78, 189; Robert J. Boyle, John Graves, and T. H. Watkins, *The Water Hustlers* (San Francisco: Sierra Club, 1971), pp. 38–62; *Great Falls Tribune,* Sept. 27, 1969; Montana, *Session Laws, 1967,* pp. 1196–97, *Session Laws, 1969,* pp. 1190–91; Montana, *House Journal, 1967,* pp. 167, 448, *House Journal, 1969,* pp. 161, 359, *House Journal, 1971,* p. 744; *Senate Journal, 1971,* pp. 67, 446; Montana Water Resources Board, *Newsletter* 1 (Dec. 1968): 3–4; House Bill No. 337, 41st Montana Legislative Assembly, 1969, Bills Introduced and Not Passed, Roland R. Renne Library; Senate Bill No. 124, 42d Montana Legislative Assembly, 1971, Bills Introduced and Not Passed, Roland R. Renne Library.

43. Montana 1972 Constitution Art. 9, Sec. 3.

44. Senate Bill No. 444, 43d Montana Legislative Assembly, 1973, MS. in Office of the Secretary of the State of Montana, Helena; Montana, *Senate Journal, 1973,* pp. 267, 515–32; *Great Falls Tribune,* Jan. 14 and Feb. 14, 1973; *Bozeman Chronicle,* Dec. 13, 1972, Feb. 18, 1973; *Helena Independent Record,* Feb. 28, 1973.

45. Montana, *Session Laws, 1977,* p. 2066.

46. Montana, *Session Laws, 1979,* pp. 1901–17; Montana, *House Journal, 1977,* pp. 455, 817, Interview with John P. Scully, Dec. 19, 1979. On Dec. 7, 1981, the state supreme court extended the filing date to April 30, 1982. *Bozeman Daily Chronicle,* Dec. 8, 1981.

47. Frank J. Trelease, "Alaska's New Water Use Act," *Land and Water Law Review* 2 (1967): 1–49.

Chapter 11

1. *Howell* v. *Johnson,* 89 Fed. Rep. 556 (1898); *Miller and Lux* v. *Rickey,* 127 Fed. Rep. 573 (1904); *Anderson* v. *Bassman,* 140 Fed. Rep. 14 (1905); *Rickey Land and Cattle Co.* v. *Miller and Lux,* 152 Fed. Rep. 11 (1907).

2. *Kansas* v. *Colorado,* 185 U.S. 125 (1902), 206 U.S. 46 (1907).

3. *Kansas* v. *Colorado,* 206 U.S. 46; Oregon State Engineer, *Third Biennial Report, 1909–1910* (Salem, Oregon, 1910), p. 87.

4. *Official Proceedings of the Fourteenth National Irrigation Congress Held at Boise, Idaho, Sept. 3–8, 1906* (Boise, 1906), pp. 80, 241; Oregon State Engineer, *Third Biennial Report*, pp. 88–89.

5. John H. Lewis, "State and National Water Laws, with Detailed Statement of the Oregon System of Water Titles," American Society of Civil Engineers, *Transactions* 76 (1913): 662–63, 670–71.

6. *Colorado* v. *Kansas*, 320 U.S. 383 (1943); Colorado State Engineer, *Seventeenth Biennial Report, 1913–1914* (Denver, 1915), p. 34, *Twenty-First Biennial Report, 1921–1922* (Denver, 1923), p. 24.

7. *Wyoming* v. *Colorado*, 259 U.S. 419 (1922).

8. *Weiland, State Engineer of the State of Colorado et al.* v. *Pioneer Irrigation Company*, 259 U.S. 498 (1922); Colorado State Engineer, *Seventeenth Biennial Report*, pp. 34–38.

9. *Who's Who in America, 1948–1949* (Chicago: A. N. Marquis, 1948), p. 397.

10. Colorado Water Conservation Board, "Interstate Compacts: A Compilation of Articles from Various Sources," 4 vols. (Denver, 1946), 1:111–37, 2:1–10; Norris Hundley, jr., *Dividing the Waters: A Century of Controversy between the United States and Mexico* (Berkeley and Los Angeles: University of California Press, 1966), pp. 17–30; Chirakaikaran J. Chacko, *The International Joint Commission between the United States of America and the Dominion of Canada* (New York: Columbia University Press, 1932), pp. 209–23, 381–94.

11. Colorado Water Conservation Board, "Interstate Compacts," 1:139; Norris Hundley, jr., *Water and the West: The Colorado River Compact and the Politics of Water in the American West* (Berkeley: University of California Press, 1975), pp. 83–109.

12. *Statutes at Large*, 42:171–72; Hundley, *Water and the West*, pp. 11–13, 130; Colorado State Engineer, *Twenty-First Biennial Report*, p. 16.

13. Hundley, *Water and the West*, pp. 138–87.

14. Ibid., pp. 187–214, 337–43.

15. Colorado State Engineer, *Twenty-First Biennial Report*, p. 16.

16. *Statutes at Large*, 45:1057–59; *Arizona* v. *California*, 292 U.S. 341 (1934), 298 U.S. 558 (1936); Hundley, *Water and the West*, pp. 215–99; Beverley B. Moeller, *Phil Swing and Boulder Dam* (Berkeley: University of California Press, 1971), pp. 67–122; N. D. Houghton, "Problems of the Colorado River as Reflected in Arizona

Politics," *Western Political Quarterly* 4 (1951): 634–43; Charles C. Colley, *The Century of Robert H. Forbes* (Tucson: University of Arizona Press, 1977), pp. 101–10.

17. Hundley, *Water and the West*, 339; Hundley, *Dividing the Waters*, 62–135.

18. Upper Colorado River Commission, *First Annual Report* (n.p., n.d.), pp. 23–42; Jerome C. Muys, "Interstate Water Compacts," National Water Commission, Report NWC–L–71–011 (Washington, D.C., 1971), pp. 20–50; Hundley, *Water and the West*, p. 301.

19. *Arizona* v. *California*, 373 U.S. 546 (1963); Hundley, *Water and the West*, pp. 303–6; Norris Hundley, jr., "Clio Nods; Arizona v. California and the Boulder Canyon Act—A Reassessment," *Western Historical Quarterly* 3 (1972): 17–51.

20. Wells A. Hutchins, *Water Rights Laws in the Nineteen Western States*, USDA, Miscellaneous Publication 1206, 3 vols. (Washington, D.C.: GPO, 1971–77), 3:87.

21. Hundley, *Dividing the Waters* (Berkeley: University of California Press, 1966), pp. 4–21; U.S. Reclamation Service, *Third Annual Report, 1903–1904* (Washington, D.C.: GPO, 1905), p. 396; U.S. Department of the Interior, Census Office, *Report on Agriculture by Irrigation in the Western Part of the United States at the Eleventh Census: 1890* (Washington, D.C.: GPO, 1894), pp. 105–7, 127–29; Herbert M. Wilson, "American Irrigation Engineering," American Society of Civil Engineers, *Transactions* 25 (1891): 174–77: Robert G. Dunbar, "History of Agriculture," in LeRoy R. Hafen, *Colorado and Its People*, 4 vols. (New York: Lewis Historical Publishing Co., 1948), 2:129.

22. Ira G. Clark, "The Elephant Butte Controversy: A Chapter in the Emergence of Federal Water Law," *Journal of American History* 61 (1975): 1015–31; Hundley, *Dividing the Waters*, pp. 21–28; U.S. Reclamation Service, *Third Annual Report*, pp. 403–25.

23. Raymond A. Hill, "Development of the Rio Grande Compact of 1938," *Natural Resources Journal* 14 (1974): 163–67.

24. Ibid., pp. 167–71; "Interstate Water Problems: Final Report of the Committee of the Irrigation Division on Interstate Water Rights," American Society of Civil Engineers, *Transactions* 104 (1939): 1842–43, 1857–59.

25. *Statutes at Large*, 53:785–92; Hill, "Development of the Rio Grande Compact of 1938," pp. 171–98; "Interstate Water

Problems," pp. 1859–61.

26. U.S. *Statutes at Large*, 63:31–43, 72:38–44; Weldon V. Barton, *Interstate Compacts in the Political Process* (Chapel Hill: University of North Carolina Press, 1965), pp. 98–103.

27. S. E. Reynolds and Philip B. Mutz, "Water Deliveries under the Rio Grande Compact," *Natural Resources Journal* 14 (1974); 200–205; *Texas* v. *New Mexico*, 352 U.S. 991 (1957); *Texas et al.* v. *Colorado*, 391 U.S. 901 (1968); New Mexico State Engineer, *Twenty-Ninth Biennial Report, 1968–1970* (Sante Fe, n.d.), p. 21.

28. Robert T. Lingle and Dee Linford, *The Pecos River Commission of New Mexico and Texas: A Report of a Decade of Progress 1950–1960* (Santa Fe: Rydal Press, 1961), pp. 60–95.

29. Ibid., pp. 121–72, 239–49; Marilyn C. O'Leary, "Texas v. New Mexico: the Pecos River Compact Litigation," *Natural Resources Journal* 20 (1980): 399–403.

30. U.S. Department of the Interior, *Documents on the Use and Control of the Waters of Interstate and International Streams: Compacts, Treaties, and Adjudications*, comp. and ed. T. Richard Witmer (Washington, D.C.: GPO, 1956), pp. 114–21.

31. Lingle and Linford, *Pecos River Commission*, pp. 175–232; Richard H. Leach and Redding S. Sugg, *The Administration of Interstate Compacts* (Baton Rouge: Louisiana State University, 1959), pp. 158–67; New Mexico State Engineer, *Thirty-Second Biennial Report, 1974–1976* (Santa Fe, 1977), pp. 18, 58–60; U.S. Congress, House, Subcommittee on Irrigation and Reclamation of the Committee on Interior and Insular Affairs, *Brantley Project, New Mexico, Part II, Hearings on H.R. 5042*, 92nd Cong., 2d sess., 1972, pp. 93–94, 98–99; O'Leary, "Texas v. New Mexico," pp. 403–10.

32. "Interstate Water Matters: Progress Report of the Committee of the Irrigation Division," American Society of Civil Engineers, *Transactions* 94 (1930): 1417–18; Montana State Engineer, "Twelfth Biennial Report, 1925–1926" (typescript), p. 9.

33. Montana State Engineer, "Thirtieth Biennial Report, 1961–1962" (typescript), p. 28; *Great Falls Tribune*, July 12, 1950; Gerald H. Robinson, "The Columbia Valley Administration Bill," *Western Political Quarterly* 3 (1950): 607–14; Harvey R. Doerksen, *Columbia River Interstate Compact, Politics of Negotiation*, State of Washington Water Research Center, Report 11 (Pullman, Wash. 1972), pp. 24–25, 33–52.

34. *Statutes at Large*, 66:737; Columbia Interstate Compact Commission, *First Annual Report, 1952–1953* ([Spokane, Wash.,]

n.d.), pp. 4–7; *Second Annual Report, 1953–1954* [Spokane, Wash.,] n.d.), pp. 6–11; *Third Annual Report, 1954–1955* ([Spokane, Wash.,] n.d.), pp. 4–7; Doerksen, *Columbia River Interstate Compact,* pp. 75–98; *Documents on the Use and Control of the Waters,* pp. 283–99. The compact was not submitted to the Wyoming legislature.

35. Columbia Interstate Compact Commission, *Fourth Annual Report, 1955–1956* ([Spokane, Wash.,] n.d.), pp. 3–7; *Columbia Interstate Compact and Proposed Federal Consent Legislation, Approved December 4, 1956,* in Folder, Dunbar—Water-Right History Papers, Special Collections, Roland R. Renne Library, Montana State University; *Great Falls Tribune,* Feb. 1, 16, 1955, Dec. 4, 1956.

36. Doerksen, *Columbia River Interstate Compact,* pp. 110–68; Montana State Engineer, "Thirtieth Biennial Report," pp. 29–30.

37. Wyoming State Engineer, *Fortieth Biennial Report, 1969–1970,* ([Cheyenne,] n.d.), pp. 41–42; U.S. Department of the Interior, *Documents on the Use and Control of Waters,* pp. 274–82; Donald J. Pisani, "The Strange Death of the California-Nevada Compact: A Study in Interstate Water Negotiations," *Pacific Historical Review* 47 (1978): 637–58.

38. *Statutes at Large,* 64:29–35, 83:86–91, 86:193–99.

Chapter 12

1. Robert G. Dunbar, "The Adaptation of Groundwater-Control Institutions to the Arid West," *Agricultural History* 51 (1977): 662–63.

2. 12 Meeson and Welsby Exchequer Reports (1843), pp. 324, 353–54. The phrase, *damnum absque injuria* means "a loss which does not give rise to an action for damages against the person causing it." (Henry C. Black, *Black's Law Dictionary,* 4th ed. [St. Paul: West Publishing, 1961], p. 470).

3. Dunbar, "Adaptation of Groundwater-Control Institutions," pp. 664–65.

4. Ibid., pp. 662–63, 665–66.

5. Ibid., pp. 666–67; *Katz* v. *Walkinshaw,* 141 Cal. 116, 70 Pac. 663 (1902); Gordon R. Miller, "Shaping California Water Law, 1781 to 1928," *Historical Society of Southern California Quarterly* 55 (1973): 30–32.

6. Petition for Rehearing, filed 26 November 1902, p. 79, and Points and Authorities, filed 19 March 1903, p. 1, *Katz* v. *Walkinshaw*, L.A. No. 967, vol. 3312, California Supreme Court Records, California State Library, Sacramento.

7. *Katz* v. *Walkinshaw*, 141 Cal. 116, 74 Pac. 766 (1903); Samuel C. Wiel, *Water Rights in the Western States*, 3d ed., 2 vols. (San Francisco: Bancroft-Whitney, 1911), 2:976–80.

8. *City of Pasadena* v. *City of Alhambra*, 33 Cal. 2d 908, 207 Pac. 2d 17 (1949); H. E. Thomas, *Water Rights in Areas of Ground-Water Mining*, USGS, Circular 347 (Washington, D.C.: USGS, 1955), pp. 9–10; California Department of Water Resources, "Watermaster Service in the Raymond Basin, Los Angeles County for the Period July 1, 1967 through June 30, 1968," Bulletin 178–68 (Sacramento, 1968), pp. 3–4; James H. Krieger and Harvey O. Banks, "Ground Water Basin Management," *California Law Review* 50 (1962): 59–61.

9. California Department of Water Resources, "Watermaster Service in the West Coast Basin Los Angeles County for Period October 1, 1972 through September 30, 1973," Bulletin 179–73 (Sacramento, 1973), pp. 7–37; Robert I. Reis, "A Review and Revitalization: Concepts of Ground Water Production and Management—the California Experience," *Natural Resources Journal* 7 (1967): 67–68; Vincent Ostrom and Elinor Ostrom, "Legal and Political Conditions of Water Resource Development," *Land Economics* 48 (1972): 9–13.

10. California Department of Water Resources, "Watermaster Service in the Central Basin Los Angeles County for Period October 1, 1974 through September 30, 1975," Bulletin 180–75 (Sacramento, 1976), pp. 7–41.

11. *City of Los Angeles* v. *City of San Fernando*, 123 Cal. Reporter 1, 537 Pac 2d 1250 (1975); Charles E. Corker, "Inadequacy of the Present Law to Protect, Conserve and Develop Groundwater Use," *Rocky Mountain Mineral Law Institute* 25 (1979): pp. 8–11.

12. [California] Governor's Commission to Review California Water Rights Law, "Final Report, December 1978," pp. 1–2, 143.

13. Ibid., pp. 145–47, 168–230.

Chapter 13

1. Edward E. Kinney et. al., *The Roswell Artesian Basin: A Study* (Roswell, N. Mex.: Roswell Geological Society, 1968),

pp. 5–28; Robert R. Lansford and Bobby J. Creel, *Irrigation Water Requirements for Crop Production—Roswell Artesian Basin: An Economic Analysis and Basic Data.* New Mexico State University Water Resources Research Institute Report 4 (June 1969), pp. 5–14.

2. *Roswell Register,* May 20, 1904; *Roswell Register-Tribune,* Aug. 6, 1908; *Roswell Daily Record,* Oct. 7, 1937; James D. Shinkle, ed., *Reminiscences of Roswell Pioners* (Roswell, N. Mex.: Hall-Poorbaugh Press, 1966), pp. 121–22; W. M. Reed, "Irrigation along Pecos River and its Tributaries," in *Report of Irrigation Investigations for 1900 under the Supervision of Elwood Mead,* USDA, Office of Experiment Stations, Bulletin 104 (Washington, D.C.: GPO, 1902), p. 69; Albert G. Fiedler and S. Spencer Nye, *Geology and Ground-Water Resources of the Roswell Artesian Basin, New Mexico,* USGS, Water-Supply Paper 639 (Washington, D.C.: GPO, 1933), pp. 191–93.

3. *Santa Fe New Mexican,* Jan. 13, Feb. 6, 1905; *Roswell Register,* March 31, 1905; Cassius A. Fisher, *Preliminary Report on the Geology and Underground Waters of the Roswell Artesian Area, New Mexico,* USGS, Water-Supply Paper 158 (Washington, D.C.: GPO, 1906), p. 25; New Mexico, *Council Journal, 1905,* pp. 58, 92, 94; New Mexico, *Session Laws, 1905,* pp. 45–48.

4. *Roswell Register,* May 12, 1905; *Roswell Tribune,* Jan. 25, 1906; *Roswell Register-Tribune,* March 12, Sept. 15, 1908, Jan. 12, 22, Feb. 12, 16, 1909; *Roswell Record,* Feb. 12, 19, 1909; New Mexico, *House Journal, 1909,* pp. 79, 200, 226, *Council Journal, 1909,* pp. 295–96; New Mexico, *Session Laws, 1909,* pp. 177–90, *Session Laws, 1912,* pp. 159–73; *Pecos Valley Artesian Conservancy Dist.* v. *Peters,* 50 N.M. 165, 173 Pac. 2d 490 (1946).

5. Robert G. Dunbar, "Pioneering Groundwater Legislation in the United States: Mortgages, Land Banks, and Institution-Building in New Mexico," *Pacific Historical Review* 47 (1978): 567–68.

6. "Pecos Valley, New Mexico-Roswell to Carlsbad: Report by John N. Kerr and W. A. Kelly, March 28, 1918," Farm Credit Administration, File Maps and Reports, New Mexico-Pecos River Drainage Area, pt. 1, RG 103, National Archives.

7. Dunbar, "Pioneering Groundwater Legislation," pp. 569–71.

8. Ibid., pp. 571–72.

9. Albert G. Fiedler, *Report on Investigations of the Roswell Artesian Basin Chaves and Eddy Counties New Mexico during the Year Ending June 30, 1926,* New Mexico State Engineer, Seventh

Biennial Report, 1925–26 (Santa Fe, [1926]), pp. 27–60. Quotation appears on p. 60.

10. Interview with Herman R. Crile, June 19, 1973; *Arizona Farmer* 30 (Nov. 10, 1951), pp. 1, 22.

11. Albert G. Fiedler to William E. Hale, Oct. 14, 1961, Files, Office of the State Engineer of New Mexico, Santa Fe; Cecil Bonney, *Looking Over My Shoulder: Seventy-five Years in the Pecos Valley* (Roswell, N. Mex.: Hall-Poorbaugh Press, 1971), p. 38; Interview with Herman R. Crile, June 19, 1973; New Mexico, *House Journal, 1927*, pp. 162, 265, 275, 332, *Senate Journal, 1927*, p. 241.

12. New Mexico, *Session Laws, 1927*, pp. 450–51.

13. Dunbar, "Pioneering Groundwater Legislation," p. 576.

14. Ibid.

15. *Yeo* v. *Tweedy*, 34 N.M. 611, 286 Pac. 970 (1929); Brief of Appellee, *Yeo* v. *Tweedy*, Case no. 3408, Office of the Clerk of the Supreme Court of New Mexico, Santa Fe. Art. 4, sec. 18 of the New Mexico Constitution reads: "No law shall be revised or amended, or the provisions thereof extended by reference to its title only; but each section thereof as revised, amended or extended shall be set out in full."

16. New Mexico, *Senate Journal, 1931*, pp. 225, 238, 348, 369, 375, 398–99, 546–47; New Mexico, *House Journal, 1931*, pp. 694, 724, 806, MS in New Mexico State Records Center and Archives, Santa Fe; Senate Bill Nos. 95 and 112, Senate Bills, 71–150, 10th State Legislature of New Mexico, 1931, MS in New Mexico State Records Center and Archives, Santa Fe.

17. New Mexico, *Session Laws, 1931*, pp. 229–31.

18. Dunbar, "Pioneering Groundwater Legislation," p. 580.

19. Ibid., p. 581.

20. New Mexico State Engineer, *Twelfth and Thirteenth Biennial Reports, 1934–1938*, (Santa Fe, [1938]), p. 254, *Sixteenth and Seventeenth Biennial Reports, 1942–1946*, (Santa Fe, 1962), p. 353; Pecos Valley Artesian Conservancy District, Minutes of the Board of Directors, Oct. 3, Nov. 3, 1934, April 6, June 7, 1935, Office of the Pecos Valley Artesian Conservancy District, Roswell, N. Mex.; Thomas M. McClure, "Conservation of the Underground Waters of the Roswell Artesian Basin, Pecos Valley, New Mexico," Association of Western State Engineers, "Proceedings, Eighth Annual Conference, Salt Lake City, Utah, November 13–14, 1935," pp. 16–27.

21. John H. Bliss, "Ground Water Problems of New Mexico," Association of Western State Engineers, "Proceedings, Twenty-

First Annual Convention, Flagstaff, Arizona, August 23–26, 1948,"
pp. 56–57; New Mexico State Engineer, *Twenty-Fourth Biennial
Report, 1958–1960* (Santa Fe, [1960]), p. 10; Interview with Fred
Henninghausen, October 24, 1974; J. S. Gatewood, Alfonso Wilson,
H. E. Thomas, and L. R. Kister, *General Effects of Drought on Water
Resources of the Southwest*, USGS, Professional Paper 372–8
(Washington, D.C.: GPO, 1964), p. 49.

22. *State ex rel. Bliss* v. *Dority et al.*, 55 N.M. 12, 225 Pac. 2d,
1007 (1950); New Mexico, *Session Laws, 1953*, pp. 108–9; Robert
Emmet Clark, *New Mexico Water Resources Law* (Albuquerque:
Division of Government Research, University of New Mexico,
1964), pp. 19–20.

23. New Mexico State Engineer, *Twenty-Third Biennial Re-
port, 1956–1958* (Santa Fe, [1958]), pp. 44, 52–53, *Twenty-Seventh
Biennial Report, 1964–1966*, (Santa Fe, [1966]), p. 11; Fred H. Hen-
ninghausen, Speech Delivered to the North Eddy Farm Bureau,
February 9, 1965, Files of the Office of the State Engineer of New
Mexico, Santa Fe.

24. *State ex rel. Reynolds* v. *Lewis*, 84 N.M. 768, 508 Pac. 2d,
577 (1973); Lansford and Creel, *Irrigation Water Requirements for
Crop Production Roswell Artesian Basin*, pp. 18–226; *Roswell
Daily Record*, Dec. 5, 6, 1965, Oct. 21, 31, Nov. 2, 1969.

25. *State of New Mexico et al.* v. *L. T. Lewis et al.* and *State of
New Mexico et al.* v. *Hagerman Canal Co. et al.*, Case no. 20294,
Court Record Box 92, pp. 379–84, Office of Clerk of the District
Court of Chaves County, Roswell, N. Mex.; *Seven Rivers Farms Inc.*
v. *Reynolds*, 84 N.M. 789, 508 Pac. 2d 1276 (1973); New Mexico
State Engineer, *Thirty-First Biennial Report, 1972–1974* (Santa Fe,
1975), pp. 21–22; Interviews with Fred H. Henninghausen, April 20,
1973, Oct. 24, 1974.

26. *City of Albuquerque* v. *Reynolds*, 71 N.M. 428, 379 Pac. 2d
73 (1962); New Mexico State Engineer, *Twenty-Third Biennial
Report*, pp. 15–28, *Twenty-Sixth Biennial Report, 1962–1964*,
(Santa Fe, [1964]), pp. 36–37; *Wall Street Journal* (May 1, 1980), p. 1.

Chapter 14

1. Nevada, *Session Laws, 1913*, pp. 192–93, *Session Laws,
1915* p. 323; Oregon, *Session Laws, 1927*, p. 579; New Mexico,
Session Laws, 1927, p. 450.

2. Oregon, *Session Laws, 1927*, pp. 576–79, *Session Laws, 1933*, pp. 389–90; D. J. McLellan, "Underground Water Code of Oregon," in Association of Western State Engineers, "Proceedings, Twenty-sixth Annual Convention, Reno, Nevada, August 17–20, 1953," pp. 41–44; Chapin D. Clark, "Survey of Oregon's Water Laws," Oregon State University, Water Resources Research Institute, WRRI–18 (March, 1974), pp. 193, 197.

3. Association of Western State Engineers, "Proceedings, Seventh Annual Conference, Salt Lake City, Utah, December 7, 1934," pp. 1, 15–20, 43–48, "Proceedings, Eighth Annual Conference, Salt Lake City, Utah, Nov. 13–14, 1935," p. 10; John C. Joyt, *Droughts of 1930–34*, USGS, Water-Supply Paper 680 (Washington, D.C.: GPO, 1936), pl. 1, facing p. 6, pp. 53–54.

4. U.S. Department of Commerce, Bureau of the Census, *Fifteenth Census of the United States: 1930, Irrigation of Agricultural Lands* (Washington, D.C.: GPO, 1932), pp. 232–35; Utah State Engineer, *Nineteenth Biennial Report, 1933–1934* (Salt Lake City, 1934), pp. 16–17; Association of Western State Engineers, "Proceedings, Eighth Annual Conference," pp. 28–29; *Salt Lake Tribune*, Feb. 3, 1935; *Deseret News*, Feb. 1, 1935.

5. Utah State Engineer, *Eighteenth Biennial Report, 1931–1932* (Salt Lake City, 1932), pp. 23–24, *Nineteenth Biennial Report*, p. 17; *Wrathall* v. *Johnson*, 86 Utah 50, 40 Pac. 2d 755 (1935); *Justesen* v. *Olsen*, 86 Utah 158, 40 Pac. 2d 802 (1935); *Horne* v. *Utah Oil Refining Co.*, 59 Utah 279, 202 Pac. 815 (1921).

6. Utah, *House Journal, 1935*, p. 14, *Session Laws, 1935*, pp. 195–200; Association of Western State Engineers, "Proceedings, Eighth Annual Conference" pp. 29–31; H. E. Thomas, *Water Rights in Areas of Ground-Water Mining*, USGS, Circular 347 (Washington, D.C.: USGS, 1955), p. 13; *Salt Lake Tribune*, Jan. 31, Feb. 1, 8, 1935; *Deseret News*, Jan. 30, Feb. 8, 1935; Utah Department of Natural Resources, Division of Water Rights, *Thirty-eighth Biennial Report, 1970–1972*, (Salt Lake City, n.d.), p. 3.

7. Penn Livingston, *Underground Leakage from Artesian Wells in the Las Vegas Area, Nevada*, USGS, Water-Supply Paper 849–D (Washington, D.C.: GPO, 1941), pp. 147–69; Bureau of the Census, *Sixteenth Census of the United States: 1940, Population*, vol. 1, *Number of Inhabitants* (Washington, D.C.: GPO, 1942), p. 655; *Irrigation of Agricultural Lands* (Washington, D.C.: GPO, 1942), p. 411; Nevada State Engineer, *Biennial Report, 1938–1940*, (Carson City, Nev., 1940), pp. 86–87; Russell R. Elliot, *History of*

Nevada (Lincoln: University of Nebraska Press, 1973), pp. 276–84.

8. Association of Western State Engineers, "Proceedings, Twenty-First Annual Convention, Flagstaff, Arizona, August, 23–26, 1948," p. 22.

9. Nevada, *Session Laws, 1939*, pp. 274–79; Nevada State Engineer, *Biennial Report, 1942–1944* (Carson City, Nev., 1944), pp. 43–44; Thomas, *Water Rights in Areas of Ground-Water Mining*, pp. 12–13.

10. Robert G. Dunbar, "The Adaptation of Groundwater-Control Institutions to the Arid West," *Agricultural History* 51 (1977): 674.

11. R. V. Smrha, "Ground Water Problems of My State," in Association of Western State Engineers, "Proceedings, Twenty-First Annual Convention," pp. 44–45; *State ex rel. Emery* v. *Knapp*, 167 Kans. 546, 207 Pac. 2d 440 (1949); Kansas, *Session Laws, 1945*, pp. 665–71; Robert B. Morton, "Ground Water Rights in Kansas," *Kansas Law Review* 5 (1957): 597–610; Washington, *Session Laws, 1945*, pp. 826–41; Association of Western State Engineers, "Proceedings, Twenty-First Annual Convention," pp. 69–71; Washington, *House Journal, 1945*, p. 623, *Senate Journal, 1945*, p. 783; Arthur M. Piper to Robert G. Dunbar, August 11, 1975, folder, Dunbar—Water-Rights History Papers, Roland R. Renne Library, Montana State University.

12. Oregon Water Resources Committee, *Report to Forty-eighth Legislative Assembly* (1955), pp. 1–2, 19–28, 58–84, 120–37; McLellan, "Underground Water Code of Oregon," pp. 41–44; Oregon, *Session Laws, 1955*, pp. 955–72; Philip D. Chadsey, "Rights to Underground Waters in Oregon: Past, Present and Future," *Williamette Law Journal* 3 (1964–65): 317–35; Piper to Dunbar, Aug. 11, 1975.

13. Wells A. Hutchins, "The Idaho Law of Water Rights," *Idaho Law Review* 5 (1968): 112–20; Wells A. Hutchins, *The Idaho Law of Water Rights* (Boise: 1956), pp. 101–8; Idaho, *Session Laws, 1951*, pp. 423–29, *Session Laws, 1953*, pp. 277–91, *Session Laws, 1963*, pp. 623–26, *Session Laws, 1967*, pp. 616–18; Association Western State Engineers, "Proceedings, Twenty-First Annual Convention," p. 42; Idaho, *Senate Journal, 1945*, pp. 462, 477–78, *Senate Journal, 1951*, p. 377, *House Journal, 1951*, p. 531; *Idaho Statesman*, Feb. 27, March 4, 1951; House Bill No. 130,

Idaho, 28th Legislature, 1945, House Bills, 1–208, (University of Idaho Library, Moscow).

14. Wyoming, *Session Laws, 1945*, p. 166, *Session Laws, 1947*, pp. 112–15, *Session Laws, 1955*, p. 375, *Session Laws, 1957*, pp. 272–83; Wyoming State Engineer, *Twenty-sixth Biennial Report, 1941–1942* (Cheyenne, n.d.), p. 33, *Twenty-seventh Biennial Report, 1943–1944* (Cheyenne, n.d.), p. 28, *Twenty-eighth Biennial Report, 1945–1946* (Cheyenne, n.d.), pp. 59–60, *Twenty-ninth Biennial Report, 1947–1948* (Cheyenne, n.d.), p. 25, *Thirtieth Biennial Report, 1949–1950* (Cheyenne, n.d.), p. 21, *Thirty-second Biennial Report, 1953–1954* (Cheyenne, n.d.), pp. 16, 22; Association of Western State Engineers, "Proceedings, Twenty-First Annual Convention," pp. 72–73, "Proceedings, Twenty-Seventh Annual Convention, Kansas City, Kansas, August 24–27, 1954," p. 114, "Proceedings, Thirtieth Annual Convention, Seattle, Washington, August 21–23, 1957," pp. 109–10; Donald A. Warner, "Ground Water in Wyoming," *Journal American Water Works Association* 41 (1949): 254–55.

15. Robert G. Dunbar, "Groundwater Property Rights and Controversies in Montana," Montana University Joint Water Resources Research Center, Report 76 (April 1976), pp. 7–15.

16. Ibid., pp. 15–22.

17. Ibid., pp. 22–41.

18. Senate Bill No. 206, Fortieth Session of the Colorado General Assembly, 1955, Division of Archives and Public Records, Denver; W. E. Code, "Colorado Needs Ground-Water Legislation," Colorado Agricultural Experiment Station, General Series Paper No. 560, mimeographed, pp. 10–13; *The Centennial: The Voice of Farm Bureau in Colorado* 11 (March 1955): 8; J. E. Whitten, "Underground Waters of Colorado," Association of Western State Engineers, "Proceedings, Twenty-Eighth Annual Convention, Denver, Colorado, September 26–28, 1955," pp. 50–51; *Greeley Daily Tribune*, Feb. 24, 1955; *Fort Morgan Times*, Feb. 26, 1955.

19. J. Bjorklund and R. F. Brown, *Geology and Ground-Water Resources of the Lower South Platte River Valley between Hardin, Colorado and Paxton, Nebraska*, USGS, Water-Supply Paper 1378 (Washington, D.C.: GPO, 1957), pp. 49, 86; W. E. Code, *Use of Ground Water for Irrigation in the South Platte Valley of Colorado*, Colorado Agricultural Experiment Station, Bulletin 483 (Fort Collins, Colo., 1943), pp. 39–40.

20. I. F. Davis, Jr., and E. J. Farmer, "74 Morgan County Farmers Interviewed," *Farm and Home Research* 7 (Jan.–Feb. 1957): 6, 8–10.

21. *Greeley Daily Tribune*, Feb. 24, March 25, 1955; *Denver Post*, Feb. 24, March 25, 1955; *Fort Morgan Times*, Feb. 26, March 16, 25, 1955.

22. Colorado, *Senate Journal, 1955*, pp. 650–51; *Fort Morgan Times*, Feb. 26, March 25, 1955; *Denver Post*, March 25, 1955; *Greeley Daily Tribune*, March 25, 1955.

23. Colorado, *House Journal, 1957*, pp. 1046–50, 1071–72, *Senate Journal, 1957*, pp. 109, 571, 624–27, 666–69, 682; Senate Bill No. 113, 41st sess. of the Colorado General Assembly, 1957, Division of Archives; Colorado, *Session Laws, 1957*, pp. 863–73; *Centennial* 12 (April 1956): 1; ibid. (May 1956: 1, 5, 13; ibid. (Aug. 1956): 1; ibid. (Jan. 1957): 3; ibid. (Feb. 1957): 1, 8; ibid. (March 1957): 1; *Denver Post*, March 12, 14, 19, 26, 27, 1957; *Rocky Mountain News*, March 19 and 27, 1957.

24. Official Water District Notice in Re: Bijou Creek Tentatively Critical Ground Water District and Minutes of the Bijou District Advisory Board Meeting, March 31, 1958, in file entitled "Tentatively Critical Ground Water District," Division of Water Resources, Colorado Department of Natural Resources, Denver; Raphael J. Moses and George Vranesh, "Colorado's New Ground Water Laws," *University of Colorado Law Review* 38 (1966): 295; *Fort Morgan Times*, Jan. 13, Feb. 17, March 6, 7, 11, April 13, 1958; *Denver Post*, March 18, April 13, 1958.

25. Felix L. Sparks to John A. Love, Dec. 21, 1964, files of Colorado Water Conservation Board, Denver; Interview with Felix L. Sparks, Sept. 14, 1973; Colorado *House Journal, 1965*, pp. 1241–62, 1320–21, *Senate Journal, 1965*, pp. 751–52, 1055–56; *Denver Post*, April 15, 28, 1965; *Rocky Mountain News*, April 15, 1965.

26. Colorado, *Session Laws, 1965*, pp. 1246–68; *Fundingsland v. Colorado Ground Water Commission*, 171 Colo. 487, 468 Pac. 2d 835 (1970).

27. Robert G. Dunbar, "The Arizona Groundwater Controversy at Mid-Century," *Arizona and the West* 19 (1977): 9–11; H. E. Thomas et al. *Effects of Drought in the Colorado River Basin*, USGS, Professional Paper 372–F (Washington, D.C.: GPO, 1963), pp. F26, F38–F43.

28. Dunbar, "Arizona Groundwater Controversy," pp. 11–12.

29. Ibid., pp. 14–15; Dean E. Mann, *The Politics of Water in Arizona* (Tucson: University of Arizona Press, 1963), pp. 50–51.

30. Dunbar, "Arizona Groundwater Controversy," pp. 13–18.

31. Ibid., pp. 19–22; *Bristor* v. *Cheatham*, 75 Ariz. 227, 255 Pac. 2d 173 (1953).

32. *Jarvis* v. *State Land Department*, City of Tucson, 104 Ariz. 527, 456 Pac. 2d 385 (1969); *Jarvis* v. *State Land Department*, 106 Ariz. 506, 479 Pac. 2d 169 (1970); *Farmers Investment Company* v. *Bettwy*, 113 Ariz. 520, 588 Pac. 2d 14 (1976); Clifford K. Atkinson, "Farmers Investment Company v. Bettwy: A Judicial Restriction of Ground Water Withdrawals, Coercing the Arizona Legislature to Act," *Natural Resources Journal* 17 (1977): 348–55; Arizona Groundwater Management Study Commission, Draft Report of Tentative Recommendations July 1979 (Phoenix, 1979), I–2–13.

33. Arizona Groundwater Management Study Commission, Final Report June 1980 (Phoenix, 1980), I–16, II–1–11; *Arizona Republic*, Oct. 6, 1979; *Statutes at Large*, 82:89.

34. Arizona Groundwater Management Study Commission, Final Report, III–1–13, Draft Report of Tentative Recommendations, III–10–20.

35. Donald E. Green, *Land of the Underground Rain: Irrigation on the Texas High Plains, 1910–1970* (Austin: University of Texas Press, 1973), pp. 171–77; Texas, *Senate Journal, 1937*, p. 59, *House Journal, 1941*, pp. 196–97, *House Journal, 1947*, pp. 717–18, 1220; E. V. Spence, "Ground Water Problems in Texas," in Association of Western State Engineers, "Proceedings, Twenty-First Annual Convention," p. 65; C. L. McGuinness, *The Role of Ground Water in the National Water Situation*, USGS, Water-Supply Paper 1800 (Washington, D.C.: GPO, 1963), pp. 843–45; H. E. Thomas et al., *Effects of Drought in Central and South Texas*, USGS, Professional Paper 372–C (Washington, D.C.: GPO, 1963), pp. C25–29.

36. Texas, *Session Laws*, 1949, pp. 559–64; Wells A. Hutchins, *The Texas Law of Water Rights* (Austin, 1960), pp. 588–92; Frank A. Raymer, "Ground–Water Basin Management on the High Plains of Texas," *Ground Water* 10 (Sept–Oct. 1972): 12–17; Stephen E. Snyder, "Ground Water Management: A Proposal for Texas," *Texas Law Review* 51 (1973): 289–99; Green, *Land of the Underground Rain*, pp. 177–88.

37. Richard S. Harnsberger, Jarret C. Oeltjen, and Ralph J. Fischer, "Groundwater: From Windmills to Comprehensive Management," *Nebraska Law Review* 52 (1973): 179–281; Carl A. P. Fricke and Darryll T. Pederson, "Ground–Water Resource Management in Nebraska," *Ground Water* 17 (1979): 544–49; Ralph R.

Marlette, and Craig L. Williams, "Nebraska Multi-Purpose Resources Districts," in *Legal, Institutional and Social Aspects of Irrigation and Drainage and Water Resources Planning and Management*, Proceedings, ASCE Irrigation and Drainage Division and ASCE Water Resources Planning and Management Division Specialty Conference, July 26–28, 1978 (New York: American Society of Civil Engineers, 1979), pp. 266–81; J. David Aiken and Raymond J. Supalla, "Ground Water Management in Nebraska," ibid., pp. 484–98; J. David Aiken and Raymond J. Supalla, "Ground Water Mining and Western Water Rights Law: The Nebraska Experience," *South Dakota Law Review* 24 (1979): 617–48; Nebraska, *Session Laws, 1959*, pp. 773–81, *Session Laws, 1969*, pp. 99–145, *Session Laws, 1975*, pp. 1145–58, Kansas, *Session Laws, 1972*, pp. 1416–30; James A. Power, Jr. to Robert G. Dunbar, March 16, 1977, Folder, Dunbar—Water-Rights History Papers, Special Collections, Roland R. Renne Library.

38. *Canada* v. *City of Shawnee*, 179 Okla. 53, 64 Pac. 2d 694 (1936); Oklahoma, *Session Laws, 1949*, pp. 641–46, *Session Laws, 1972*, pp. 529–34; Joseph F. Rarick, "Oklahoma Water Law, Ground or Percolating in the Pre-1971 Period," *Oklahoma Law Review* 24 (1971): 403–26; Wells A. Hutchins, *Water Right Laws in the Nineteen Western States*, USDA, Miscellaneous Publication 1206, 3 vols. (Washington, D.C.: GPO, 1971–77), 3:436–38.

39. North Dakota, *Session Laws, 1955*, p. 579; South Dakota, *Session Laws, 1955*, pp. 521–28; *Knight* v. *Grimes*, 80 S.D. 517, 127 N.W. 2d 708 (1964); Hutchins, *Water Right Laws*, 3:410–12, 498–500; *Dakota Farmer* 75 (May 7, 1955): 8.

40. Frank J. Trelease, "Alaska's New Water Use Act," *Land and Water Law Review* 2 (1967): 11–39; Hutchins *Water Right Laws*, 2:660, 3:256–58.

41. M. Craig Haase, "The Interrelationship of Ground and Surface Water: An Enigma to Western Water Law," *Southwestern Nevada Law Review* 10 (1978): 2083–85; Arthur M. Piper, *Interpretation and Current Status of Ground-Water Rights*, USGS Circular 432 (Washington, D.C.: USGS, 1960), 7–8.

Chapter 15

1. *United States* v. *Rio Grande Dam and Irrigation Company*, 174 U.S. 690 (1899); *California* v. *United States*, 438 U.S. 645

(1978); Ira G. Clark, "The Elephant Butte Controversy: A Chapter in the Emergence of Federal Water Law," *Journal of American History* 61 (1975): 1015–33.

2. U.S. Congress, Senate, *Congressional Record,* 55th Cong. 3d sess., 1899, 32, pt. 2:1445, pt. 3:2269; Anne C. Hansen, "The Congressional Career of Senator Francis E. Warren from 1890 to 1902," *Annals of Wyoming* 20 (1948): 42.

3. *Statutes at Large,* 32:380; Donald J. Pisani, "State vs. Nation: Federal Reclamation and Water Rights in the Progressive Era," *Pacific Historical Review* 51 (August 1982): 268–69; Samuel P. Hays, *Conservation and the Gospel of Efficiency: The Progressive Conservation Movement, 1890–1920* (Cambridge: Harvard University Press, 1959), p. 19.

4. *California* v. *United States,* 438 U.S. 645 (1978).

5. *Winters* v. *United States,* 207 U.S. 564 (1908); *Conrad Investment Co.* v. *United States,* 161 Fed. 829 (1908); Norris Hundley, jr., "The Dark and Bloody Ground of Indian Water Rights: Confusion Elevated to Principle." *Western Historical Quarterly* 9 (1978): 460–65; Edward E. Barry, "The Fort Belknap Indian Reservation: The First One Hundred Years, 1855–1955," MS in Special Collections, Roland R. Renne Library, Montana State University, Bozeman, Mont., pp. 81–92, 123–28, 278–82; Norris Hundley, jr., "The 'Winters' Decision and Indian Water Rights: A Mystery Reexamined," *Western Historical Quarterly* 13 (1982): 17–42.

6. *Wyoming* v. *Colorado,* 259 U.S. 419 at 443–55; Pisani, "State vs. Nation," pp. 273–75; John H. Lewis, "State and National Water Laws, with Detailed Statement of the Oregon System of Water Titles," American Society of Civil Engineers, *Transactions* 76 (1913): 664.

7. U.S. Congress, Senate, Subcommittee on Irrigation and Reclamation of the Committee on Interior and Insular Affairs, *Water Rights Settlement Act: Hearings on S. 863,* 84th Cong., 2d sess., March 19–29, 1956, pp. 24–25, 75; *California Oregon Power Co.* v. *Beaver Portland Cement Co.,* 295 U.S. 142 at 163–164 1935).

8. *Nebraska* v. *Wyoming,* 325 U.S. 589 at 611–16 (1945); Wells A. Hutchins, *Select Problems in the Law of Water Rights in the West,* USDA, Miscellaneous Publications 418 (Washington, D.C.: GPO, 1942), pp. 421–27; National Reclamation Association, *Proceedings Seventh Annual Convention, Reno, Nevada, October 11–12–13, 1938* (n.p., n.d.), pp. 147–48. The National Reclamation

Association in convention in 1942 authorized the appointment of a committee to draft a statement of the states' position on water rights. The committee, chaired by Clifford H. Stone of Colorado, prepared the desired statement, which it issued in 1943 under the title of *Preservation of Integrity of State Water Laws.*

9. National Reclamation Association, *Proceedings of the Twenty-first Annual Meeting, Long Beach, California, November 12, 13, 14, 1952* (n.p., n.d.), p. 181; *Statutes at Large,* 66:560; *Water Rights Settlement Act: Hearings on S. 863,* p. 62; *California v. United States,* 438 U.S. 645 (1978).

10. *Federal Power Commission v. Oregon,* 349 U.S. 435, (1955).

11. Ibid. at 457; *United States v. New Mexico,* 438 U.S. 696 (1978); Heidi Topp Brooks, "Reserved Water Rights and Our National Forests," *Natural Resources Journal* 19 (1979): 436.

12. *Water Rights Settlement Act: Hearings on S. 863,* pp. 62, 78–79, 81–86; *Nevada ex rel. Shamburger v. United States,* 279 Fed. 2d, 699 (1960).

13. *Ivanhoe Irrigation District et al. v. McCracken et al.,* 357 U.S. 275 at 292 (1958); *City of Fresno v. California,* 372 U.S. 627 at 630 (1963); U.S. Congress, Senate, Committee on Interior and Insular Affairs, *Federal-State Water Rights; Hearing on Problems Arising from Relationships between the States and the Federal Government with Respect to the Development and Control of Water Resources,* 87th Cong., 1st sess. June 15 and 16, 1961, p. 61; Timothy J. Beaton, "Breathing New Life into Section 8 of the 1902 Reclamation Act: California v. United States," *University of Colorado Law Review* 50 (1979); 212–13.

14. *Federal-State Water Rights: Hearings on Problems,* pp. 4–9, 163.

15. *Arizona v. California,* 373 U.S. 546 at 564–94 (1963); Frank J. Trelease, "Federal-State Relations in Water Law," National Water Commission Report NWC–6–71–014, dated Sept. 7, 1971, p. 86.

16. *Arizona v. California,* 373 U.S. 546 at 595–601; Harold A. Ranquist, "The *Winters* Doctrine and How it Grew: Federal Reservation of Rights to the Use of Water," *Brigham Young University Law Review* 1975: 639–724.

17. *Water Rights Settlement Act: Hearings on S. 863,* pp. 1–62; Eva Hanna Morreale, "Federal-State Conflicts Over

Western Waters — A Decade of Attempted 'Clarifying Legislation'," *Rutgers Law Review* 20 (1966): 464–78, 512–15.

18. *Federal-State Water Rights: Hearings on Problems*, pp. 68, 78, 122–24, 157; *Water Rights Settlement Acts: Hearings on S. 863*, pp. 151, 167; Morreale, "Federal-State Conflicts," pp. 459–63, 478–82, 517–18.

19. Morreale, "Federal-State Conflicts," pp. 482–512. U.S. Congress, Senate, Subcommittee on Irrigation and Reclamation of the Committee on Interior and Insular Affairs, *Federal-State Water Rights: Hearings on S. 1275*, 88th Cong., 2d sess., March 10–13, 1964, pp. 3–19; Wesley A. D'Ewart, "Water Problems Won't Wait for a Solution," *Montana Farmer-Stockman* 54 (Jan. 19, 1967): 9.

20. *United States v. District Court in and for the County of Eagle*, 401 U.S. 520 (1971); *United States v. District Court in and for Water Division No. 5*, 401 U.S. 527 (1971).

21. *Cappaert v. United States*, 426 U.S. 128 (1976).

22. *Colorado River Water Conservation District v. United States*, 424 U.S. 800 (1976).

23. U.S. Congress, House, *Congressional Record*, 95 Cong., 1st sess., 1977, vol. 123, p. 4800, 2d sess., 1978, vol. 124, p. 5047; *Federal Register* 42 (July 15, 1977): 36792–94; Association of Western State Engineers, "Proceedings, Fiftieth Annual Convention, Lincoln, Nebraska, September 20–23, 1977," pp. 37–41, 63–70; Scott M. Matheson, "President Carter's Water Policy: Partnership or Preemption?" *Rocky Mountain Mineral Law Institute* 25 (1979): 1–25; *Great Falls Tribune*, July 29, 1977; *Denver Post*, October 23, 1977; *Montana Water News*, September 1977, p. 3; *New York Times*, April 19, 1977, p. 20.

24. *United States v. New Mexico*, 438 U.S. 696 (1978); *California v. United States*, 438 U.S. 645 (1978); Brooks, "Reserved Water Rights and Our National Forests," pp. 433–43; Alan E. Boles, Jr. and Charles M. Elliott, "*United States v. New Mexico* and the Course of Federal Reserved Water Rights," *University of Colorado Law Review* 51 (1980): 209–35; Beaton, "Breathing New Life into Section 8 of the 1902 Reclamation Act: *California v. United States*," pp. 207–29.

25. Helen Ingram, Nancy Laney and John R. McCain, "Water Scarcity and the Politics of Plenty in the Four Corners States," *Western Political Quarterly* 32 (1979): 298; Richard A. Simms, "National Water Policy in the Wake of United States v. New Mexico," *Natural Resources Journal* 20 (1980): 1–16; Frank J.

Trelease, "Uneasy Federalism—State Water Laws and National Water Users," *Washington Law Review* 55 (1980): 758–75; Robert D. Dellwo, "Recent Developments in the Northwest Regarding Indian Water Rights," *Natural Resources Journal* 20 (1980): 101–20; Tim Gebhart, "Who owns the Missouri? South Dakota and the Sioux battle for a river," *Progressive* 44 (October 1980): 44–45; Michael F. Lamb, "Adjudication of Indian Water Rights; Implementation of the 1979 Amendments to the Montana Water Use Act," *Montana Law Review* 41 (1980); 73–95.

Chapter 16

1. *Proceedings Concerning Adjudication of Priorities under Irrigation Act of 1881, in Water District No. 3, Cache la Poudre District* (Denver: Clark and Reid, n.d.), pp. 20–21, 31–32, 67–68; Arthur Maass and Raymond L. Anderson, . . . *and the Desert Shall Rejoice: Conflict, Growth, and Justice in Arid Environments* (Cambridge: MIT Press, 1978), pp. 293–96; Robert G. Hemphill, *Irrigation in Northern Colorado*, USDA, Bulletin 1026 (Washington, D.C.: GPO, 1922), pp. 13–42. Actually the situation is more complicated than the illustration indicates. Because of enlargements, ditches like the Larimer and Weld Canal have several priorities.

2. U.S. Department of Commerce, Bureau of the Census, *Sixteenth Census of the United States: 1940, Population, vol. 1, Number of Inhabitants* (Washington, D.C.: GPO, 1942), p. 34, *1980 Census of Population and Housing, Advance Reports, California and Colorado, Preliminary Report, Arizona* (Washington, D.C.: Bureau of the Census, 1981); Gerald D. Nash, *The American West in the Twentieth Century; A Short History of An Urban Oasis* (Englewood Cliffs, N.J.: Prentice-Hall, 1973).

3. *Strickler* v. *City of Colorado Springs*, 16 Colo. 61, 26 Pac. 313 (1891). See also *Farmers Highline Canal and Reservoir Co.* v. *City of Golden*, 129 Colo. 575, 272 Pac. 2d 629 (1954).

4. Roderick Nash, *Wilderness and the American Mind* (New Haven: Yale University Press, 1967), pp. 161–81; Elmo R. Richardson, *The Politics of Conservation: Crusades and Controversies 1897–1913* (Berkeley: University of California Press, 1962), pp. 43–44, 72, 110, 123, 154; Kendrick A. Clements, "Engineers and Conservationists in the Progressive Era," *California History* 58 (1979–80): 282–303.

5. Abraham Hoffman, *Vision or Villainy: Origins of the Owens Valley-Los Angeles Water Controversy* (College Station: Texas A & M University Press, 1981), pp. 3–203; Remi A. Nadeau, *The Water Seekers* (Garden City, N.J.: Doubleday 1950), pp. 15–115; William L. Kahrl, *Water and Power: The Conflict over Los Angeles' Water Supply in the Owens Valley* (Berkeley: University of California Press, 1982), pp. 7–317; William L. Kahrl, "The Politics of California Water: Owens Valley and the Los Angeles Aqueduct, 1900–1927," *California Historical Quarterly* 55 (1976): 2–25, 98–120; William K. Jones, "Los Angeles Aqueduct: A Search for Water," *Journal of the West* 16 (1977): 5–21; Vincent Ostrom, *Water & Politics: A Study of Water Policies and Administration in the Development of Los Angeles* (Los Angeles: Haynes Foundation, 1953), pp. 9–14.

6. Nadeau, *Water Seekers*, pp. 197–240; Ostrom, *Water & Politics*, pp. 14–20, 179–93; Norris Hundley, jr., *Water and the West: The Colorado River Compact and the Politics of Water in the American West* (Berkeley: University of California Press, 1975), pp. 282–306.

7. Courtland L. Smith, *The Salt River Project: A Case Study in Cultural Adaptation to an Urbanizing Community* (Tucson: University of Arizona Press, 1972), pp. 97, 101, 112; A. S. Andrews, "Denver Water Supply System," in Maurice L. Albertson, L. Scott Tucker and Donald C. Taylor, eds., *Treatise on Urban Water Systems* (Fort Collins: Colorado State University, 1971), pp. 810–23; Earl L. Mosley, "Western Slope Water Development for Denver," *Journal American Water Works Association* 49 (1957): 251–62; *Engineering News-Record* 115 (Sept. 12, 1935): 357–58, 153; ibid. (Nov. 4, 1954): 28, 155; ibid. (Oct. 20, 1955): 26; *City and County of Denver* v. *Northern Colorado Water Conservancy District*, 130 Colo. 375, 276 Pac. 2d 992 (1954); U.S. Congress, Senate, Subcommittee on Irrigation and Reclamation of the Committee on Interior and Insular Affairs, *Water Rights Settlement Act; Hearings on S. 863*, 84th Cong., 2d sess., 1956, pp. 345–47, 370–71; *Denver Post*, Oct. 6, 1955.

8. Wells A. Hutchins, *Water Right Laws in the Nineteen Western States*, USDA, Miscellaneous Publication 1206, 3 vols., (Washington, D.C.: 1971–77), 2:145–71; Robert Emmet Clark, "The Pueblo Rights Doctrine in New Mexico," *New Mexico Historical Review* 35 (1960): 265–83.

9. George W. Pring and Karen A. Tomb, "License to Waste: Legal Barriers to Conservation and Efficient Use of Water in the

West," *Rocky Mountain Mineral Law Institute* 25 (1979), article 25; Wyoming Territorial Engineer, *Second Annual Report, 1889* (Cheyenne, 1890), pp. 25–32; U.S. Department of Agriculture, *Yearbook, 1903* (Washington, D.C.: GPO, 1904), pp. 93–94; George E. Radosevich, "Western Water Laws and Irrigation Return Flow," U.S. Environmental Protection Agency (Ada, Okla, 1978), pp. 53–54; Mead, *Irrigation Institutions*, pp. 110–42.

10. *Water Policies for the Future: Final Report to the President and to the Congress of the United States by the National Water Commission* (Washington, D.C.: GPO, 1973), pp. 260–70; *Federal Register* 42 (July 15, 1977): 36793; Richard M. Alston, "Commercial Irrigation Enterprise: The Fear of Water Monopoly and the Genesis of Market Distortion," Ph.D. diss., Cornell University, 1970.

11. A. Dan Tarlock, "The Recognition of Instream Flow Rights: 'New' Public Western Water Rights," *Rocky Mountain Mineral Law Institute* 25 (1979): 1–46; J. David Aiken, "The National Water Policy Review and Western Water Rights Law Reform: An Overview," *Nebraska Law Review* 59 (1980): 336–38; *McClellan* v. *Jantzen*, 26 Ariz. Appeals, 223, 547 Pac. 2d 494 (1976); Corinne C. Sherton, "Preserving Instream Flows in Oregon's Rivers and Streams," *Environmental Law* 11 (1981): 390–401; Washington, *Session Laws, 1971*, pp. 1020–26; Montana, *Session Laws, 1973*, p. 1134; Jim Posewitz, "A Free-Flowing Yellowstone: No Longer Just a Dream," *Montana Outdoors* 10 (March–April, 1979): 34–37.

Index